T0298643

Leadership Lessons from the Trump Presidency

This book seeks to demonstrate that we can learn from both 'good' and 'bad' leaders. Part One looks at President Trump's behaviour from inauguration to impeachment. The ancient Greek concepts of Kairos and Chronos are used to indicate that Trump was almost a natural fit for the US of 2017. Part Two considers the consequences of his behaviour on the US, the world at large, and for leadership overall.

There is a temptation to consider only 'good' leaders when asking what we can learn from others. This book explores the issue of what can be learned from any person in a leadership role, no matter what the value judgement we make of them. Part One explores Trump's behaviour up to the moment of impeachment and the longer-term residual impacts this will have once his term as President is over. It shows that our value judgements tend to be based on perception and a priori assumptions. Part Two explores what we can learn from the Trump event no matter what our leadership role.

Disruption is endemic in today's world. Today, it often seems that we are born, live, and die, in three quite different worlds. Yet, at its core, things have changed very little. Oligarchy has been a reality since time immemorial. Unless we are first 'unfrozen' from the status quo, change tends to be more cosmetic than actual. Donald Trump's presidency has the potential to be the thawing agent that could enable 'real' change through which new forms of both democracy and capitalism might emerge across the world.

Douglas Long, PhD, teaches in the University of New South Wales School of Management in Sydney, Australia. He is the author of three previous books published by Routledge-Gower.

Leadership Lessons from the Trump Presidency

Douglas Long

LONDON AND NEW YORK

First published
by Routledge
2 Park Square, Milton Park, Abingdon, Oxon OX14 4RN

and by Routledge
52 Vanderbilt Avenue, New York, NY 10017

Routledge is an imprint of the Taylor & Francis Group, an informa business

British Library Cataloguing-in-Publication Data
A catalogue record for this book is available from the British Library

Library of Congress Cataloging-in-Publication Data
Names: Long, Douglas G., author.
Title: Leadership lessons from the Trump presidency / Douglas Long.
Description: Abingdon, Oxon ; New York, NY : Routledge, 2020. |
Includes bibliographical references and index. |
Identifiers: LCCN 2020003839 (print) | LCCN 2020003840 (ebook) |
ISBN 9780367862374 (hardback) | ISBN 9781003018469 (ebook)
Subjects: LCSH: Trump, Donald, 1946- | Leadership--Case studies. |
Presidents--United States--Case studies.
Classification: LCC HM1261 .L66 2020 (print) |
LCC HM1261 (ebook) | DDC 303.3/4--dc23
LC record available at https://lccn.loc.gov/2020003839
LC ebook record available at https://lccn.loc.gov/2020003840

ISBN: 978-0-367-86237-4 (hbk)
ISBN: 978-1-003-01846-9 (ebk)

Typeset in Times New Roman
by Taylor & Francis Books

Contents

Figures

About the author

Douglas G. Long was born in New Zealand but has lived in Australia for most of his adult life. His tertiary education was in New Zealand, Australia, England and the United States, culminating in 1985 with a PhD in Organisational Psychology.

For many years, he taught in universities in Australia and the United States including, in Melbourne, Preston Institute, David Syme Business School, and RMIT Graduate School of Management and, in the USA, Drexel University. From 1988 to 2001 he was associated with Macquarie Graduate School of Management in Sydney where he researched, designed and delivered the programme Leadership in Senior Management. From 2002 to 2012 he was with Australia's Southern Cross University Graduate College of Management where he supervised doctoral candidates. Since 2013 he has taught in the Management Department at the University of New South Wales Business School in Sydney.

He is the author of eight books on leadership, ethics, and values.

Part One

'The Trump Decapitalise'

Part One explores leadership issues relating to the presidency of Donald J. Trump.

1 Promises and early activities

'Every French soldier carries in his cartridge pouch the baton of a marshal of France'

Napoleon Bonaparte

Everything in Donald Trump's past makes it clear that, first, he has always been ambitious for power and wealth, and, second, that he views the world in a polarity of 'winners' versus 'losers' – and he hates to lose. His books and history show that he will do almost anything to make others appear to be losers in this quest to be 'top dog'. In 2016, Trump finally acknowledged the presence of the baton in his cartridge pouch and, in 2017, he put it on full display by nominating for the US Presidency.

Until he nominated as a candidate for the presidency, across the world Donald Trump was known primarily for his real estate deals, his aggressive use of bankruptcy law to further his own ends, and for being a reality TV star. Even in the US, his was not a household name unless one was considering staying in certain up-market hotels or had seen his television show, *The Apprentice*. The result was that, in the very early stages, few took his candidacy seriously and he was subjected to much negative commentary from Republican and Democrat alike. History shows that the magnitude and ferocity of his ambition were seriously underestimated, as was his ability to develop and implement a winning strategy that was vastly different from any previously seen. The assumption seemed to be that any marshal's baton that Trump might possess would prove to be plastic rather than gold. Hillary Clinton was perhaps the most prominent, but certainly not the only person, to ridicule both Trump and his supporters.

It has long been known that there are two key contributing factors to a person's make-up: nature and nurture. It is debated as to the influence each of these has on our mature selves, but the fact that both contribute is indisputable. These factors were largely ignored by Trump's commentators and competitors in the months leading up to the 2016 election. Assumptions and prejudice supplanted data and analysis. It was a classic example of what, for many years, has been labelled 'PHOG Management'. PHOG Management is where decisions and subsequent actions are made on Perception, Hearsay, Opinion and Guess rather than on facts and analysis. It is a prime cause of the all-too-often encountered reality where today's solutions become tomorrow's problems. The result is that we end up in a vicious, downward spiral of reacting to the undesirable impacts of poorly considered decisions and actions.

Donald Trump's grandfather, Friedrich Trump, immigrated to the US from Bavaria in 1885 and he became a US citizen in 1892. Around this time he also anglicised his name to Frederick. From all accounts he was one of many immigrants who made their way to the US in the late nineteenth and early twentieth centuries in the hope of making a fortune in the new world. Frederick Trump was one of many who succeeded. It appears that his wealth arose primarily from running hotels and restaurants for those who were seeking their fortunes from goldfields. The information also shows that the drive shown by Frederick Trump was replicated in his sons; John became a prominent engineer and inventor and Fred, Donald's father, became one of New York's major real estate developers. Nature and nurture combined to make Donald both ambitious and goal orientated. The issue of ethical behaviour, of course, is a different subject.

On Frederick's death in 1918, his wife and family inherited a significant fortune of around $32,000. Frederick's wife, Elisabeth, and elder son, Fred, used this to continue in real estate development, while the younger son, John, developed his own path as an engineer and inventor. On Fred's death in 1999 it appears that Donald inherited between $100 million and $200 million. Prior to this, Fred seems to have provided significant help to his son although this is disputed, with Donald Trump stating that his father only helped him with 'a small loan' in 1975. Others claim that this loan was the somewhat larger figure of around $14 million.

It is important to note that although Donald Trump is invariably spotlighted on the world stage, his siblings have all been successful in their chosen careers. The benefits of nature and nurture in the Trump family were not confined to Donald. By the time he became President, Donald Trump had amassed a fortune of between around $3 billion (external valuations) and $10 billion (his own valuation).

Now, whether the original support provided by his father was a small loan or $14 million, and whether or not his fortune at the time of nominating for the presidency was around $3 billion or $10 billion, is largely irrelevant. The fact remains that between 1975 and 2016 Donald Trump amassed a vast fortune. Not many people, even those who start out with financial means, grow their wealth by a factor in excess of 200 in a period of around 40 years. Valuable, available information was ignored by his detractors in favour of assumption and prejudice.

It begs the question as to how this was achieved.

Trump's early works in print provide examples from his business in real estate investing and appearances on television. These indicate that everything tends to be reduced to a zero-sum game in which there are only winners and losers. His record shows that he has been a frequent user of the bankruptcy laws in order to minimise or annul claims from creditors and that, along with this, he has repeatedly employed the legal system to enforce payment from debtors. This reflects a Darwinian world; the weak are tolerated and supported only insofar as they can further the aims and ends of the rich and powerful. There is, of course, nothing illegal in this behaviour and it is a frequently used approach. Whether or not it is ethical is a different question altogether.

In the business arena, Trump seems to have been abrupt and abrasive. He appears to have demonstrated very little real concern for his employees or contractors, and always concentrated on doing deals that would be ultimately to his personal benefit. Perhaps he was even able to confuse fear with respect – people doing what he asked because they feared dismissal rather than people doing their jobs because of their commitment to him and his organisation. Between 1991 and 2009 his hotel and casino businesses used Chapter 11 bankruptcy protection six times in order to re-negotiate debt. Trump was quoted by *Newsweek*[1] in 2011 saying, ' I do play with the bankruptcy laws – they're very good for me.'

By 2016, Trump and his businesses had been involved in more than three thousand five hundred state and federal legal actions. It appears that Trump or one of his companies was the plaintiff in 1,900 cases and the defendant in 1,450. With Trump or his company as plaintiff, more than half the cases have been against gamblers at his casinos who had failed to pay off their debts. With Trump or his company as a defendant, the most common type of case involved personal injury cases at his hotels. In cases where there was a clear resolution, Trump's side won 451 times and lost 38.[2]

To quote Donald Trump, 'I've used the laws of this country to pare debt … We'll have the company. We'll throw it into a chapter. We'll negotiate with the banks. We'll make a fantastic deal. You know, it's like on *The Apprentice*. It's not personal. It's just business.'[3]

It is clear that Donald John Trump measures his success by the accumulation of personal wealth, power and influence, rather than how these actions have impacted on the organisation or anything else overall. Given this available evidence there must clearly be questions as to why his opponents so seriously underestimated him.

Part of the reason seems to lie in the issue of personality and background. It seems to be that Trump has always marched to the beat of his own drum. He has not been closely identified with any one political party. Over the years he seems to have changed political allegiance several times, and certainly has never held political office at any level of US government. It is unclear whether he has ever been closely linked to any Washington lobbyists in order to influence federal government decisions, partly because, in areas where he was acquiring and developing property, key people he needed to influence were at administrative or, at best, state government levels.

Some have suggested that his political rise and intention to shake the establishment has similarities with John F. Kennedy and/or Ronald Reagan. This is certainly not the case. Prior to becoming President, John F. Kennedy had been a US Congressman – he was a political insider in Washington D.C. Although the fathers of both JFK and Donald Trump were, in many ways, self-made men in terms of serious wealth creation, unlike Joseph Kennedy (the father of President John F. Kennedy) Trump's father (a contemporary of Joseph Kennedy) does not appear to have been politically active in any overt way. Also, as a recent immigrant in the early twentieth century, Frederick Trump was most unlike Joseph Kennedy who came from a well-established, highly influential, New England family. Ronald Reagan came from a poor, mid-western family. He had been a trade union leader who had campaigned for better working conditions and remuneration for actors and, for him, acting was always his primary activity. Prior to becoming President, Reagan had established his political credentials by becoming Governor of California. Perhaps the only similarity between Trump and Reagan is the presence of their brass stars on the Hollywood Walk of Fame.

Comparisons with previous Presidents meant that Donald Trump was largely considered 'an outsider' whose audacity in seeking the presidency was, even if unconsciously by some, resented by many in the establishment. Wealth alone is not enough to gain 'real' respectability! In addition, other wealthy, 'respectable' businessmen, such as Ross Perot (who had strong, long-term connections to the Republican Party) had been unsuccessful previous contenders for the presidency, therefore, Trump was not to be taken seriously.

Another possible reason for this underestimation seems to lie in the audiences Trump sought. Although every politician claims to be interested in the grassroots voting public, it has become increasingly uncommon for them to speak at town hall style campaign functions that are targeted largely at undecided, or inactive, enrolled voters. And where such town hall style campaign functions are held, the audience is largely stacked with vocal supporters of the speaker. Although, as Trump's campaign advanced, this stacking was increasingly obvious, in the early stages, it was not obviously on show. Trump's original appeal was to use his reality TV image to attract a wide audience.

So, against all early odds, Trump became President. And the closer he came to achieving his goal, the more promises he made. Now, all politicians make promises and most people realise that they could be described as 'core' and 'non-core' – in other words, there are promises that they may try to keep and others that they really have no intention of following through. The track records of past US Presidents (like all other politicians), makes it clear that promises are made to win elections, and sometimes are actually best left unfulfilled. Consequently, no-one should be surprised that Trump has not kept (and is not likely to keep), all the promises he has made.

Depending the source you trust, the first 36 or so months of the Trump presidency has either resulted in a total failure to keep significant promises, or it has meant that, despite the best intentions and efforts of Trump and the Republican Party, the fulfilment of promises has been thwarted, or at least delayed, by Democratic intransigence, obstructing judges, and bureaucratic red tape. Those promises that have clearly been kept, such as significant reduction in tax rates, withdrawal from the Trans-Pacific Trade Partnership, withdrawal from the Paris Agreement on the reduction of carbon emissions and the like, are seen by his supporters as evidence that Trump is on track to achieve his targets, and his failures are blamed on factors beyond his control. Trump's detractors point out that defeats or delays are viewed as 'victories' in maintaining a vibrant democracy and any Trump successes are seen through the light of unfavourable consequences. In relation to Trump's possible re-election, it is highly likely that the views of his supporters will prove more powerful than those of his detractors. We will explore the reasons for this in Chapter 2.

Trump's promises, and the degree to which he has implemented or sought to implement them, is important. As already shown, Trump sees everything as a nett sum game. There are only winners and losers and, if he is going to win, then it follows that others must lose. The concept of a win-win outcome seems to be totally foreign to him. In 2016, the 'win' was to become President. Now the 'win' will be re-election. He is very conscious of the voter base that gave him the win in 2016.

In many countries, the President or Prime Minister is the person gaining most votes overall, or is the leader of the political party that gains the most seats in that country's parliament. In the US, however, every state has a set number of 'electoral college' votes and it is these that ultimately determine who becomes President. There are well-documented instances where the President has gained office despite receiving less popular votes than his competition, the famous loss of Al Gore to George Bush was but one of them. Similarly, in 2016, Hillary Clinton may have gained more individual votes, but Donald Trump took the prize. The Electoral College votes of mid-western and southern states were key. This is where manufacturing and mining jobs had been lost because of international trade barriers being lowered or removed and/or because of a reduction in demand for coal as a key fuel. Such economic factors were highly influential in this result. So, too was the impact of conservative, evangelical Christians and those allied to the far-right wing of political thought. Those states with large numbers of voters in such categories responded positively to Trump's promises to rebuff political correctness, to place tariffs on imports, to reduce immigration, to wind back environmental safeguards, to aggressively assert US dominance in world politics, to support narrow conservative agendas, relocate the US Embassy in Israel to Jerusalem, and so on. The geopolitical, socio-economic, environ-mental, human rights, and even religious implications and ramifications of these promises were (and are) seen to be totally irrelevant.

Trump's claim was that he would 'Make America Great Again' and that only he could do that. No matter that he was an extremely wealthy man whose path to riches may have involved questionable ethical practices that pushed the boundaries of legality, to those who saw or who had seen businesses close, jobs disappear, and their 'American Dream' fading into a dissipating chimera, Trump offered hope across many areas. In a manner like those with little money who constantly buy lottery tickets in the hope of winning financial security, people felt that things could hardly get much worse and there was a vague possibility of them actually improving. These voters were not 'deplorables' as Hilary Clinton so offensively labelled them: they were people who wanted to be rid of the despair and difficulty they currently faced, and Trump offered an almost messianic option. Similarly, for those who wanted a return to the previous status quo of male dominance, realisation of a narrow, fundamentalist Christian view of the world, rejection of the increasing secularisation of society with its acceptance of multiculturalism and widespread tolerance of religions, sexual orientations, etc., Trump offered the potential that their wishes could be, at least, promoted and, at best, fulfilled. Trump's behaviour in 2017 and 2018 therefore makes sense to these people.

In 1957, the American journalist Vance Packard, published *The Hidden Persuaders*.[4] In this book, he explored the rise of market research and the use of psychological concepts in order to make marketing more effective so that people were increasingly orientated to buy what manufacturers wanted to produce and that sales organisations wanted to sell. Rather than manufacturing being driven by consumer demand, consumers responded to what was produced. He explained the influence of unconscious motivators on the rise of the consumer society. He went on to discuss the way in which, from the 1950s, these same forces were then developed into the political arena, with the rise of image and brand becoming vital to the election of candidates and their parties. Presentation and promotion increasingly supplanted substance as the basis for votes. Effective political manipulation had arrived.

The forces of which Packard wrote were not new. For centuries, leaders and politicians of all persuasions have known that voters could be influenced. Public speeches, tracts of various sorts, and mass meetings have been common practice across the ages. The difference now was that insights from people such as Freud, Pavlov, Riesman and others helped us understand '*why*' this was so and, with this understanding, came the ability to improve the '*how*'. The craft of public relations had arrived. Political campaigning changed forever. Donald J. Trump, however, has taken this to a new level.

A key insight of public relations was that the so-called 'hidden persuaders' were not equally effective with everyone; for some people, the views they held were so fixed and ingrained that nothing could convince them to consider an alternative perspective. There are indeed people so locked into the position of 'my mind's made up: don't confuse me with the facts', that no different thought can penetrate. These people seek only confirmation as to the 'rightness' of their views. The potential for influence is found among those who are at neither extreme end of any continuum. Fortunately, this middle group is the vast majority of every population – consequently, it is to this segment of society that all political campaigns are really addressed.

All politicians understand that there is widespread cynicism and mistrust of them and their profession. The 'professional politician' is widely despised – especially among people who are not actively identified with any political party. We have seen corruption, cronyism, pandering to special interest groups, lying, obfuscation, and the promotion of self-interest so often that we sometimes consider it to be the norm. Trump took this cynicism about politicians and used it to his advantage.

Closure and reduction in large scale manufacturing had hit the American Midwest particularly hard. Imported steel, aluminium and other core construction and industrial materials had impacted the mining regions, while the growth in demand for key energy sources other than coal and other fossil fuels, had affected additional regions as well. People who relied on mining, smelting, manufacturing and related support services had found their jobs disappearing and their incomes dropping. The global financial crisis of 2007/8 had destroyed the 'American Dream' for thousands who had lost their homes and seen their communities decimated. The Democratic Party and the Obama Administration, previously supported by many of these people, had not delivered on significantly improving the plight of these sections of societies while the Republican Party was widely considered to be a key aspect of the cause for their situation.

In 1987, key members of the Republican Party sought to persuade Trump to run for President, even though he was a registered Democrat voter. However, it was not until 1999 that Donald Trump actually took his first steps towards that role – and then it was not for either the Democrats or Republicans. He was persuaded to consider seeking the 2000 presidential nomination of the Reform Party, which had once featured businessman Ross Perot as its candidate. Trump set up an exploratory committee to consider this and focused his campaign on the issues of fair trade, eliminating national debt, and achieving universal healthcare. Although Trump never advanced beyond this exploratory phase, he did prove that he had the ability to attract attention and to win supporters. Later, having gained greater fame as the host of *The Apprentice*, he seriously considered running in the 2012 presidential election but later decided against it.

In 2015, having re-joined the Republican Party, using the motto 'Make America Great Again', Trump finally stood as a Republican candidate. It was a direct appeal to those who felt themselves to be victims of unfair international practices. In his announcement speech in June 2015, he took a tough stance against illegal immigration and promised to build a wall on the US–Mexico border if elected President. Trump styled himself as the candidate of anti-establishment Republicans. It was soon obvious that voters favoured the purported honesty of Trump's message and his abrasive approach. His populist position in relation to international affairs and trade, border security, criticism of political correctness, opposition to illegal immigration and various trade agreements, such as the Trans-Pacific Partnership, earned him support especially among voters who were male, white, blue-collar and/or those without college degrees – many of whom, if they voted at all, had been traditional Democratic Party supporters.

He was also active in wooing the influential Jewish and evangelical Christian electoral base. Claiming membership of the Presbyterian Church, Trump appealed to the broader Christian community by stating that the Bible was his favourite book. In September 2015, he also solicited the support of religious leaders by inviting dozens of Christian and Jewish leaders to his New York City offices for a prayer meeting. He gained further conservative Christian support by nominating a conservative Christian as his running mate – the Governor of Indiana, Mike Pence. Activities such as this drew high levels of evangelical support despite Trump exhibiting behaviours at odds with the stated beliefs of many evangelicals. In July 2016, the Pew Research Center found 78 per cent of white, evangelical Christians said that they would vote for Trump.[5]

The rest, as they say, is history. We may debate the issue of whether a factor may have been that some people actually voted for 'someone who was not Hillary Clinton', but little is gained from this. Although he lost the popular vote in terms of numbers of people actually voting for either the Republican or Democratic parties, Trump won the majority of votes in the Electoral College and became President of the United States in January 2017.

In ancient Greek there were two words for time – *Kairos* and *Chronos*. Kairos indicates an opportune time for action while chronos refers to chronological, or sequential time. Kairos has a qualitative nature, while chronos is quantitative. In the presidential elections of 2017 these two coincided. A series of events had created the kairos under which Donald Trump could fulfil his presidential ambitions.

Donald Trump's marshal's baton has been taken from his cartridge pouch and is now being proudly waved aloft. Up to this mid-way point, his supporters can claim he is doing exactly what he said he would do in relation to international relations, trade, immigration, and political correctness. Any failures to implement promises are therefore, not his fault.

Notes

1 Howard Kurtz, 'The Trump backlash', 24 April 2011. Available at http://www. newsweek.com/kurtz-trump-backlash-66503.
2 Nick Penzenstadler and Susan Page, 'Trump's 3,500 lawsuits unprecedented for a presidential nominee', 23 October 2017. Available at https://www.usatoday.com/story/news/politics/elections/2016/06/01/donald-trump-lawsuits-legal-battles/84995854/.
3 Amy Bingham, 'Donald Trump's companies filed for bankruptcy 4 times', 20 April 2011. Available at http://abcnews.go.com/Politics/donald-trump-filed-bankruptcy-times/story?id=13419250v. See also http://fortune.com/2016/03/10/trump-hotel-casinos-pay-failure/.
4 Vance Packard (1957), *The Hidden Persuaders: An Introduction to the Techniques of Mass-Persuasion Through the Unconscious.* London: Longmans Green.
5 Pew Research Center, 13 July 2016; 20 August 2016.

2 'The medium is the message'

In 1964, a Canadian professor of English literature, Marshall McLuhan, proposed that a medium itself, not its content, should be the focus of study.[1] He held that a medium affects the society in which it plays a role, not only by the content delivered through that medium, but also by the characteristics of the medium itself: there are personal and social consequences of any medium. McLuhan says, in Chapter 1, '... the "message" of any medium or technology is the change of scale or pace or pattern that it introduces into human affairs ... it is the medium that shapes and controls the scale and form of human association and action.' Better than any politician of recent years, this was understood and used by Donald Trump.

McLuhan used his book title to draw attention to his claim that 'a medium is not something neutral, it does something to people, it takes hold of them, it roughs them up, it massages them, it bumps them around in the same way that a chiropractor manipulates a body in order to reposition muscles.' His view was that the general 'roughing up' that any society gets from a medium, especially a new one, is that on which we should focus. It is a lesson Trump learned well and of which he shows a greater mastery than most.

It has already been shown that, at the time of nominating for the Presidency, Trump was worth at least around $3 billion (even if he did claim it was in excess of $10 billion). The question then arises as to how this very wealthy captain of capitalism could be viewed by many as the champion of the poor. McLuhan may help us find the answer.

Donald J. Trump knows the power of words to influence – and to injure. He is a past master of using social media, especially Twitter, to promote himself and to denigrate those with whom he disagrees. There is no doubt that this was a key factor in his political success and in the on-going loyalty of his die-hard supporters. Coupled with this, was his denigration of traditional media channels which he accused of promulgating 'fake news' if they presented him and his campaign in anything other than a highly favourable light. Portraying traditional media as 'losers', enhanced his projected self-image as a 'winner'.

There is a sense in which Trump has revolutionised political communication. This was first seen in his election campaign and has continued during the first two years of his presidency. Although President Obama used social media in both his campaigns and in his presidency, it was as a supplement to his use of traditional media. Donald Trump eschewed traditional media – writing off anything with which he disagreed as 'fake news' – and concentrated on direct communication to his vast number of Twitter followers. In short spurts of 280 or so characters he cut to the core of what he wanted to say and ensured he tapped into the concerns and prejudices of his followers. History shows that this approach succeeded to a level previously unimagined.

When challenged by those who were concerned that this approach lacked any of the usual checks and balances, Trump's response was to say, 'This is the new Presidential'. He's right. Because of Trump, political campaigning has changed forever – and not only in the US. Donald Trump knows that he is delivering his chosen message to the people who matter – the everyday American voter who will determine how the US Electoral College will vote in the next election. The 'elite' may complain and try to maintain a balanced approach, but in a society that now responds to superficial soundbites rather than to in-depth analysis and discussion, Trump is clearly winning the communications war. Whether or not others like it, President Trump has ascertained the best medium for communicating with his target audience.

Returning to the McLuhan statement with which this chapter started: *a medium affects the society in which it plays a role not only by the content delivered over the medium, but also by the characteristics of the medium itself*, it is clear that social media (Twitter especially), has changed the source of news and opinion.

In the Introduction to the first edition of his book, McLuhan wrote:

> In the mechanical age now receding, many actions could be taken without too much concern. Slow movement insured that the reactions were delayed for considerable periods of time. Today the action and reaction occur almost at the same time. We actually live mythically and integrally, as it were, but we continue to think in the old fragmented space and time of the pre-electric age.

McLuhan wrote this in 1964, when the world was still in the relatively early stages of embracing telephones, radio and television, as essential everyday items that could be owned and/or accessed by everyone. How much more prescient are his words in these early decades of the twenty-first century – this digital age? Today, we live in a society where almost everyone (at least in first-world and frequently in the developing world), has some form of communications device that connects to the internet of things and gives instant access to everything happening and being said everywhere in the world.

In the Introduction to the second edition, McLuhan makes the point that 'any technology gradually creates a totally new human environment. Environments are not passive wrappings but active processes.' Again, in this digital age we have ample evidence of the truth of his statement. Every day, in virtually every place on earth people are moving around, paying more attention to their mobile communication devices than they are to anything else. This includes, all too often, failure to pay attention to their own personal safety and well-being. The result is often tragic when such behaviour is accompanied by interaction with motor vehicles and the like. McLuhan made the point that any medium has the power of imposing its own assumption on the unwary! He says: 'The effects of technology do not occur at the level of opinions or concepts but alter sense ratios or patterns of perception steadily and without any resistance.'

In the 1930s, it was Joseph Goebbels who made transformational use of media. He was particularly adept at using the relatively new media of radio and film for propaganda purposes. Aware of the value of publicity (both positive and negative), he deliberately provoked beer-hall battles and street brawls, including violent attacks on the Communist Party of Germany. Goebbels adapted recent developments in commercial advertising to the political sphere, including the use of slogans and subliminal cues. He formulated the strategy that fashioned the myth of Hitler as a brilliant and decisive leader. He convened massive political gatherings at which Hitler was presented as the saviour of a new Germany. In a major new approach, Goebbels oversaw the erection of movie cameras and microphones at key locations in order to accentuate Hitler's face and voice. Such events and manoeuvrings played a major role in convincing the German people that their country would regain its honour only by pledging unwavering support to Adolf Hitler. Goebbels was an expert communicator who ensured that the use of media would never again rely only on print for its major impact.

When McLuhan speaks of the 'electric media' he is talking primarily of film, wireless technology, radio, television, the telephone, teleprinters, and the relatively early stages of computer use. However, as he points out, these 'electric media' ensured that complex data could be processed faster than at any previous period in history; that stories could be accompanied by recent film of events; and that information from one location could be available virtually anywhere else in the world within a matter of hours, or days, rather than weeks. What was more, when desired, this material could be edited and reused easily so that particular political messages could be emphasised. The news cycle was reduced from weeks to days and currency of information became a competitive advantage. Through the insights of Goebbels, media had changed.

At that time McLuhan did not see the rise of the internet and social media. However, everything he says regarding 'the electric' media is even more pertinent today. As we have moved from 'the electric age' through 'the electronic age' to 'the information age', our quest for information immediacy has accelerated from days or weeks to micro-seconds. Today, something happening anywhere in the world can be viewed in real time by anyone in any other part of the world. And this dissemination of events can be performed by any individual without the need for sophisticated recording and broadcasting resources – the attack on the Twin Towers of the World Trade Center in New

York on 11 September, 2001 and, more recently, the terrorist attack of 15 March 2019 in Christchurch, New Zealand that resulted in the tragic deaths of some 50 people provide clear evidence of that. Our news cycle is continuous. With the widespread use of social media, stories can be promulgated without any of the previous checks and balances which were designed to ensure balanced, honest and accurate reporting. 'Fake news' can be promulgated along with 'real news' and, for many, the only criterion for assessing veracity lies in the frequency and vehemence with which a story is broadcast. This climate created the perfect time for Donald Trump to make his pitch for the Presidency.

In trying to make sense of what we see today, it has been suggested that Trump is creating chaos and uncertainty in order to bring about a situation in which no-one is sure of who to trust, or of the direction in which to move.[2]

For any real change to be possible, there is abundant evidence that some form of 'unfreezing' or destabilising of the status quo is necessary. This unfreezing of the present state moves the system out of balance so that change can be pursued until a new state of equilibrium comes into existence. Of course, the 'unfreezing' required is usually more complex than a single event – it is more akin to the effect of earthquakes where the impact of the initial event can be horrific, but the subsequent aftershocks are capable of increasing the damage to total devastation. Some people may be able to ignore the initial effect of the earthquake, but the cumulative ongoing impact commands attention and action from the broadest spectrum of individuals and emergency agencies.

If Trump does not succeed in 2020, his 'unfreezing' may well come to nought. The critical issue is to continue 'unfreezing' until the organisation does not fall back into its previous position. As in all change initiatives, there is an initial, often prolonged, period where the system waits for the disruptor to go, so it can return to where it has always been.

Everyone involved in bringing about change knows, too, that the effectiveness of this unfreezing event is crucial. Like good comedians, really effective change agents know that 'timing is everything'. If the intervention is poorly timed, the probability of success is low. Trump's supporters argue that this is now the right time for President Trump to be a powerful agent of change who, in the early days, is intent on unfreezing the establishment so that a better US and world can emerge.

The key question here relates to Trump's ability to create a new and more inclusive society. There is an old joke in which a man complains that his dog has a bad habit of chasing cars. His friend responds that this is normal canine behaviour. The first man then comments that he understands this, however, the problem is that the dog doesn't know what to do with the cars after he catches them. Some who support Trump as a disrupter, who is unfreezing the status quo, suspect there is a parallel between the dog and Donald J. Trump: seeking to disrupt the status quo is not abnormal behaviour. The question relates to whether Trump can now do anything positive in rebuilding the US. Today's media can facilitate the unfreezing. Can it also facilitate the necessary reconstruction?

In late 2019, this question as to the ongoing loyalty of his initial supporters was again raised with industrial action being taken against General Motors. In the 2016 campaign, Trump claimed to be a champion of the working class, standing up for American jobs. However, when, in mid-September 2019, approximately 50,000 General Motors workers went on strike to get what they saw as their fair share of profits and to prevent further lay-offs. Trump showed little or no concern for the employees. He commented that it was 'sad to see' it and that he hoped it would be short, and said he did not want General Motors to build plants outside of the US, but made no attempt to suggest that GM should increase wages and working conditions for its employees. It is estimated that the strike is impacting General Motors' operating income by somewhere around between $50 million and $100 million a day. What will be the impact if the strike or its aftermath eventually threatens the jobs at General Motors' suppliers, c.10,000, and triggers a recession in the Midwest where most of those suppliers are based?

Corporate profits may have reached record levels, but most Americans have not benefited. Profits now constitute a larger portion of national income, and wages a lower portion, than at any time since the Second World War. These profits are generating higher share prices (fuelled by share buybacks) and higher executive pay, resulting in wider inequality. The richest 1 per cent of Americans own about 40 per cent of all shares of stock; the richest 10 per cent, around 80 per cent. There has been a power shift from workers to shareholders. This has brought about a dramatic increase in inequality that has had an unfortunate and lasting consequence for the system. Today, the issue of stagnant wages, abandoned communities, and a working class vulnerable to exploitation, has become the norm. To those in the lower socio-economic strata, Donald Trump is increasingly being seen as a champion of the rich. This could have ramifications if Trump's preferred medium, Twitter, starts to be challenged by those negatively impacted by the economy.

Donald Trump has relied on direct messages and on support of media such as Fox News to portray himself and his administration in a positive light. Problems could arise should any chink appear in this protective armour. Towards the end of 2019, those chinks began to appear. In October 2019, a long-serving Fox News anchor, Shep Smith stepped down and stated that 'intimidation and vilification of the press is now a global phenomenon. We don't have to look far for evidence of that.' This was followed in December 2019 by another leading Fox News host, Chris Wallace, directly attacking the President for his messages on press freedom. At a media function in Washington, D.C., Wallace said:

> I believe that President Trump is engaged in the most direct sustained assault on freedom of the press in our history. He has done everything he can to undercut the media, to try and delegitimise us, and I think his purpose is clear: to raise doubts when we report critically about him and his administration that we can be trusted. Back in 2017, he tweeted

something that said far more about him than it did about us: "The fake news media is not my enemy. It is the enemy of the American people."

Wallace then continued:

> Let's be honest, the president's attacks have done some damage. A Freedom Forum Institute poll, associated here with the Newseum, this year found that 2 per cent of Americans, almost a third of all of us, think the first amendment goes too far. And 77 per cent, three quarters, say that fake news is a serious threat to our democracy.

Wallace went on to point out that not all of Trump's criticisms are without foundation. He stressed that much of the mainstream media's coverage of Trump could be seen as emotional rather than rational. He reminded his listeners:

> I think many of our colleagues see the president's attacks, his constant bashing of the media as a rationale, as an excuse to cross the line themselves, to push back, and that is a big mistake. I see it all the time on the front page of major newspapers and the lead of the evening news: fact mixed with opinion, buzzwords like 'bombshell' and 'scandal'. The animus of the reporter and the editor as plain to see as the headline.

Criticism, even if it is qualified, by two representatives of Trump's main media supporter does not mean that Donald Trump has lost the support of Fox News. However, given that any criticism of the President is extremely rare from Fox News, the examples of Smith and Wallace may have an impact on others who seek to provide an impartial political commentary. If this extends to raising questions as to equitable treatment of all people, it could have an impact on the 2020 elections.

Notes

1 Marshall McLuhan (1964), *Understanding Media: The Extensions of Man.* New York: Mentor. Second edn, 1994, Cambridge, MA: MIT Press.
2 Naomi Klein, 'Now lets' fight back against the politics of fear', 10 June 2017. Available at https://www.theguardian.com/books/2017/jun/10/naomi-klein-now-fight-back-against-politics-fear-shock-doctrine-trump?CMP=share_btn_link.

3 Success: perception or reality?

There is a well-known axiom that 'perception is reality'. To an extent this is true. We respond to things as we perceive them – not necessarily as they are – and that is a key reason why so many arguments and conflicts arise. The question is, just whose perception actually is the reality? Police and other authorities have been known to comment that 'no-one lies like an eyewitness'. What they mean is that, depending on the vantage point from which something is seen, different opinions as to 'facts' can lead to totally different accounts of what actually occurred.

Where different people see the same situation from different personal perspectives, to what extent can we claim that our subjective view (even if unconsciously subjective), is objectively more accurate than that of others? To Donald Trump, it appears as though this is a redundant question. In his mind, his perception is always 'right' and as many who once worked for, or with him, have discovered, he brooks no denial. This approach also enables him to actively influence the perceptions of others.

There is no doubt that Donald Trump has mastered the art of communicating the messages he wants to send to the recipients he believes will be most responsive. His portrayal of any media he does not like as 'fake news' is a prime example of this.

In no way has this influence of others' perceptions been more prolonged and consistent than in his portrayal of himself as 'a winner'. Right now, this portrayal is of vital importance for his re-election. It has however, been suggested that Trump is already finished as president. One commentator Robert Reich, says:[1]

> When the public fires a president before election day, as it did Jimmy Carter, Nixon and Herbert Hoover, they don't send him a letter telling him he's fired. They just make him irrelevant. Politics happens around him, despite him. He's not literally gone but he might as well be. It has happened to Trump. The courts and House Democrats are moving against him. Senate Republicans are quietly subverting him. Even Mitch McConnell told him to end the shutdown. The Fed is running economic policy. Top-level civil servants are managing day-to-day work of the

agencies. Isolated in the White House, distrustful of aides, at odds with intelligence agencies, distant from his cabinet heads, Trump has no system to make or implement decisions. His tweets don't create headlines as before. His rallies are ignored. His lies have become old hat.

While much of what is said may be true, there is a very real sense in which this primarily appears to be wishful thinking.

First, in the case against Reich's proposition, is that, as history shows, losing the popular vote does not mean that one fails to become president. The important factor in presidential elections is the Electoral College votes – and there are instances where these have been different from how the majority of people in a particular state may have voted. So long as Trump's core constituency believe in him and his promises and, coupled with this, he maintains all or most of the States that propelled him to power in 2016, he will win.

Second, never ignore the power of symbolism. Donald J. Trump *is* President of the United States and, as such, he treads the world stage and is feted by national leaders no matter how much they may dislike him or disagree with his policies and/or behaviour. A case in point was the 2019 World Economic Forum in Davos, Switzerland. Trump may not have attended, but his economic pronouncements certainly impacted that congregation. It is further seen in Trump apparently being nominated by Japan for the Nobel Peace Prize for initiating dialogue with North Korea. It matters little whether such a nomination has actually occurred (confirmation of nominations is never made public – only the final determination). Nor does the reality of any results from the discussions with North Korea matter – or even the breakdown of the February 2019 summit in Vietnam. What does matter among both his supporters and some waverers is the perception of Trump as a major influence on the international stage. Additionally, Trump is now backed by a Republican party that reflects his own image, very significant funding, and a newly sophisticated political data operation. These things have great power. Whereas some regard him as an accidental president who was lucky to win the White House in 2016, his lieutenants are ensuring that, with all the advantages of incumbency, nothing will be left to chance in securing a second term.

This is also true for his interactions with China over trade sanctions and tariffs. He has taken a hard line. Initially he refuted the time-honoured concept of the Memorandum of Understanding (MoU) and the Chinese delegates agreed that they, too, wanted a signed agreement rather than an MoU. Then his actions of February 2019, implying sanctions against China might not come into effect early in March (or even later), was able to be portrayed as strength in negotiation rather than as response to pressure from a wide range of vested interests who saw sanctions and tariffs as being potentially detrimental to both the US and to their own wealth. His eventual decision to impose sanctions and then to present this as detrimental to China and beneficial to the US is believed by many, despite economic realities.

Donald Trump, the man who reinvented Presidential Communications, knows that so long as he can maintain the aura and mystique he has projected to date, probability of re-election remains strong. The same is true for Trump's declaration of an emergency in order to finance the wall between the US and Mexico. The United States Congress has voted to disallow the declaration (there were sufficient opponents to the declaration in both Houses), and Donald Trump has vetoed this vote. Now the saga will go on. The declaration may or may not ultimately be overturned by either politicians or the courts but, either way, Trump wins – if the declaration is finally approved then he gets his wall. If it is overturned, then it's not his fault – evil forces beyond his control must have intervened.

The third reason why Reich's comments may reflect wishful thinking is found in Trump's self-belief. While all who aspire to high office are strongly driven by ego, few, if any, exhibit this egocentricity to the extent that we see in Donald Trump. Whether or not Richard Nixon or Herbert Hoover ever experienced self-doubt will probably never be known, although Jimmy Carter and, perhaps, Barack Obama may well have the humility to confess, if asked. However, there is absolutely no indication from any source that self-doubt is, or ever has been, even a miniscule part of Donald Trump's persona. In times of uncertainty and disruption, people seek certainty. This is recognised by all autocrats and dictators. Create uncertainty and disruption then present yourself as the strong saviour: 'Only I can resolve this mess and give you what you want'. The reality of who started the uncertainty and disruption is lost and/or ignored. The strong, self-confident, ego-driven leader creates a self-fulfilling myth.

The issue of 'confirmation bias' is relevant here. Whenever a person has developed a view that something is the absolute fact, then this a priori opinion impacts everything they see, read, hear or otherwise are confronted about that issue. So it is that a person with an a priori view that a particular book such as the Bible, the Koran, the Book of Mormon, the Upanishads, etc., is (or at the very least 'contains') ultimate truth then they are predisposed to discount any message that contradicts that view, while accepting any message that reinforces that view. And this no matter the strength of the evidence available.

So it is with Donald Trump. For those who get their news reports unfiltered by fact checking or source validation, Trump's portrayal of mainstream media as 'fake news' is a far stronger factor of influence than any research, or even assertion, that the mainstream media may be correct, especially if it provides a contradictory message from that sent by Donald Trump. To the core Trump supporter, one is either 'for Trump' or 'against Trump'. There is no middle ground and no room for even the smallest element of doubt as to his authenticity and direction.

This creates difficulties for those who hope that the Donald J. Trump we see today is different from the Donald J. Trump that could emerge post the 2020 elections. Can you teach an old dog new tricks? Absolutely. The question is not one of possibility, but of probability. Given the resources available and the motivations involved, is it probable that change can and/or will be effected in the time available? Almost certainly the answer is 'no'.

Whatever the result, subsequent to the 2020 elections Donald Trump will have no motivation to change. If he is re-elected, then his approach will have been validated. If he loses, then change is irrelevant. He will still promote the myth of 'Donald J. Trump – Winner' because of his success in 2016 and, as he rides off into the sunset to continue the pursuit of wealth, he will blame all failures on his opponents. As already indicated, the concept of a self-fulfilling prophecy is important here.

A self-fulfilling prophecy occurs when results are commensurate with the expectations a person and/or their family, teachers, supporters and so on, hold in relation to that person. In education it often reflects the views teachers have about their students because these views impact, either consciously or unconsciously, with how the teacher relates to that student. In the workplace, the performance of individuals and work groups often tends to reflect the expectations of their manager or supervisor. In terms of personal success, one's self-image tends to impact on one's overall performance and life success.

Napoleon Hill came to fame in 1937 with his book *Think and Grow Rich*. His argument was that riches begin with a state of mind, with definiteness of purpose. Hill's message was later repeated by Norman Vincent Peale who, in his book *The Power of Positive Thinking* (1952) echoed Hill by arguing that our mental attitude strongly influences both what happens to us and our responses to these events. The emphasis is that your self-image dictates your future success. Donald Trump attended Peale's church in New York while growing up, as well as marrying his first wife, Ivana, there. The concept of self-fulfilling prophecies is well-ingrained in Trump's psyche and underlies much of his behaviour to date.

In the 1989 movie, *Dead Poet's Society*, there is a powerful scene in which the teacher, John Keating (as portrayed by Robin Williams), asks his students to stand on their desk and to look around them. His point is that looking at things from different vantage points provides a different perspective. This new perspective opens the possibility to new insights. It is highly unlikely that many of Trump's 'rusted-on' followers are willing to consider Trump from any vantage point other than that which they already have. This limits their opportunities for obtaining a different perspective. It also limits their potential for new insights.

As long as Donald Trump continues to exude the self-belief shown to date, only his perception will matter, and the probability of his re-election is high.

Note

1 Robert Reich, 'You're fired! America has already terminated Trump', 24 February 2019. Available at https://www.theguardian.com/commentisfree/2019/feb/24/youre-fired-america-has-already-terminated-trump?CMP=share_btn_link

4 Which brings us to Machiavelli

In *The Prince*, Machiavelli described immoral behaviour, such as dishonesty and the killing of innocents, as being entirely normal and highly effective in the sphere of politics. He even appeared to encourage it in some situations. He stated that 'it would be best to be both loved and feared. But since the two rarely come together, anyone compelled to choose will find greater security in being feared than in being loved.'[1] In much of Machiavelli's work, it seems that a ruler must adopt unsavoury policies for the sake of maintaining his regime. This has given rise to the term 'Machiavellian' to denote unscrupulous behaviour and 'an end justifies the means' approach in all areas of life.

Bob Woodward is one of the journalists who broke the Watergate story that eventually led to the resignation of President Nixon in 1974. The title of Woodward's book, *Fear: Trump in the White House* (2018), comes from a remark that Trump made to Woodward and another reporter in 2016 'Real power is through respect. Real power is, I don't even want to use the word, fear.'[2] Trump uses his power in order to create fear in others so that he obtains a negotiating advantage. It gives him a winning edge. It is the embodiment of Machiavelli's axiom.

Some years ago, David McClelland, a Harvard Professor, identified three motivators that he believed we all have: a need for achievement (or 'inhibition'), a need for affiliation, and a need for power.[3] All three drives exist in everyone, but each person will have different characteristics depending on their dominant motivator.

People who have a need for affiliation prefer to spend time creating and maintaining social relationships, enjoy being part of groups, and have a desire to feel loved and accepted. People in this group tend to adhere to the norms of the culture in that workplace and typically do not change or even challenge the norms of the workplace for fear of rejection. This person favours collaboration over competition and does not like situations with high risk or high uncertainty.

People who have a need for achievement prefer working on tasks of moderate difficulty, prefer work in which the results are based on their effort rather than on anything else, and prefer to receive feedback on their work. Achievement-based individuals tend to avoid both high-risk and low-risk situations. Low-risk situations are seen as too easy to be valid and the high-risk situations are seen as based more on the luck of the situation rather than the achievements of the individual. These people tend to achieve results because of the trust, respect, and rapport they have with those among whom they work. They are able to inhibit negative drives and exhibit high self-control in order to focus on what is to be achieved (hence the alternate term of 'inhibition'). For these people, positions in a hierarchy, titles, and the trappings of power are of secondary importance. People with this approach seem more likely to be able to adapt to changes in organisational structure and to concentrate more on enabling people to perform than on controlling people. It is not however, that they eschew positional power. When required, they are ready and able to wield it. Rather, the difference is that this is an ultimate fall-back position instead of being the normal mode of operating. Their authority tends to come not from the organisation or job per se. Instead, it comes from within because of their expertise, their communicative ability and the overall trust they both engender and demonstrate.

The need for power is the desire within a person to hold control and authority over another person and to influence and change another's decision in accordance with his or her own needs or desires. In McClelland's view, the need to enhance self-esteem and reputation drives these people and they desire to have their views and ideas accepted and implemented over the views and ideas over others. People who have a need for power enjoy work and place a high value on discipline. While the positive side of the need for power is that these people can be very good organisers, who will refocus and restructure an organisation, the downside to this motivational type, is that group goals may become zero-sum in nature. For one person to win, another must lose. Those who are motivated by power enjoy competition and winning arguments. They aspire to status and recognition but they do not like to lose. They are self-disciplined and demand that same characteristic from peers and teams. The need for power is accompanied by a drive for personal prestige. Being driven by a need for power is a hallmark of egocentricity which may indicate a lack of emotional growth. It is quite different from the person driven by a need for achievement, who recognises that the apparatus of power must not be abused.

In relation to power, it must be recognised that there are two key types: personal power and positional power and, in each of these, it can be exercised in either an adversarial or collaborative fashion. Personal power depends on the trust, respect and rapport that an individual has established among those being influenced, while positional power is based on one's position in the hierarchy – the more senior one is in the hierarchy, the more positional power one tends to have. Both these forms of power can be (and often are), abused.

McClelland recognised that the balance between the three power bases can vary with life circumstances and also discussed the possibility that, overall, an equitable balance between all three could be attained in a well-rounded personality.

Such a balance does not seem obvious in the character of President Trump. McClelland argues that in organisations there is a need for power, but not necessarily a desire for it, except where it enables an individual to exercise leadership and vision. This is different from Trump's desire for power. It would appear that Trump is motivated primarily by power for its own sake to the extent that relationships are encouraged only if they recognise and heed his power and authority.

The role of US President requires power but Trump desires it in order to satisfy his ego; whether his supremacy can be then directed to work for the benefit of the country as a whole is somewhat questionable. McClelland and Burnham (2008),[4] argue that effective and positive use of power motivation requires a person to have high self-control or 'inhibition' (closely related to 'achievement') so that responses are not primarily reactive to emotional stimuli. The point is made that:

> … In our earlier study, we found ample evidence that [persons lacking in self-control] exercise their power impulsively. They are more often rude to other people, they drink too much, they try to exploit others sexually, and they collect symbols of personal prestige such as fancy cars or big offices.

They make the point that the very best power motivated managers are mature. While, as a teetotaller, Donald Trump clearly does not 'drink too much', it may still be possible that President Trump lacks maturity.

In *The Prince*, Machiavelli treads a fine line between the need and desire for power. In order to be effective, he says, a leader needs the power to take whatever action is necessary to achieve goals. What he does not address, is the stage at which the desire for power is stronger than the need for power. Does a person seek leadership roles because of a desire for power or does a desire for power emerge and/or strengthen once a leader has seen what can be achieved by the exercise of that power?

The U.S. Constitution recognised this conundrum and, as a result, instituted checks and balances to try and ensure that no one person (or small group of people), could accumulate so much power that they were above the law. This is one reason why the Executive Branch of US politics is separate from the Administrative Branch.

Despite this separation of powers (or, perhaps, because of it), one of the characteristics of both major US political parties is that they seek to influence appointments to the Supreme Court – the highest court of the federal judiciary of the United States. With the advice and consent of the United States Senate, the President of the United States appoints the members of the Supreme Court. Because nominations to the Court are the prerogative of the President, it follows that when the Senate is controlled by the President's political party, the President has the opportunity to try and ensure that the make-up of the Court is sympathetic to his views. Invariably, at least in recent years, the dominant political party has ensured that judges with similar views to their own are appointed when vacancies occur. Once appointed, justices have lifetime tenure unless they resign, retire, or are removed from office. This means that an existing president's real influence can actually extend long after a new president has been elected. This has the potential to reduce the impact of the protections set out in the Constitution. Machiavelli would highly approve. Donald Trump is no exception to his predecessors in utilising this loophole.

Towards the end of President Obama's presidency, a vacancy arose on the Supreme Court with the death, in February 2016, of Associate Justice Antonin Scalia. The Republican-controlled Senate delayed the appointment of a new justice until after the election. After taking office, Donald Trump nominated Neil Gorsuch to succeed Scalia, and Gorsuch was confirmed in April 2017. In June 2018, Associate Justice Anthony Kennedy announced his retirement, creating a second vacancy on the Supreme Court. In early July 2018, Trump nominated Brett Kavanaugh as his replacement, Kavanaugh was confirmed on 6 October 2018. The dominant political allegiance of the Supreme Court is now orientated towards the Republican Party.

The appointment of Kavanaugh was controversial because of an allegation of sexual assault against him. The accusation delayed the scheduled 20 September vote. Following the accusation, Kavanaugh indicated he would not withdraw, even though initial allegations were followed by a further accusation of sexual assault by a one-time classmate of Kavanaugh at Yale, and a further allegation that dated back to high school days. These were investigated at a short enquiry. Subsequent to this enquiry the Judiciary Committee voted to approve Kavanaugh and he was sworn in.

This restructuring of the Supreme Court increases the probability that, no matter who is elected President in 2020, the Supreme Court will probably overrule decades of progressive precedents. This could be particularly problematic in the event of a Democratic president as there is the possibility that the majority of Justices could be philosophically aligned to a non-progressive agenda.

Donald Trump has history in attempts to influence the courts. He has displayed a clear pattern of attacking judges and courts for rulings with which he disagrees. This pattern began during his presidential campaign and has continued into his presidency. Consider these examples:

- Between February 2017 and May 2017, various courts around the US stopped the enforcement of Donald Trump's 27 January executive order limiting immigration from seven predominantly Muslim countries and halting the admission of refugees from elsewhere. Trump responded by making a series of tweets and public statements attacking the ruling judges personally, questioning the authority of federal courts in reviewing his orders, suggesting that the court was biased, and that the judges and the court system would be responsible for future terrorist attacks.
- In January 2018, District Court Judge William Alsup temporarily blocked the Trump administration from ending the Deferred Action for

Childhood Arrivals (DACA) program, maintaining protections for 'Dreamers', US-born children of illegal immigrants. Trump then claimed that this decision showed that the US Court system was broken and unfair.

- Following the issuing of new rules that would limit the ability of people entering the US to then seek asylum, in November 2018, Judge Jon Tigar of the U.S. Court of Appeals for the Ninth Circuit ordered the administration to accept asylum claims regardless of where migrants entered the country. This was labelled 'a disgrace' by President Trump who went on to imply that the Ninth Circuit was biased.

Of course, when considering the likely long-term impact of Trump's Supreme Court appointments, it must be noted that any attempts to influence judicial decisions does not mean that Justices toe party lines when making decisions. Many past presidents can attest to this. Accordingly, no-one should believe that the Justices will necessarily side with Trump should any appeals about his activities reach the Supreme Court or in relation to the consideration of future progressive legislation. History indicates that, in the main, Justices of the Supreme Court make their decisions according to law rather than to political allegiance. That is a key reason why they are in the administrative rather than the executive branch of government. Members of the Supreme Court have often shown that they are as aware of Machiavelli as any president!

However, there are also some disquieting (from Trump's perspective), elements happening among Trump's most vocal political supporters – the Republicans in Congress and the Senate. On 11 December 2019 legislation to stop Donald Trump from withdrawing the US from the North Atlantic Treaty Organization (NATO) was approved for a Senate vote – a chamber dominated by the Republican Party. The Senate foreign relations committee voted unanimously for the bipartisan bill which will now await a slot to go to the Senate. It was stated that this was a response to fears that the Trump administration is actively considering withdrawal from NATO. This was quickly followed by the US Senate voting unanimously to recognise the genocide of Armenians by the Ottoman empire. The Senate resolution formally acknowledges the mass killing of an estimated 1.5 million Armenians between 1915 and 1922 as an act of genocide. This resolution was in defiance of both Donald Trump and the Turkish president, Recep Tayyip Erdoğan.

It is possible that Donald Trump does not really command the fear and/or respect he thinks he does.

Notes

1 Niccolò Machiavelli (1532), *The Prince*. Trans and ed. Tim Parks (2014). London: Penguin.

2 Bob Woodward (2018), *Fear: Trump in the White House.* New York: Simon & Schuster.
3 David C. McClelland (1961), *The Achieving Society.* New York: Van Nostrand Company Inc.
4 David C. McClelland and David H. Burnham (2008), *Power is the Great Motivator.* Boston: Harvard Business School Publishing. First published in *Harvard Business Review*, 1976.

5 The US and the world in 2019

At the end of 2019, the world is a far less safe and secure place than it was only four years ago. While it is certainly not true that the actions of Donald J. Trump have created this negative change, it is certainly true that he has made a major contribution to it.

Consider some of the changes that have occurred internationally since Trump became president.

When Barack Obama completed his final term as President, the threat posed by Iran, in the development of nuclear weapons, was under control. An international agreement was in place under which, in return for destruction of enrichment tools and the right of United Nations personnel to monitor activities in Iran, the path was open for reduction of international sanctions and for resumption of partial trade with Iran. Today, Iran has returned to uranium enrichment beyond what had previously been agreed and there has been hostile action in the Strait of Hormuz, including the seizure of a British oil tanker in retaliation for Britain's seizure of an Iranian vessel suspected of breaking EU sanctions.[1] The single, most significant contributor to this increase in tension has been Donald Trump's unilateral decision to abrogate the international agreement, despite all evidence from the intelligence agencies of both the UN and the US that showed Iran was totally compliant with the agreement.

At the end of Obama's presidency, the nuclear non-proliferation agreement was still in force prohibiting the development and testing of new nuclear weapons. This had been in place since 1968 and, although largely ignored by countries that included Israel, Pakistan, India and North Korea and partially ignored by Russia, it had been a key factor in reducing the threat of a nuclear holocaust. Today, we have active testing of weapons by North Korea (and probably by Russia), and President Trump has announced that the US is withdrawing from the Treaty. The door is ajar for a renewed nuclear arms race between both major and minor powers. Before Trump became President, international trade was continuing to benefit both developed and developing countries through the use of multinational supply chains in which goods manufactured worldwide were, at least in part, dependent upon components supplied by other countries. Boeing, for example, might assemble the final aircraft, but it used components from myriad other countries and, in turn, sold its completed aircraft back to those countries. Stock markets across the world had tended to rise consistently because of generally buoyant economic conditions and consumers everywhere had found that the price of goods meant that replacement was preferable to repair for old and broken items. Today, trade agreements between the US and Mexico, Canada, most Pacific Nations, and the EU are either in trouble, or are facing renegotiation that will almost certainly be biased in favour of the US. Most worrying, at the present time we are in the middle of a Trump-initiated trade war between the US and China with economists around the world warning that the potential for global recession (and possible depression) is increasingly likely. The core dispute may be between the US and China, but the collateral damage will be experienced globally.

At the start of 2017, international terrorism seemed to be potentially in decline and extremist views tended to be marginalised. Donald Trump has however, provided the oxygen to fuel extremism. Although he has not directly advocated extremist views and actions, his failure to condemn them has encouraged their growth and promulgation. He has deliberately conflated Islam with terrorism and refugees with invaders while allowing despotic leaders and governments to be recognised and, all too often, rewarded. North Korea is a prime example, with the various well-publicised meetings between Kim Jong-Un and Trump, including the President's symbolic crossing of the military demarcation line into North Korea to shake hands with the North Korean president. Trump is reported as saying about the history-making event: 'Stepping across that line was a great honor'. It certainly did nothing to lessen Kim Jong-Un's international reputation.

Of course, Barack Obama did not create the situation inherited by Donald Trump. An argument can be made that, in many ways, Obama was a 'NATO' president – in other words, in terms of global politics, he was a 'No Action Talk Only' president. Many commentators make the point that Obama inherited a global system that was largely working well, and he simply ensured that it continued that way (although he is probably better known for authorising the operation to raid Osama Bin Laden's compound and either capture or kill him),[2] Obama's major geopolitical contribution was brokering the agreement with Iran. This, as is well known, garnered him the Nobel Peace Prize – something to which, at least at this stage, Trump may aspire but probably has little likelihood of achieving. In late 2019, the perception of the US as a reliable friend and ally took another blow with Trump's decision regarding Turkey, Syria and the Kurds.

Early in October 2019, the White House announced the US would withdraw troops from northern Syria. This was an abrupt foreign policy change that effectively abandoned the Kurds who had been key military partners with the US in the fight against ISIS. The statement read that, after a telephone conversation between Donald Trump and the Turkish president, Recep Tayyip Erdoğan, Turkey would advance into the territory and take custody of captured ISIS fighters. It was made very clear that US troops would no longer provide a buffer between Turkish forces and the Kurds, despite the fact that Turkey had long considered the Kurdish forces to be a serious security threat. It appeared that this was a unilateral decision by Trump without consultation with, or knowledge of, US diplomats dealing with Syria, or the UK and France, the main international partners of the US. Trump also stated, 'I was elected on getting out of these ridiculous endless wars, where our great military functions as a policing operation to the benefit of people who don't even like the USA.'

Within the US this decision was met with dismay across the political divide. The Kurdish forces bore the brunt of the US-led campaign against Islamic State militants, and Republicans and Democrats warned that allowing a Turkish attack would send a troubling message to American allies across the globe. Republican Senator Lindsey Graham, one of Trump's most loyal allies in Congress, said: 'This decision to abandon our Kurdish allies and turn Syria over to Russia, Iran, and Turkey will put every radical Islamist on steroids. Shot in the arm to the bad guys. Devastating for the good guys.' Following the outcry, Trump twittered: 'If Turkey does anything that I, in my great and unmatched wisdom, consider to be off limits, I will totally destroy and obliterate the economy of Turkey'. The response from Turkey was equally blunt. Turkey's Foreign Minister, Mevlüt Çavuşoğlu, hit back at the threat to economically devastate the country if it followed through on a planned operation against Kurdish forces in northern Syria, saying that Ankara would not be intimidated by its NATO ally.[3]

Around the world, the fallout from this has been highly vocal. Trump's decision to abandon the Syrian Kurds is being seen by allies as a compelling piece of evidence to prove that they should not vest any faith in Donald Trump. The Kurds had been reliable partners with the US in the fight against ISIS with the loss of over 11,000 Kurdish-led Syrian Democratic Forces. They had provided unquestioning support to the US and its allies. Removing the US military presence at some point might actually be the right call, but doing it in a manner that left a void to be filled by Russia and its allies did not advance any cause for the US. The reaction was also strong in Israel – America's closest partner in the Middle East. A headline in *Yedioth Ahronoth*, Israel's largest daily newspaper, described it as, 'A knife in our back'. Before going on to say, 'The conclusion we draw needs to be unequivocal: Trump has become unreliable for Israel. He can no longer be trusted'.[4]

Trump then moved to ensure that at least some US troops remained in Syria. However, it quickly became clear that their purpose was not to assist Turkey or any other country in the fight against ISIS. When U.S. Secretary of Defence Mark Esper announced that their mission was the enduring defeat of ISIS, adding that about 500 to 600 troops would remain in place, Donald Trump was very quick to disagree. Almost immediately, he repeated his assertion that the US should take possession of the oil in the region and went on to say: 'We are keeping the oil. We have the oil. The oil is secure. We left troops behind only for the oil.' Support of long-term loyal allies was unimportant. Only the oil mattered!

In regard to the internal situation of the US, consider the following:

Racism and prejudice

In July 2019, President Trump denigrated four Democratic congresswomen of colour by 'saying that they hated America and that one of the first two Muslim women elected to Congress sympathised with Al Qaeda'.[5] He later put pressure on Benjamin Netanyahu, Prime Minister of Israel, to ban two women, Ilhan Omar and Rashida Tlaib, from visiting Israel on a fact-finding tour of conditions in the West Bank. Donald Trump has previously condemned black athletes kneeling during the national anthem, lobbed at developing countries, and defended protesters participating in a white supremacist march.

Racism seems to be rearing its ugly head again. As in many other first-world countries, prisons in the US are disproportionally populated by people of colour. In August 2019, the widely disseminated photograph of two white police officers on horseback leading a black prisoner on foot, and tethered by a rope brought back images of slavery that most believed were long gone. Also, in August 2019, the comments by Jean Cramer, a city council candidate in Marysville, St. Clair County, Michigan that she wanted to keep her community white 'as much as possible' would have been totally unimaginable only a few years ago. But it is not only black people who are targets of racism. Trump's denigration of people from Latin America and his comments about 'invasion' by refugees and potential migrants has enabled once quiescent voices to become increasingly vocal. Racist attacks and racist comments are increasing and, far too often, are defended by conservative commentators under the guise of being 'freedom of speech' – a strategy for diverting attention away from the content of what is said.

This racist picture was seen in a domestic attack in El Paso, Texas on 5 August 2019. The suspect, who came from Dallas, 600 miles away, said the mass shooting was a 'response to the Hispanic invasion of Texas'.[6] Only a few days earlier, it appears that the Governor of Texas, Greg Abbott, had sent a fundraising letter to Republicans in which he complained about the number of illegal immigrants coming into Texas and went on to say 'If we're going to defend Texas, we'll need to take matters into our own hands'. The gunman's manifesto included the statement: 'Hispanics will take control of the local and state government of my beloved Texas, changing policy to better suit their needs'. It added that politicians of both parties are to blame for the United States 'rotting from the inside out,' and that 'the heavy Hispanic population in Texas will make us a Democrat stronghold.'[7] He killed 20 people and injured a further 26, yet all 46 people were simply doing normal everyday shopping at their local mall.

Following this attack, a wide range of media reported that law enforcement officials across the country said that they had thwarted similar white supremacist attacks and mass shootings from potential gunmen who espoused far right and racist viewpoints. Residents of El Paso are reported to have blamed Trump's escalating attacks on immigrants and racist campaign speeches for creating a climate that encouraged this kind of violence. They make the point that, prior to this tragedy, El Paso was rated as one of the safest cities in the US.

Human rights

In its World Report 2019, Human Rights Watch stated:

> The United States continued to move backward on human rights at home and abroad in the second year of President Donald Trump's administration. With Trump's Republican party controlling the legislative branch in 2018, his administration and Congress were able to pass laws, implement regulations, and carry out policies that violate or undermine human rights.

It went on to say:

> The Trump administration also continued to support abusive governments abroad militarily, financially, and diplomatically. Though it has expressed support for some international initiatives aimed at sanctioning individuals and governments committing human rights abuses, overall administration policy undermined multilateral institutions and international judicial bodies seeking to hold people accountable for egregious human rights violations.

In July 2019, the Trump administration announced that they would establish a 'Commission on Unalienable Rights' to examine the meaning of human rights. Secretary of State, Mike Pompeo said this would determine 'which rights are entitled to gain respect.'

For a great many years, the world has become used to people such as Russia's Vladimir Putin and China's Xi Jinping decrying human rights groups as insidious initiatives and a means to implement a liberal democratic agenda. Their denigration of human rights is an attempt to deflect attention from their own gross human rights abuses. The clear message from the Secretary of State is that only certain rights will continue to be considered important by the Trump administration. There seem to be strange (and worrying) echoes here of what we now hear from Russia, Saudi Arabia, North Korea, and China.

The environment

In February 2019, *National Geographic* magazine listed 15 ways in which the Trump administration has changed environmental policies. Their list is as follows:

1 U.S. pulls out of Paris Climate Agreement
2 Trump EPA poised to scrap clean power plan
3 EPA loosens regulations on toxic air pollution
4 Rescinding methane-flaring rules
5 Trump announces plan to weaken Obama-era fuel economy rules

6 Trump revokes flood standards accounting for sea-level rise
7 Waters of the U.S. Rule revocation
8 NOAA green lights seismic airgun blasts for oil and gas drilling
9 Interior Department relaxes sage grouse protection
10 Trump officials propose changes to handling the Endangered Species Act
11 Migratory Bird Treaty Act reinterpretation
12 Trump unveils plan to dramatically downsize two national monuments
13 Executive order calls for sharp logging increase on public lands
14 Trump drops climate change from list of national security threats
15 EPA criminal enforcement hits 30-year low[8]

National Geographic state they have been tracking the decisions that will impact America's land, water, air, and wildlife. They argue that what started with curtailing information when the president took office in 2017 has evolved into actions like executive orders that open public land for business. The article goes on to demonstrate that States, municipalities, and NGOs have been forced to respond to these changes by filing lawsuits to block the administration's breakdown of environmental protection but that only some of these blocking initiatives have been successful.

The 2019, G7 Summit took place in Biarritz, France, while in Brazil, devastating forest fires were destroying the Amazon rainforests; there was some evidence supporting the claim that this was a co-ordinated effort by Brazilian farmers and business interests to further their own financial objectives. Well before the outbreak of these fires, The French President, Emmanuel Macron, had placed the climate emergency and protection of biodiversity at the heart of the summit – something that led senior Trump aides to comment that Macron was seeking to embarrass his US counterpart by making the summit focus on 'niche issues' such as climate change or gender equality. It was noteworthy that, when the issues of forest fires came up for discussion, Trump was not present, and he expressed little concern to explain his absence.

The poor and disadvantaged

When high levels of inequality are discussed, a common response is that the 'politics of envy' are being deployed. However an enormous amount of research shows how harmful inequality is for people. A range of studies show that high levels of inequality damage our health and well-being, harm social cohesion and levels of trust, and act as a brake on economic performance.[9]

Countries with high levels of inequality are more stressed and anxious, less happy and healthy, and have lower feelings of solidarity or trust across society. Research indicates that in societies with high levels of inequality there is an ever-increasing cachet to being rich and it becomes more shameful to be poor. This heightens anxiety over social status. When this happens, money – and what one does with it – becomes increasingly important to social status.

As a result, inequality brings out the worst aspects of consumerism and leads to feelings of entitlement for those at the top and shame for those at the bottom. It reduces social mixing, trust and social cohesion. In 2015, Christine Lagarde, then heading the International Monetary Fund, said: 'Reducing excessive inequality … is not just morally and politically correct, but it is good economics.'[10]

It has been argued that the (re)emergence of a 'patrimonial' society in which wealth, particularly inherited wealth, is the crucial determinant of life chances.[11] Although this study was done in Australia, its message is not geographically specific. It is considered that studies in other countries would reveal very similar data. Thomas Piketty[12] looked at growing inequality in incomes in the US, Britain and France, with particular emphasis on the share going to the top one per cent. The point was made that society's real division is increasingly not between the old and the young, but between those who own and control capital and those who rely on wages. Because labour's share of income is declining, accumulating wealth by saving from personal income becomes less and less feasible. Data from the US show average household wealth has grown strongly, nearly doubling in the last 30 years. But median wealth (that of a household in the middle of the income distribution), is lower than it was in the 1980s, and barely changed from the 1960s. All of the gains have gone to households in the top 20 per cent of the income distribution, and the vast majority has gone to those in the top one per cent.[13]

While it may be true that 'the best form of welfare is a job', it is equally true that the job needs to provide the worker with sufficient income to flourish, rather than to simply survive. There are sound economic reasons why this is so.

First, a 'consumer society' can only exist when potential consumers have adequate resources to be able to purchase what is available at a price that provides a fair return to all vested interests. The law of supply and demand makes it clear that if there is over-supply because of insufficient demand, prices drop and, eventually, the producer loses revenue, profit, and in the worst-case scenario, the business itself. This is a situation where, in the long term, there are no winners. We know that those at the lower end of the socio-economic spectrum tend to spend all their income, while those closer to the upper end of the same spectrum tend to save a proportion of it. To a large extent, a consumer society depends on the spending of those who save little.

Second, those at the lower end of the socio-economic spectrum tend not to have health insurance and when medical issues arise, treatment is either not sought (and the situation exacerbated) or, if treatment is sought, the cost must be met by public health funding. Pickett and Wilkinson (2011), make it clear that those at the lower end of the socio-economic spectrum therefore, tend to be the main users of public health services.[14] Public health funding must be provided by government sources, which means either that the quality of healthcare falls, in order to operate within existing financial constraints, or that taxes of one or another source must be levied from the more affluent (even if they are only 'more affluent' because their income has moved them into a higher tax bracket), in order to maintain services at an acceptable standard. Ensuring that people have adequate economic sources is an effective (and far less expensive) way of providing 'a fence at the top of the cliff rather than an ambulance at the bottom'.

Third, while privatising probation and prison services has provided businesses with increased opportunities to make profits, 'law and order' themes with their high rates of imprisonment must be paid from somewhere. Clearly, those who are imprisoned are not able to pay for that incarceration so, again, taxes must be levied from the more affluent. In addition, those who are incarcerated are not earning money (even if they would like to), and therefore not contributing to the nation's Gross Domestic Product (GDP). While this is not of concern in relation to those who have committed serious criminal offences, for those whose offence is the inability to pay a fine, or some other relatively minor misdemeanour, this can be a major social concern with serious economic implications.

There is no evidence that Trump's attempts to wind back the Obama health initiatives or that the much-lauded tax cuts promoted by Trump have done anything to alleviate problems such as these.

Political lobbying

David Koch died on 23 August 2019, aged 79. As discussed in Long (2018),[15] David Koch, along with his brother Charles, controlled Koch Industries and, for more than 30 years, they used a significant proportion of their vast wealth (currently in excess of $US 50 billion) to transform politics in the US by supporting free market and libertarian ideals epitomised by the neoliberal approach to economics and management. They became known as the face of the right-wing, super-donor class in the modern era. They sponsored twice-yearly gatherings of top conservative figures in order to shift the Republican party further to the right, through the attendance of senior figures in the party, major donors and even US Supreme Court justices. This enabled them to push many of the policies that have become pillars of today's American conservatism, including promotion of the early Tea Party in 2010, opposing Barack Obama's expanded healthcare provision, Obamacare, and waging a sustained attack on government regulation, including attempts to combat the climate crisis. Central to their operation is a lobby group, initially largely funded by Charles and David Koch, known as 'Americans for Prosperity'. Since 2004, this lobby group has expanded into every state across the US.

Of course, Americans for Prosperity (AFP) are only one among many lobbyists. There are over 20,000 lobbying organisations with about 600 having a permanent presence in Washington to directly contact their targets. Best known among these include National Rifle Association, Sierra Club, Blue Cross and Blue Shields. Since a decision by the Supreme Court in 2010, permission for lobbying has been extended to election campaigns up to 60 days before the election and it has been decided that lobbying can be done not only by individuals but, as an element of 'free speech' it can also be done by corporations per se.

In the US, as in almost all countries, lobbying tends to be closely linked to financing. Politicians and political parties need funds. Supplying those funds in large enough quantities buys influence. The main objective of a lobbyist is to influence decision-making, whether at an executive, legislative, federal or state level. Their influence can also be applied to hinder or block the decision-making process. Therefore, influence is created on the long term by forming strong contacts with politicians and is often accompanied by financial benefit relating to electoral campaigns. Clearly this means that the influence of a lobbying organisation is not proportional to its size, but rather to its financial resources. For instance, the National Rifle Association (NRA) is extremely active and influential, despite the call by people of all political persuasions and socio-economic levels for increased restrictions on the purchase of, especially, military grade firearms – a reaction across the US to the rise of mass shootings and domestic terrorism.

When he stood for president in 2008, Barack Obama stated his intention to contend with the influence of lobbying but, following his election, he not only failed to do this, but even maintained links with some lobbying groups. On several occasions, in response to mass shootings, Donald Trump has implied that some additional restrictions should be placed around the purchase of firearms but, invariably, after lobbying from bodies such as the NRA, he has always backed down.

In September 2019, the influence of the NRA was again highlighted when the San Francisco Board of Supervisors passed an official resolution that declares the National Rifle Association (NRA) a 'domestic terrorist organisation'. Their declaration stated:

> The National Rifle Association musters its considerable wealth and organisational strength to promote gun ownership and incite gun owners to acts of violence. ... The National Rifle Association spreads propaganda that misinforms and aims to deceive the public about the dangers of gun violence. ... The leadership of the National Rifle Association promotes extremist positions, in defiance of the views of a majority of its membership and the public and undermines the general welfare. ... The NRA exists to spread pro-gun propaganda and put weapons in the hands of those who would harm and terrorise us. ... Nobody has done more to fan the flames of gun violence than the NRA. ... Every country on earth has video games, movies and mental health issues, and yet only the US has gun violence at elementary schools, at the movies, at Walmart.

Understandably the NRA responded. 'NRA is the fabric of American society. We are teachers, doctors, cops and everyone who fights for America's freedoms. ... San Fran should be ashamed.' Later it was announced that the NRA was taking legal action in regard to this declaration. Lobbying is very big business in the USA (and most other countries)!

Notes

1 'Stena Impero: Seized British tanker leaves Iran's waters', 27 September 2019. Available at https://www.bbc.com/news/world-middle-east-49849718.
2 'Death of Osama bin Laden Fast Facts', *CNN Library*, Updated 18 April 2019. Available at https://edition.cnn.com/2013/09/09/world/death-of-osama-bin-laden-fast-facts/index.html.
3 Robin Wright, 'Turkey, Syria, the Kurds and Trump's Abandonment of Foreign Policy', 20 October 2019. Available at https://www.newyorker.com/magazine/2019/10/28/turkey-syria-the-kurds-and-trumps-abandonment-of-foreign-policy.
4 'Israelis watch Trump abandon Kurds and worry: who's next?', 10 October 2019. Available at https://jmedia.online/2019/10/10/israelis-watch-trump-abandon-kurds-and-worry-whos-next/.
5 Julie Hirschfield Davis, 'After Trump Accuses Four Democratic Congresswomen of Hating U.S., They Fire Back', 15 July 2019. Available at https://www.nytimes.com/2019/07/15/us/politics/trump-go-back-tweet-racism.html.
6 Alexandra Hutzler 'GOP sent fundraising letter asking supporters "to defend" Texas', 23 August 2019. Available at https://www.newsweek.com/texas-governor-asked-supporters-defend-state-illegal-immigration-1455874.
7 'Walmart Shooter Manifesto', 3 August 2019. See https://drudgereport.com/flashtx.htm.
8 See Sarah Gibbens, '15 Ways the Trump administration has changed environmental policies', 1 February 2019. Available at https://www.nationalgeographic.com/environment/2019/02/15-ways-trump-administration-impacted-environment/
9 See, for example, Kate Pickett and Richard Wilkinson (2011), *The Spirit Level: Why More Equal Societies Almost Always Do Better*. Harmondsworth: Penguin Books.
10 Christine Lagarde, 'Lifting the Small Boats', 17 June 2015. Available at https://www.imf.org/external/np/speeches/2015/061715.htm?hootPostID=f097bb9b76ffcc5c19c18ac65ac504bf.
11 Danielle Wood and Kate Griffiths, 'Generation gap: ensuring a fair go for younger Australians', 18 August 2019. Available at https://grattan.edu.au/report/generation-gap/.
12 Thomas Piketty (2017), *Capital in the Twenty-First Century*. Cambridge, MA: The Belknap Press of Harvard University Press.
13 Edward N. Wolf, 'Household wealth trends in the United States, 1962–2016. Has middle class wealth recovered?', *NBER Working Paper, No. 24085*, November 2017. Available at https://www.nber.org/papers/w24085.
14 Pickett and Wilkinson, *The Spirit Level*.
15 Douglas G. Long (2018), *Donald John Trump: Villain or Hero?*, London: Austin Macauley Publishers Ltd.

6   What could impact on re-election?

Impeachment

On 18 December 2019, Donald J. Trump became the third President of the United States of America to be impeached. There were two charges:

- The first article, which charged the President with abusing his power as President by asking a foreign power, Ukraine, to investigate his political rival, passed 230 votes to 197.
- The second article, which charged the President with obstructing Congress by stonewalling witnesses from participating in the impeachment inquiry, passed 229 votes to 198.

In 2020, attention moved from Congress to the Senate as Mr Trump faced a trial on these two charges. The Senate refused to call any witnesses and, as expected, the President was acquitted of both charges. On 5 February 2020 the US Senate voted *not guilty* by a margin of 52-48 on the first article of impeachment. It voted *not guilty* by a margin of 53-47 on the second article of impeachment.

Almost from the start of his presidency, there have been those who have sought to have Donald Trump removed from office. They argue that, for a variety of reasons, he is an inappropriate person to be hold the high office of President of the United States. Beneath the surface, the issue of impeachment has been like a quiescent volcano that could erupt at any time. Advocates of impeachment have referred to a range of possible reasons, including claims of unethical behaviour (the use of his own facilities, like hotels and golf clubs, for official business), and other such actions.

At the end of 2019, polls showed that, although previously a majority of Americans did not support impeaching the President, the situation has changed. A Washington Post–Schar School poll released on 8 October found nearly half of those polled approved of the inquiry into impeachment and wanted Trump removed from office, while six per cent approved of the proceedings but did not want him removed and 38 per cent totally disagreed with the proceedings.[1] A Quinnipiac University poll, also released on 8

October, found slightly lower support for impeachment than the *Washington Post* – 45 per cent of those polled said the President should be impeached and removed from office, 49 per cent said he should not. Quinnipiac's poll was among registered voters, rather than all adults, but this poll specifically referenced Trump's removal from office. More (53 per cent) approved of the House's formal impeachment inquiry, according to the same poll. A third poll, by NBC and *Wall Street Journal*, was released on the same day found even less support for impeachment and the removal of Trump – 43 per cent of those polled said they were in favour and 49 per cent said they were against both impeachment and removal. While Trump condemned these polls as 'fake news', on 3 November 2019, even Fox News stated that the top three Democrat contenders ranked higher than Donald Trump in the preferred President stakes. On the eve of the impeachment vote in Congress, the average of polls by polling website FiveThirtyEight showed an almost even split in public opinion, with 47.4 per cent of Americans in favour of impeachment and 46.6 per cent opposed.

The possibility of impeachable activity by President Trump had begun to be seriously investigated early in 2019. However, it was an event of late September 2019 that brought the issue of impeachment to the fore. Information had come to light about a telephone conversation between Donald Trump and the president of Ukraine, Volodymyr Zelensky, in which President Trump appears to have asked Zelensky to investigate the activities of Hunter Biden, son of Democratic presidential aspirant Joe Biden, for possible corrupt activities. Hunter Biden had been named a paid board member of Burisma Holdings in April 2014. The founder of Burisma Holdings was a political ally of Viktor Yanukovych, who was then Ukraine's Russia-friendly president. Although stories about Trump's conversation had been available for several weeks, it was not until 25 September that a summary of the telephone discussion was released by the White House. This document appeared to imply that Donald Trump was enlisting the help of a foreign power to assist him in his re-election campaign.

In March 2019, the House Judiciary Committee announced that they had initiated a probe into possible obstruction of justice, corruption and abuse of power by the President. It was stated that the panel had sent document requests to 81 people linked to the president and his associates. Subsequent months saw much of the information obtained published in the media. When the information about Ukraine became available in September 2019, this was grist to the mill.

Televised public hearings on impeachment commenced in November 2019. The investigative committee was clearly divided on partisan lines with the Republicans attempting to refute or cloud evidence by attacking the character of the witnesses and/or the quality of their information. This approach was seriously damaged when evidence was given by people who were direct witnesses or who were actually involved in discussions with both the president and with Ukrainian authorities. One in particular, Gordon Sondland, U.S.

Ambassador to the European Union, was a major Trump supporter who had donated $1million to Donald Trump's inauguration celebration. Sondland stated very specifically that there was a quid pro quo required if assistance to Ukraine were to be provided. Another Trump appointee, Fiona Hill, a former National Security Council official, testified that it was 'very clear' that US officials had made a White House meeting for the President of the Ukraine contingent on an announcement of investigations into Joe Biden and 2016 election interference.

The last of the scheduled public impeachment hearings came to a close towards the end of November 2019. The 12 witnesses who testified before cameras had corroborated, in detail, each other's evidence. That evidence was based on conversations, meetings, text messages and emails between those who were doing the negotiating over several months. However, the decision on impeachment would be decided on political, partisan lines because there was little indication that the Republicans would support any action against Trump.

To the independent observer, however, three things now seemed clear.

1   The Trump Administration clearly sought a 'quid pro quo' from Ukraine.
2   The diplomats and staffers involved were trying to save themselves.
3   President Donald Trump and his personal lawyer, Rudy Giuliani, were at the centre of the scheme.

But three key questions remained unanswered:

1   Was any of this an impeachable offence?
2   Did the hearings change the minds of voters? and,
3   Would the final outcome advantage Democrats or Republicans?

Impeachment is a very long and complex process involving both houses of the U.S. Federal Government. Prior to 2019, Republicans controlled both houses and, in 2019, the Senate is still controlled by Republicans.

The Democrats believed that the testimony of Ambassador Gordon Sondland, that the President did seek a quid pro quo from Ukraine, had parallels with the 1973 Senate testimony of John Dean, the White House lawyer who spectacularly turned against Richard Nixon, however, there were significant differences. Key among these differences is change in the media climate. In the Nixon era, most Americans received their information from newspapers, radio and nightly television broadcasts. Media outlets played to the centre, meaning that Republicans and Democrats could operate with a shared set of facts.

Today, the US media is fragmented and highly partisan: progressives and conservatives largely live in their own information bubbles. Chief among Trump's supporters is Rupert Murdoch-controlled, Fox News, which is a prime source of information for conservative voters. While mainstream media outlets focused on Sondland's belief there was a quid pro quo, conservative commentators looked elsewhere. Conservative commentators homed in on Sondland's testimony about a September telephone call in which Trump told him: 'I want nothing, I want nothing, I want no quid pro quo. I want Zelensky to do the right thing.' While to the Democrats, this was a self-serving statement that only came *after* Congress was notified about the whistleblower complaint, and it revealed that Trump was trying to cover his tracks; to conservative commentators this was the real bombshell of the day – they saw it as definitive proof that Trump had done nothing wrong.

On 5 December 2019, quoting from the United States Declaration of Independence regarding the possibility that a President might one day betray his country to foreign powers, the House speaker, Nancy Pelosi, announced that she was directing the judiciary committee to draft articles of impeachment against Donald Trump. 'The president leaves us no choice but to act,' Pelosi said. 'Sadly, but with confidence and humility, with allegiance to our founders and a heart full of love for America, today I am asking our chairman to proceed with articles of impeachment. ... If we allow a president to be above the law, we do so surely at the peril of our Republic. In America, nobody is above the law.'[2]

These articles of impeachment were completed, the House impeached Donald Trump, and, as already indicated, the Senate then acquitted the President on 5 February 2020.

The Republicans control 53 votes of the 100 members in the Senate. To remove a president there must be a two-thirds majority vote in the Senate – 67 seats. At least 20 Republican senators would have needed to find Mr Trump guilty of the impeachment charges in order to remove Mr Trump from office. As a two-thirds majority guilty verdict was not reached then Trump was acquitted because the impeachment vote have failed to get the required majority. The current situation is that Donald Trump is still considered to be impeached, but such a declaration has no functional effect. In other words, he continues to be President of the United States and will almost certainly stand for re-election in 2020.

As at March 2020 one is left with the feeling that nothing has really changed. The Democrats may well feel that the evidence strongly supports their decision to initiate impeachment proceedings and they may also have felt that, despite the impeachment being blocked in the Senate, the evidence could sway undecided voters in the 2020 elections. The hearing may not have been a disaster for Democrats, but neither has it provided the showstopper moment they will need to convince Republicans to abandon Trump. No matter what may be wanted or not wanted by pro-Trump or anti-Trump forces, the fact remains that, without a direct and compelling link between Trump and some totally undeniable seriously illegal behaviour, the probability of Trump being removed from office is remote.

The reality that, in the Senate, political affiliation would supersede evidence, was highlighted even prior to the vote in Congress when Lindsey

Graham, a South Carolina Republican and close Trump ally, stated he would not try to 'pretend to be a fair juror' should Donald Trump face an impeachment trial in the U.S. Senate. He said he was 'trying to give a pretty clear signal I have made up my mind. I'm not trying to pretend to be a fair juror here. What I see coming, happening today, is just a partisan nonsense.'[3] This statement indicates probable legal and ethical issues that should have confronted both Democratic and Republican senators when the matter came to the Senate. Prior to any Senate trial (at which the Chief Justice of the Supreme Court presided), every single senator took an oath to render 'impartial justice'. To be 'impartial' a person must try to put aside any personal prejudice and bias so that facts can be differentiated from fiction and decisions made on the facts themselves. Graham and others, on both sides of the political divide, seem to have subverted this concept of impartiality through the appearance of having already reached their decision.

The sad fact of all politics is that, no matter the best of motives and intentions with which most people enter politics, the reality of 'politics is the art of the possible' all too often seduces people away from their personal values and ethics to a situation in which the party dictates values, ethics, and behaviour. There is a sense in which the very existence of political parties indicates breakdown in the democratic process – the will of the party all too often becomes more important than personal values and ethics, or anything else.

Throughout this entire process, there is no evidence that a single mind has been changed. Almost certainly this saga will continue to evolve throughout 2020 but, unless far more dramatic information becomes available and is widely disseminated, the ultimate probability of any impeachment process being successful in terms of removing Trump from office continues to be extremely low. It is likely to prove only a relatively minor speedbump on Trump's road to re-election.

Patriotism

This is possible but, again, unlikely to impact negatively. It is claimed that around 1775, the English writer, Samuel Johnson stated that patriotism is the last refuge of a scoundrel. Whether or not Johnson was right, Donald Trump has played the patriotism card extensively over recent years. His slogan, 'make America great again' is an obvious indicator of this.

In Western countries, the US is well known for its patriotic fervour. From their earliest days, children are taught The Pledge of Allegiance and recite this at the start of each school day. The American flag flutters proudly from American homes in far greater numbers than does the flag of any other nation. Although the US is not unique in sustaining such rituals, there is a level of patriotic enthusiasm in the country that citizens of other countries find difficult to comprehend and of which many non-Americans are sometimes envious. It transcends both left and right of the political spectrum.

This is both a powerful and a dangerous thing. Those at either extreme end of the spectrum use the issue of loyalty to the US as a weapon with which to attack. Those towards the centre of the spectrum see it as a unifying force. Trump has especially appealed to those trending towards the far right and, short of Trump doing something so egregious that it cuts through every bias and prejudice, there is no way that they will allow any issue of patriotism to negatively impact on his re-election.

These are the people to whom Trump appeals when he conflates globalism with nationalism. Like the mercantilists of yesteryear, Trump sees everything as a zero-sum game and he seems to lack the conceptual ability necessary to see that you can be fiercely patriotic while supporting multilateral trade agreements and apparent trade deficits if, as is patently the case with the US, your country overall benefits and continues to be the world benchmark for democracy and capitalism.

Building 'the wall'

This, too, is unlikely to impact negatively. In February 2019, following an acrimonious argument about federal funding, Trump finally signed off on a bill to ensure there was no repeat of the December debacle in which federal employees were either required to work without pay, or were stood down without pay because the necessary finance approbation bills had not passed. Almost simultaneously with signing the bill – which did not give him the finance he sought to build a wall on the border with Mexico – Trump declared a state of emergency in order to take money from other programs and apply it to his pet project.

Immediately subsequent to this declaration, the Democratic-controlled Congress stated that they would act to annul the declaration and a number of states joined together in order to challenge it in the courts. Among the reasons for opposing the declaration are the comments made by Trump during his declaration speech (in which he seemed to suggest no real emergency actually existed) and the fact that surveys indicate a significant majority of US citizens (some sources claim close to 70 per cent) do not believe that the wall is either necessary or will be effective.

It seems increasingly clear that, because of the actions of Congress and legal activities, the wall will not be built prior to the 2020 Presidential elections, but this will not seriously impact Trump's probability of re-election. His supporters will see the declaration as proof that Trump is trying to fulfil his promises and that it is only the actions of others that is proving problematic. There is a sense in which Trump has effectively wedged his opponents into a 'no win' situation. This 'wedging', however, has not stopped those opposing the wall from flexing their muscles.

On 26 February 2019 it was announced that the Democratic-controlled House of Representatives had advanced a resolution to terminate Donald Trump's national emergency declaration at the US-Mexico border, in a bid to block the president from beginning construction on a border wall without approval from Congress. The vote was 245–182 with 13 Republicans joining the Democrats. The Bill now goes to the Senate where it is expected the vote will be far closer, but only a handful of Republican defections are needed for it to pass in what would mark a major rebuke to the president because virtually no other promise is as symbolic of Trump's agenda as that of building a wall along the Southwestern US border. Trump has vowed to veto the measure if it reaches his desk and this is important because Republican leaders have said they did not anticipate the measure would earn a veto-proof majority of a two-thirds supermajority of both houses.

Opposition to the border wall from the House of Representatives is, of course, only one stage in the campaign by those opposing the use of a Presidential Declaration of an Emergency – the progression of opposition through the courts is still to come and will take a long time. Of course, Donald Trump may not wait for these legal niceties.

As at August 2019, the U.S. Army Corps of Engineers has completed just about 60 miles of 'replacement' barrier during the first two-and-a-half years of Trump's presidency, all of it in areas that previously had border infrastructure. In light of this, apparently the President has told senior aides that a failure to deliver on the signature promise of his 2016 campaign would be a let-down to his supporters and an embarrassing defeat. With the election still months away and hundreds of miles of fencing plans still in blueprint form, various media report that Trump has held regular White House meetings for progress updates and to hasten the pace.

In 2018, Trump, in an immigration meeting with lawmakers, conceded that a wall or barrier is not the most effective mechanism to curb illegal immigration, recognising it would accomplish less than a major expansion of US enforcement powers and deportation authority. But he told lawmakers that his supporters want a wall and that he has to deliver it.

This issue took a further twist in December 2019. On 6 December, the federal government filed its first land acquisition case to obtain more than five hectares of private property in the Rio Grande Valley. The owner was offered $US93,449 in compensation. As the government pushes to accelerate construction of what Trump has promised will be a total of 800 kilometres of new barrier by the end of 2020, local families are in the way. This then pits local Texans against Trump, who has long said he wants to take whatever land he needs to build his wall. Landowners, including some who support Trump, are preparing a legal fight that could stall the wall-building effort and lead to lengthy court battles. It could possibly impact their voting in 2020.

Trade wars

In many ways this is 'a sleeper'. During his campaign, Donald Trump threatened to impose a tariff on imported goods, and he has fulfilled this promise this with tariffs now impacting on a broad range of imports from the

European Union, China, Turkey and other countries. The initial promise seemed to ignore or fail to understand that the businesses importing these goods are owned by both private individuals and by corporate stockholders. Increasing tariffs means either lower returns for these owners and/or increased prices to end consumers. Without increased remuneration, increased prices on goods such as consumer goods and household capital items mean lower profits and thus less disposable income for workers and lower levels of employment. In turn, this means people concentrate on essentials rather than optional purchases.

Most economists, indicate that a trade war has the potential to result in a shrinking economy and further job losses. Donald Trump's key economic advisor disagrees. Peter Navarro, a professor of business with a PhD from Harvard University, initially joined the Trump campaign as its chief economic adviser. He is now Assistant to the President, and Director of Trade and Manufacturing Policy. It is Navarro who has provided academic underpinning for the three main planks of Trumpian economics: the belief that tariffs make the US economy stronger; the view that trading relationships are a zero-sum game and that one country can only prosper at the expense of another; and the third, is a fixation on the loss of traditionally masculine manufacturing jobs, while ignoring the rise of jobs in the service sector. Navarro has himself stated that he sees his role as listening to what Donald Trump wants to do and then finding underlying analytics that will support it. He starts from the assumption that the President's intuition is correct and that his role is to find justification for implementing policies based on that intuition. An interesting example of an a priori position influencing 'impartial' advice, perhaps?

Virtually everything manufactured in the US and most other first-world countries relies on some imported inputs, even if it is raw materials, such as rare earths rather than finished goods. Accordingly, it is highly likely that every area of the US economy will eventually be affected by tariffs imposed by President Trump. Indeed, as at March 2019, the data showed the US deficit in goods and services with the world topped $US600 billion in 2018 which means Trump's presidency had seen the US trade shortfall – the main metric by which he judges countries to be winning or losing – grow by more than $US100 billion. By Trump's own benchmark, the US was about 20 per cent worse off than it was at the end of 2016, just before he took office.

The impact of trade wars is not just one way. While the tariffs currently imposed certainly impact, the retaliatory effect in which affected countries respond by imposing their own tariffs on goods imported from the US exacerbates the situation. Eventually the impact will be felt by farmers and other suppliers within the US who face the prospect of lower prices or reduced international markets for their products. This, coupled with rising prices for electronic and other imported goods, may lead to many one-time Trump supporters becoming disillusioned.

Although people, like White House economic adviser Larry Kudlow, see tariffs as a temporary measure for achieving greater market access for US companies and for getting China to play by international rules, Peter Navarro has a different view. For Navarro, tariffs are not a negotiating tool but an end in themselves. Because he supports a zero-sum approach to trade, his argument is that the US is better off not trading with countries who have a trade surplus with them. This appears to be basically a reformulating of the mercantilist approaches that dominated economic thought in the 15th to 18th centuries. It largely ignores the reality that international trade is at the core of the modern global economy; that international trade will help resolve the China–US trade war; and that international trade makes a new Cold War less likely. Disentangling the economies of China and the US would be very hard to do. It would also be incredibly costly in economic terms. But it would have another, even more important, consequence: it would make military conflict between America and China more likely.

One of the issues often overlooked in a discussion about trade wars, is the reality that growing interdependence between countries and powers has been a key factor in the peace we have all experienced over the past 70 years. History shows that wars are all about power and control. They are fuelled by nationalist philosophies which seek to enlarge influence and, usually, territory. Ultimately, might is seen as being right, and the goal is to ensure no state is larger than your own. Even if we ignore all conflicts up to 1945, this can still be seen in all the post-World War II conflicts. The fact is that interdependence of trade may well have been far more powerful a force in developing a largely peaceful world than has been the impact of military might by the US or any other nation.

Global trade in which end-user products are built from components sourced from across the world has encouraged a feeling of interdependence. As previously stated, a company such as Boeing may assemble aircraft in the US but, in order to control costs, it will source almost all the necessary parts from outside of the US. In return for this international supply chain, Boeing will gain increased influence with international airlines who are the ones who will purchase the finished aircraft. A similar story pertains with virtually every product sold in across the world. Over some 60 years, national markets have morphed into one huge marketplace as firms are basing individual productive activities at the optimal world location for that activity. National borders have become less important as, with the neoliberal emphasis on growth of GDP, the quest for national wealth through trade has largely supplanted a quest for national wealth through physical domination. There are international corporations today (mainly in the US) whose annual revenues exceed the total GDP of many nations.

By initiating trade wars, Trump has tapped into the angst of those who see the benefits of globalism as being heavily skewed to favour the rich and powerful. While this is arguably true, Trump argues a different view. Trump argues that globalism has negatively impacted the US because of exploitation by other countries.

GDP is the market value of all final goods and services produced within a country in a given time period. The quest for constant increase of GDP generally ignores the fact that this measure captures only the market value of goods and services produced and that it specifically excludes those goods and services produced by and for households and by society at large in the course of everyday living. Simon Kuznets, whose 1934 work on Gross National Product was the precursor of the concept of GDP, highlighted this key factor when cautioning against such measures being the sole measure of economic success. In other words, GDP is good as a measure of economic wellbeing and volume of economic activities, but there are limitations, particularly with regards to human wellbeing and sustainability.

Data from the World Bank in March 2019 showed that the GDP of the US is around $19 trillion – well above China in second place at around $12.5 trillion. However, when the spread of benefits from this GDP is analysed (what is known as 'The GINI Coefficient' – a tool often used as a gauge of economic inequality, measuring income distribution or, less commonly, wealth distribution among a population), the reason for discontent with living standards becomes apparent.

OECD data in March 2019 showed that income inequality in OECD countries is at its highest level for the past half century. The average income of the richest 10 per cent of the population is about nine times that of the poorest 10 per cent across the OECD, up from seven times 25 years ago. A report from Credit Suisse to the 2019 World Economic Forum at Davos in Switzerland stated that global wealth in 2018 was $US 317 trillion, that there were 42,000,000 millionaires worldwide, and that the average 2018 wealth per adult was $US 63,100 – all of which looks quite good until one considers the spread of this wealth both across countries and in specific countries. Across countries, the report showed that Switzerland ($US 530,240), Australia ($US 411,060) and the United States ($US 403,970) headed the league table according to wealth per adult with 60 per cent of total household wealth held by just 17 per cent of the worldwide adult population.

When the spread of wealth across the population is considered, the data are similar. A very small minority of people – somewhere between 50 and 70 depending on the source used – have more wealth than the bottom 50 per cent. In the US (as in most other countries), the inequality of this wealth spread is exacerbated when factors such as geographic location, race, education etc., are taken into account. So, if I live in a region where my job has been (or is in danger of being) outsourced to some third country and, as a result, I see my income falling and job opportunities vanishing, I am very much in favour of any professed endeavour to introduce trade barriers and to regenerate employment opportunities for me. This is the key demographic to whom Trump addresses his messages. 'If America is great again, there will be jobs for all and less of wealth inequality – and only Trump can make this happen.' Many of those who see no change in their job and/or remuneration prospects may now be questioning this message.

For many years, economists such as the 2001 Nobel Laureate in economics, Joseph Stiglitz, have expressed concern about the primacy of GDP as a measure. He sees this problem – the gap between what our metrics show and what they need to show – as an urgent one. He is increasingly worried about how our main economic measures fail to take into account environmental degradation and resource depletion. If our economy seems to be growing but that growth is not sustainable because we are destroying the environment and using up scarce natural resources, our statistics should warn us. But because GDP does not include resource depletion and environmental degradation, we typically get a very unbalanced picture. Stiglitz holds (as do many others), that there is something fundamentally wrong with the way we assess economic performance and social progress. He argues that, even worse, our metrics frequently give the misleading impression that there is a trade-off between the two; that, for instance, changes that enhance people's economic security, whether through improved pensions or a better welfare state, come at the expense of national economic performance. Stiglitz makes it clear that, in fact, the social obligation to enhance people's economic security actually improves the overall national economic performance of a country.[4]

Another equally concerned person, Kate Raworth, is also very aware of these factors. As an economist she originally subscribed to traditional approaches but, having then worked in the developing world, she realised that a different approach was needed. She now teaches at Oxford University and has developed what she calls 'Doughnut Economics'.[5] She argues that humanity's challenge this century is to meet the needs of all within the means of the planet. In other words, to ensure that no one falls short on life's essentials (from food and housing to healthcare and political voice), while ensuring that collectively we do not overshoot our reliance on Earth's life-supporting systems, on which we fundamentally depend – such as a stable climate, fertile soils, and a protective ozone layer. Raworth presents her concept as a doughnut in which social and planetary boundaries provide a viable approach to framing that challenge, and it acts as a compass for human progress this century. In my terms, her approach is clearly a post-capitalist one because it shows how we can achieve economic growth while still caring for people and the environment.

These comments by Stiglitz and Raworth are pertinent because the GDP of the US is a primary reason why Donald Trump has initiated the current trade war with China and why he has withdrawn from a variety of international trade agreements. GPD is also a key factor in his decision to withdraw the US from the World Trade Organization.

Media reports indicate that right now in America, there are some 140 million people living in poverty or just one pay cheque or emergency away from poverty. Apparently 37 million people live without healthcare and 62 million are paid less than a living wage. It is said that 14 million families cannot access clean water and millions are living in insanitary conditions. In other words, the US has degenerated into a polarised 'democracy' in which, it is claimed, because of various gerrymanders and disenfranchisement of those who lack the resources to fight voter restrictions, much of the population has fewer voting rights today than it did before the 1965 Voting Rights Act was passed.

It is argued that there is a national emergency of systemic racism, poverty, ecological devastation and the defence economy. Of course, this did not start with President Trump, although he is certainly exacerbating it. The truth is, neither party has done what is needed to address this real emergency, even though the deepest religious and constitutional values (to which most legislators would claim allegiance), compel care for the vulnerable, welcome to the immigrant, fair pay and assistance for the poor. So much for the declaration on the Statue of Liberty: 'Give me your tired, your poor, Your huddled masses yearning to breathe free, The wretched refuse of your teeming shore, Send these, the homeless, tempest-tossed to me, I lift my lamp beside the golden door!'

In the areas where Trump wants to build his wall, reports indicate that, along the border in Texas, hundreds of thousands are being denied health care because their home state refuses to expand Medicaid. Workers make $7.25 per hour and struggle to support their families. Unaccompanied minors who cross the border seeking asylum are sent to federal detention centres until caseworkers can find them a home. If they turn 18 before that, they graduate to adult detention facilities.

Consistently, a range of media reports shows there is a crisis at the border just as there is a crisis across areas such as Appalachia, the Mississippi Delta, inner cities, small towns and rural areas, and along the coasts. While the data is strenuously disputed, some authorities claim that in North Carolina alone, 2 million people live in poverty. In Lowndes county, Alabama, families without proper wastewater treatment infrastructure live with raw sewage pooling in their yards; and that 45 per cent of people in Alabama are poor or low-income – a total of 2.1 million residents. This last figure is said to include 53 per cent of children (589,000), 47 per cent of women (1.1 million), 60 per cent of people of colour (976,000), and 37 per cent of white people (1.1 million). In West Virginia, it is claimed that data shows over 53,300 veterans (33 per cent of the state's veteran population) have incomes below $35,000 a year. Even if these figures are not totally accurate, there certainly seems to be some compelling evidence that serious social problems exist across many parts of the US and that these are having a negative impact on the overall economy.

The reality is that, globally, both national and international economies are broken, with hundreds of millions of people living in extreme poverty while huge rewards go to those at the very top. This is as much so in the US as it is in most other countries – the difference is that the US is a 'first world' country in which such disparity is not supposed to be the norm.

Trade wars in which, because of tariffs, prices rise and/or low-cost consumer essentials become less available, do absolutely nothing to help those in the lower end of the pyramid – the vast majority of people. The rich, of course, are largely insulated from such inconvenience! Of course, the rich seem to have very few problems in ensuring they have full voting rights in presidential elections.

As at late 2019, concern over a trade war is increasing rather than dissipating. According to the Tax Foundation, if the tariffs already announced by Trump go into effect, they will amount to a $US200 billion annual tax increase which is larger than the $US165 billion average annual reduction provided by the Tax Cut and Jobs Act of 2017. When campaigning for the presidency, Donald Trump pledged to renegotiate America's 'horrible trade deals' and reinvigorate US manufacturing. When those negotiations failed and a trade war broke out, Trump assured Americans that trade wars were good and easy to win. That appears to be more hope than fact. The trade war has been raging for nearly 18 months, the trade deficit continues to increase, and manufacturing growth is beginning to slump. Meanwhile, the White House continues to assure Americans that the trade war is only temporary. Which begs the question 'how long is temporary?' There are few, if any, credible signs that the trade war will end any time soon and it may well continue through the 2020 presidential campaigning season. It is clear that tariffs are still rising, and the trade war is taking an increasing toll on the broader economy both because of importers needing to pass on the additional costs, and because of retaliatory tariffs. If consumer spending starts to slip, then economic growth is under very serious threat – and all this was before the impact of the corona virus!

On 24 August 2019, Donald Trump threatened to invoke The International Emergency Economic Powers Act (IEEPA) – a drastic action far in excess of the reciprocal tariff skirmishes currently being fought. It is the Trump Administration's most extreme trade weapon and could effectively block China's access to all US markets if deployed. It would mean not just blocking goods and services, it would target Chinese investments and probably close the door on China's access to US financial markets and banks. Once invoked, the U.S. Treasury can block assets without proving any wrongdoing, nor can the target of the action appeal against the decision through the courts. At the same time, Trump ordered US companies to move any operations from China to third countries – a symbolic, rather than a lawful edict, but one which implies they should look for countries that could not incur further tariff increases. This, understandably, fuels fears that more increases could be on the way.

Rather than calming markets, all this heightens the fear that a global recession is in the offing. Economists around the world point to warning signs they see and of which they hope President Trump will take heed. Some of these are:

First, an escalation in the trade war between US and China. As already indicated, in reality there are no winners in a trade war, and it seems that most countries are being negatively impacted by this event. Although the trade war is certainly having a material impact on China's economy and global growth, as at September 2019 it is also starting to show up in reduced business investment and waning business confidence in the US.

Increasingly, global concern about this trade war is turning toward the possibility that, from a technological perspective, the world may evolve into an eastern zone versus a western zone. Because, at present, the operating systems for mobile technology tend to be universal (either iOS or Android), there are few barriers to using the one device across international borders. There are grounds for believing Donald Trump is trying to take China out of the telecommunications supply chain with his harsh stance on manufacturer Huawei. Trump blacklisted the Chinese company in May 2019 and, more recently said that the US is 'looking really not to do business with Huawei.' This could see Huawei's next smartphone released with a totally different operating system and, depending on a variety of factors, could either mean a serious challenge to both iOS and Android, or it could impact on compatibility between the systems if political actions are taken to further limit Huawei's growth. This could then spill over into action against other Chinese aspects of western supply chains with additional costs incurred or new Western suppliers needing to be found. Either of these scenarios will have economic ramifications.

Second, decreasing US growth. The U.S. Bureau of Economic Analysis released figures showing that economic growth in the US had slowed from around 3.0 per cent in the first quarter of 2019 to 2.1 per cent in the second quarter. This was despite any boost provided by earlier tax cuts and indicates that the US manufacturing sector is in decline for the first time in a decade. Growth in capital expenditures is running at about a quarter of the rate it was in 2018 and, as at September 2019, in the latest US quarterly earnings reporting season, about half the companies referred to the negative impact of the conflict on their earnings outlooks. Federal Reserve chairman, Jerome Powell, has linked the deterioration in the outlook for global growth and weak US manufacturing and capital spending to US trade policies.[6]

During a recession, people pull back and reassess a wide variety of the things in their lives. Consumers spend less, avoiding purchases that can be postponed: a new car, home renovations and expensive holidays. Businesses spend less on new factories and equipment and put off recruiting. They don't have to explain their reasons for doing this – their gut feelings and emotions can be enough. If US growth deteriorates further into a decline, then a recession is possible. A severe recession could be Donald Trump's Achilles heel. While he is correct in saying that many other nations depend more on trade than does the United States, it is not the full story. Exports account for about 13 per cent of the US economy, while domestic consumer spending makes up about 70 per cent.

The big question relates to whether the United States can stand alone as trouble spots grow around the world. The United States economy is primarily a service economy that feeds off domestic demand, which provides some insulation to problems overseas. But there are limits to that buffer. As other countries falter, global investors are buying up U.S. Treasury bonds, causing the yield curve to invert in the United States, a warning sign of recession and a reminder that there are ways that panic felt abroad spills over. As the consumer becomes more cautious, so business becomes more cautious in terms of investment plans and this will impact across the world.

Third, potential of an imminent recession in Germany. As at August 2019, analysts are predicting two consecutive quarters of negative growth, which is the technical definition of a recession. Germany's economy shrank during the April–June period of 2019. A decline in exports dampened growth which came amid concerns of a global slowdown. Gross domestic product (GDP) fell by 0.1 per cent compared with the previous quarter, according to the Federal Statistics Office. That took the annual growth rate down to 0.4 per cent. Germany, Europe's largest economy, narrowly avoided a recession in 2018, but it seems unlikely that this will continue. It must be noted, though, that Chancellor Angela Merkel's government still believes the economy will grow slightly this year and does not think further stimulus is necessary.

Fourth, the Chinese debt crisis. As at August 2019, industrial production growth in China is at a 30-year low at 4.8 per cent. State industries are said to have borrowed heavily and so have consumers. Banks are weighed down by loans that some analysts fear will never be repaid, and this has potentially detrimental consequences for the global market.

China's debt was a key factor in its economic success in riding out the global financial crisis, due to a large, government-financed boost to its economy. However, that boost mostly led to China having one of the highest corporate debts in the world, only second to the Special Administrative Region of Hong Kong. Adding to this concern, the Hong Kong economy is also under serious threat as at September 2019, because of civil unrest arising from opposition to new policies that are considered to impact negatively on traditional freedoms.[7]

Forecast figures by several global financial institutions do not look positive for the global superpower and adding to the debt fears is an opaqueness and inability for analysts to completely obtain information and understand the full extent or impact of the potential looming problem. A 2016 International Monetary Fund (IMF) report found 38 out of 43 economies whose national debt was 30 per cent higher than its GDP experienced 'severe disruption' in the form of financial crises and a decline in growth.[8] It also found the probability of a 'bad outcome' was imminent if the boom lasted for more than six years – these are all worrying criteria that the Chinese economy meets.

Fifth, Brexit. Brexit is the withdrawal of the United Kingdom (UK) from the European Union (EU). Following a referendum held on 23 June 2016 in which 51.9 per cent of those voting supported leaving the EU, the Government invoked Article 50 of the Treaty on European Union, starting a two-year process which was due to conclude with the UK's exit on 29 March 2019. That deadline was later extended to 31 October 2019. Most economists believe that if the UK leaves the EU without a deal the damage will be severe. The IMF, OECD and World Bank also warned that leaving without a deal would negatively impact global growth because the UK is the world's sixth largest economy after France.

In July 2019, Boris Johnson became Prime Minister of Great Britain after the previous Prime Minister, Theresa May, failed to negotiate a deal acceptable to the EU and the British Parliament. Johnson argued that, despite all comments to the contrary from the EU, he would be able to negotiate a better deal than could be achieved by May. In the event of not getting a suitable deal, Johnson stated he would implement the result of the Brexit referendum in October without any deal defining what would happen post 31 October. The threat of a 'no deal' Brexit had economists and many in the UK very concerned. If this had happened, the UK would have left the single market and customs union overnight – arrangements designed to assist trade between EU members by eliminating checks and tariffs (taxes on imports). Of course, Brexit did *not* eventuate at the end of October 2019, because Johnson was forced to call a General Election. This took place in December and Boris Johnson was elected with a large majority after promising to 'get Brexit done'

Under former Prime Minister Theresa May's deal – which was voted down three times by the UK Parliament – the UK would have entered a 21-month transition period. This would have provided some breathing space, maintaining much of the status quo, while the two sides tried to negotiate a trade deal. Under a no-deal Brexit, there would have been no time to initiate a UK–EU trade deal. Trade would initially have to be on terms set by the World Trade Organization (WTO), and, if this happens, tariffs would apply to most goods UK businesses send to the EU. Some companies worried that could make their goods less competitive. Additionally, food prices could rise in the UK – a possibility highlighted by a government assessment – which would have an obvious impact on individuals across the UK. The Office for Budget Responsibility – which provides independent analysis of the UK's public finances – believed a no-deal Brexit would cause a UK recession. As indicated above, this would add to the risk of a global recession given the UK is the world's sixth largest economy. The politician, Phillip Lee (who supported a second EU referendum) released a strongly worded statement announcing that he had joined the centre-left Liberal Democrats. He went on to say that the Conservative Government was 'putting lives and livelihoods at risk unnecessarily and it is wantonly endangering the integrity of the UK. ... More widely, it is undermining our country's economy, democracy and role in the world'.

At 23:00 GMT on 31 January 2020, the UK stopped being a member of the European Union (EU). Brexit became a reality. As at March 2020 there is no agreement regarding the new relationship between the EU and Great Britain. Trade talks between the two officially started on 2 March[9] and every indication is that the talks will be extremely contentious. There is a deadline by which negotiations are supposed to be completed (26 November 2020)[10] and, although there will be on-going discussions, there could be major complications if no agreement is in place.

Sixth, a string of countries is currently in recession or have recently suffered a contraction. Economists nominate Argentina, Iran, South Africa, Turkey and Venezuela as being of concern with South Africa and Turkey being the major worries. In addition, Italy, Mexico, Brazil, Russia, Germany, China, Singapore, South Korea, Australia and the US have slowing economies while what is happening in the UK post-General Election is of keen interest. Many of the countries slowing down or in recession have a common problem: They are heavily dependent on selling goods overseas. And this is not a good time to have an export-driven economy. China's slump and President Trump's trade war are undercutting the global exchange of goods that had helped power the global economy for decades, and some of these countries are seeing sharp declines in exports. The corona virus pandemic is a further complication.

Seventh, wide fluctuations in financial markets. Although stock markets in the US and Germany remain at historically high levels, they are experiencing a rollercoaster of falls and rises (with some daily falls being in the region of three per cent), as they respond to tweets from President Trump and uncertainty as to further trade war skirmishes.

The Trump Administration strongly rejects any connection between these events and a recession. They claim that the US economy is very strong and that, if there are negative factors at play, it is because the Federal Reserve is failing to reduce interest rates sufficiently. Donald Trump, himself, weighed in on this claim in August 2019, stating that the Federal Reserve Chairman Jerome Powell is an enemy of equal concern as President Xi Jinping of China. This was the most personal attack Trump has made against his own pick to run the Federal Reserve and highlights what many see as attempts by Trump to undermine the independence of the Reserve and to make it subject to political influence. Of course, the fact that further reductions in interest rates could well be of benefit to Trump's own companies is purely incidental and will have had no influence on the call. (But it is widely known that in the five years before he became president, Trump borrowed more than $360 million via four loans from Deutsche Bank for his hotels in Washington, D.C. and Chicago, as well his 643-room Doral golf resort in South Florida.)

At the end of November 2019, messages on the trade wars were confused. Donald Trump says that the possibility of an agreement with China is very real and he implies that it could occur soon, but the message from China and other sources are not so positive. Although President Xi Jinping has said 'We want to work for a "phase one" agreement on the basis of mutual respect and equality,' he has also stated 'When necessary we will fight back, but we have been working actively to try not to have a trade war. We did not initiate this trade war, and this is not something we want.' Donald Trump has also made it very clear that the US would have to come out on top in any deal.

At the end of 2019, any hope that there might be a resolution of this issue in the near future was dashed. While visiting London for the recognition of 70 years of the NATO alliance, Donald Trump warned that a trade deal with China could be more than a year away. These comments sent shares in Britain's top 100 companies and US stock markets tumbling. Trump went on to say that the US was doing 'very well' from the trade war and he was in no hurry to sign an agreement before he runs for re-election next November. He added: 'In some ways it's better to wait until after the election for the China deal. But they want to make a deal now.'

Trump's comments about China being keen to make a deal do not seem to be supported from the Chinese end. China has made it clear it will not be satisfied with a US promise that it would not go ahead with the final round of tariffs on 15 December 2019. It also wants a rollback of the existing tariffs while the US wants to retain them as an enforcement mechanism to ensure China delivers on its promises. China has also taken a hard line against the U.S. Government's resolution of support for the demonstrators in Hong Kong who are still opposing Hong Kong legislature and, which for some months, had brought Hong Kong to a standstill. When President Trump signed into law the Hong Kong Human Rights and Democracy Act of 2019, he sought to dampen its impact with a conciliatory message, expressing hope that China and Hong Kong could 'amicably settle their differences leading to long-term peace and prosperity for all'. This statement was rejected by China, who accused the US of trying to meddle in China's internal affairs.

Wall Street reflects this uncertainty in its fluctuations. There is no particularly strong evidence to show that the economic position of the average American is significantly better than it was before Trump came into power. How this may be reflected in the 2020 elections is impossible to predict. Certainly many economists are predicting the economy of the US (and the rest of the world) is in a questionable state.[11]

In November 2019, the Australian operations of News Corporation raised the issue of environmental concern and linked it to economic decline.[12] This is of particular note because News Corporation is Rupert Murdoch's holding company for such organisations as *The Wall Street Journal*. Neither Murdoch, nor *The Wall Street Journal* could be labelled 'anti-Trump'. Fox News – the preferred media channel for Donald Trump – was founded by Rupert Murdoch and is still controlled by the Murdoch family.

In an interview with Paul Ehrlich, whose 1968 book *The Population Bomb* triggered international debate and Flinders University ecologist Professor Corey Bradshaw, the history of environmental impacts on society was discussed from an historical perspective. Reflecting on 3,200 years, Ehrlich and Bradshaw considered societies such as the Egyptians, the Hittites, and the prosperous city-state of Ugarit, that were impacted by waves of refugees escaping circumstances caused by drought and other climate disasters. Economies failed and rulers were overthrown because of societal inability to combat natural disasters. The statement is made that the issue of major waves of economic refugees is becoming all too familiar in our own world of the 21st century. Bradshaw points to statistical modelling showing a two-to-five-fold increase in African refugees for every one per cent increase in population. He goes on to say: 'If you tried to take that through and extrapolate it to the end of the century ... you're looking at between 80 and 120 million refugees coming out of Africa every year alone. Just Africa.'

The message from Ehrlich and Bradshaw is that failure to address environmental issues will have a serious economic impact and such an impact could be disastrous. They make the point that moves towards nationalistic societies with the associated neo-mercantilism are more likely to exacerbate, than alleviate the problem. Perhaps the ideas of people such as Stiglitz and Raworth really do have relevance!

The Democrats

This is, of course, where most people are directing their focus. There is understandably much interest in those who are nominating to be the Democrat candidate in the 2020 presidential election, however, as already indicated, this is only one factor.

As of late 2019, the list of Democratic presidential candidates has comprised Former Governor of Colorado John Hickenlooper, Governor of Washington Jay Inslee, Senator Bernie Sanders, Senator Amy Klobuchar, Senator Elizabeth Warren, Senator Cory Booker, Senator Kamala Harris, Senator Kirsten Gillibrand, ex-San Antonio Mayor Julian Castro, Representative Tulsi Gabbard, former Representative John Delaney, former three-term Representative Beto O'Rourke, author Marianne Williamson and former tech executive Andrew Yang. Since then, former Vice President Joe Biden has joined declared his intention to run. Of these, the frontrunners are generally considered to be Biden, Sanders, Warren and Harris. Late contenders in the race include Pete Buttigieg, mayor of South Bend, Indiana and former mayor of New York, Michael Bloomberg. As of late 2019, Buttigieg had emerged as one of the frontrunners.

All of this changed once the Primaries commenced in 2020. Going into the 'Super Tuesday' Primaries, the field had been reduced to four major contenders: Sanders, Biden, Warren and Klobuchar with Sanders and Biden being the most heavily supported. Following Super Tuesday, the contest appears to be down to just Sanders and Biden, with Biden having the greater momentum following his very strong results he achieved.

Whether any Democratic contender has the ability to counter Trump's communication skills and the offensive that he is sure to launch remains to be seen. The current indicators are not particularly positive. Based on comments made across the spectrum, it could be argued that the Democrats are still lost in a frenzy of anti-Trump indignation and the eternal outrage of identity politics.

In February 2019, John Podesta who had been the chairman of Hillary Clinton's unsuccessful 2016 presidential election campaign, was interviewed by Australian media about the 2020 presidential elections. He said: 'I think that what the Democratic candidates need to do is two things: one is to continue to make the case that [Donald Trump] is temperamentally unfit and unqualified to be president, that he's made bad judgments, that he ran as a populist, but he governs as a plutocrat … I think it's kind of easy in his case because he proves it every day. Then you have to a provide a positive alternative, that you can get the economy going for the middle and for the bottom ... But ultimately I think what Democratic voters are looking for is "who can take this guy on?", "who can get him out of the Oval Office?", "who can get the country back on the path of inclusive values", and we have some exciting candidates who I think are going to be able to do that.'[13] His comment about the quality of Democrat candidates awaits validation.

Possibly of more importance than who becomes the Democrats' nominee is, however, the investigations that have been initiated and/or are likely to be initiated by the House of Representatives. As already shown, the House of Representatives has started prying deeply into Donald Trump's entire world – his White House, his inauguration committee, his 2016 campaign, his 2020 campaign, his organisation, and his family. They are seeking documents from people such as Trump Organisation chief financial officer Allen Weisselberg, former chief strategist Steve Bannon, former press secretary Sean Spicer, publisher of the *National Enquirer* David Pecker, his sons, Donald Trump Jr and Eric Trump, and son-in-law Jared Kushner. Understandably, both Trump's supporters (including most Republican politicians) together with Trump's family and close associates are furious. Almost certainly many of these requests (or demands) will be resisted and this might lead to protracted court actions. The unknown around this relates to whether such court action, especially if it extends into 2020, will influence the way people vote.

On 26 November 26, a federal judge, Ketanji Brown Jackson destroyed the Trump Administration's argument that the president had the power to compel 'absolute immunity' to block former senior White House aides from having to testify before Congress. Judge Jackson's ruling stated that the White House's legal argument had 'startling and untenable implications' and is incompatible with 'our constitutional scheme' It went on to say:

> Stated simply, the primary takeaway from the past 250 years of recorded American history is that Presidents are not kings. This means that they do not have subjects, bound by loyalty or blood, whose destiny they are entitled to control. Rather, in this land of liberty, it is indisputable that current and former employees of the White House work for the People of the United States, and that they take an oath to protect and defend the Constitution of the United States. Moreover, as citizens of the United States, current and former senior-level presidential aides have constitutional rights, including the right to free speech, and they retain these rights even after they have transitioned back into private life.[14]

This ruling is likely to have much broader implications – including for former national security adviser John Bolton.

The Republicans

To many, the idea of the Republican party entertaining the nomination of an alternative candidate to Donald Trump is a far-fetched fantasy. But mounting a challenge to a sitting president is not unknown – even if it is highly unlikely to be successful.

While, as of March 2020 there did not seem to be confirmed candidates to campaign against Trump, there had been some who, in the recent past, indicated they could consider such action. The first of these was William Weld, a former Massachusetts governor who ran for vice president on the Libertarian Party ticket in 2016, while there has also been speculation that others might challenge him, including Senators Mitt Romney and Ben Sasse together with Maryland Governor, Larry Hogan. In September 2019, Mark Sanford, the former South Carolina governor and congressman, joined the Republican race against President Donald Trump. His rationale was that the Republican Party had lost its way and Sanford stated that he wanted his nomination to facilitate a discussion on what it means to be a Republican. Fifty-nine-year-old Sanford has long been an outspoken critic of Trump, frequently questioning his motivations and qualifications during the run-up to the 2016 presidential election and calling Trump's candidacy 'a particularly tough pill to swallow.' Although it seems unlikely that any well-known Republican will eventually seek to supplant Trump, this is very much a case of 'watch this space'.

In August 2019, Joe Walsh, a former Illinois congressman who is now a radio talk show host announced that he would challenge President Donald Trump for the Republican Party nomination at the 2020 election. Walsh described Trump, 'He's nuts. He's erratic. He's cruel. He stokes bigotry. He's incompetent. He doesn't know what he's doing.'[15]

A further unknown in this regard is the long-term impact of the decision by some Republicans to support the House-initiated motion to disallow Donald Trump's declaration of 'An Emergency' in order to fund the border wall. While the motion passed both Houses without sufficient support to prevent the President from exercising his veto, it is possible that this could indicate increasing unhappiness with Donald Trump among Republicans. There is no evidence at present to suggest a Republican revolt, it is a possibility that will need to be monitored.

Adding to the uncertainty around Republican support levels was Donald Trump's renewed personal attacks on the late Senator John McCain. John McCain died of brain cancer in August 2017 and, prior to his death, had opposed Trump-initiated legislation when he believed such legislation was inappropriate. The most famous instance of this was when McCain's vote stopped repeal and replacement of Obamacare. But the animosity between them started long before this. Trump first clashed with McCain, a decorated veteran, during the 2016 campaign, after he mocked the senator for being held as a prisoner of war in Vietnam. McCain, who faced re-election in the Senate the same year, declined to endorse Trump even after he became the Republican presidential nominee. and Utah senator Mitt Romney expressed disbelief at Trump's denigration of McCain.

Following Trump's remarks of March 2019, there was an upsurge of denunciation of Trump from Republicans in Congress, who defended McCain as a 'hero'. Senator Johnny Isakson, from Georgia was scathing in his comments; Senator Martha McSally who became McCain's replacement in the Senate was ardent in her support for McCain. The impact of these comments on both veterans and those still serving in the US military remains to be seen but, given the sense of 'family' that exists between military personnel, Trump's comments could negatively impact the level of support he receives from the broader military.

In September 2019, there was an unexpected new voice calling for opposition to Trump's re-election – Anthony Scaramucci who served for just 11 days as White House communications director before being sacked for derogatory comments about some of Donald Trump's inner circle. Scaramucci claimed that Trump is unable to believe he could ever be wrong about anything or ever to apologise for anything and said this basically had to do with very low self-esteem. Scaramucci was widely reported as saying of Donald Trump: 'I mean the poor guy has the self-esteem of a small pigeon.' He went on to state: 'Remember, he's such a malignant narcissist that he needs the spotlight at all times.' It must be noted, of course, that the ill-feeling is mutual. In the past Mr Trump has called Mr Scaramucci an 'unstable nut job'[16] whose 11 days as director of communications were marked by gross incompetence.

Hubris

This is probably the strongest factor that could negatively affect Trump's re-election.

Greek legend tells of Icarus, whose attempt to escape from Crete, using wings constructed of feathers and wax. He is warned not to fly too close to the sun as its heat will melt the wax and the feathers will fall off. When that happens Icarus will crash and die. Icarus becomes so caught up in his power to fly that he ignores the warnings, flies too close to the sun, and falls to earth and dies. The issue is one of hubris – or excessive pride and belief in one's own powers and abilities. If there is one single thing that could impact negatively on his re-election it is Donald Trump's excessive self-confidence that borders on (or extends into) hubris.

There can be absolutely no doubt that Donald Trump has tremendous pride in his own abilities. He is totally convinced that he is always right and that he has the ultimate answer to both America's and the world's problems. Read any of his books and his self-promotion is obvious. Read any of his presidential tweets and his self-opination is blatant. 'Trump is in his White House and all is right with the world'. As recently as August 2019 this was apparent in Trump's claim to be 'the Chosen One' to repel the economic and geopolitical ambitions of China.

True self-confidence doesn't mean being brash and constantly letting others know how good you are. Neither does it mean being aggressive or offensive. Rather, it means having a realistic sense of one's strengths and weaknesses coupled with a determination to make a positive contribution to one's world wherever possible. From the perspective of a national leader, it involves recognising that neither they, nor their Party, are omnipotent. There is no simple answer to the complex issues facing every government in every country. Simplistic answers such as those often propounded by various pressure groups tend to be short term and single issue specific. They fail to deal with the degree of complexity involved in national leadership. This is especially true for the US under President Trump.

The antithesis of hubris was seen in New Zealand in relation to the terrorist attack in Christchurch during March 2019. In the aftermath of 9/11, President Bush called for a 'War on Terror' and emphasised the might of the US would be brought against those who attacked. Subsequent Presidents have all re-emphasised the testosterone-empowered, 'might is right' approach. This is the macho, ego-driven hubris that, all too often, impels us into escalating rather than containing violence. New Zealand Prime Minister Ardern took a diametrically opposite approach. She eschewed hubris for leadership.

Since a self-proclaimed white supremacist burst into two mosques in the South Island city Friday, killing at least 50 people and wounding dozens more, Ardern has become the face of her nation's sorrow and grief, and its resolve.

Observers hailed the calm and compassion she has shown in the wake of the worst mass killing in her country's modern history. She led a multiparty delegation from the country's capital, Wellington, to Christchurch, donning a black headscarf and mourning with relatives and friends of the victims. She also promised to cover the funeral costs of all those slain. A photographer who covered her visit marveled at the prime minister's composure and empathy.

'Ardern's performance has been extraordinary – and I believe she will be strongly lauded for it both domestically and internationally,' political commentator Bryce Edwards of Victoria University in Wellington told Reuters.[17]

This was humility. This was strength. This was leadership. This was a set of behaviours we are unlikely to see from Donald John Trump. In the coming months, President Trump needs to ensure he doesn't fly too close to the sun. Jacinda Ardern has set a new benchmark.

President Trump's statement of 21 August 2019 seems to endorse the belief that hubris might be his downfall. At an informal, driveway press conference, when speaking of the trade conflict with China, he told reporters that previous presidents should have confronted China. He went on to say that he was confronting them because he, Trump, was the 'Chosen One'. Only a few hours earlier he had, apparently, also referred to himself as the 'King of Israel'. He had, of course, only the day before questioned the 'loyalty' of Jews who support Democratic politicians!

Trump is supported in this view by many of his supporters. On 26 November 2019, it was reported that U.S. Secretary of Energy, Rick Perry, believes that President Donald Trump was chosen by God to lead the country and that he has handed the President a one-page description of morally flawed biblical kings as inspiration. Perry said he told the President that this posturing as 'the Chosen One', which some critics took as egotistical or even blasphemous, was correct. Perry reflects a common view among some evangelical Christians. Some of Trump's loudest evangelical defenders, like Franklin Graham, often compare him to sinful, but important biblical kings, especially King David – who wrote some Psalms and slayed Goliath, but who also impregnated Bathsheba and then plotted to have her husband killed.

Further evidence of this hubris may be found in Trump's comments about purchasing Greenland.

The Arctic is estimated to hold about 13 per cent of the world's undiscovered oil reserves and 30 per cent of its natural gas reserves, plus huge deposits of minerals such as zinc, iron and rare earth metals[18] but for a very long time, Canada, Denmark, Finland, Iceland, Norway, Sweden, Russia and the US – those nations having territory within the Arctic region have emphasised peaceful co-operation rather than strenuous competition for these resources. Under international law, the North Pole and the Arctic Ocean are not owned by any country. But all coastal states share 200 nautical-mile exclusive economic zones. They also maintain overlapping claims to extended continental shelf resources. There appears to be some suggestion that China is seeking to gain influence in the area and Greenland has been mentioned as a target for them.

Over recent years, climate change has brought about significant changes in the area. Various studies indicate that the region is warming at a rate vastly exceeding that of the global average. This means that, should this change continue (and especially if it should accelerate), it is possible that new sea lanes could open with the result that sea trade between China and Europe could be significantly faster and, consequently, far less expensive. The major players – US, Russia, China – are all jockeying for dominance in both the military and mining arenas. Their aim is to exploit the resources before any other power can do so. Under those circumstances, it is understandable that the US would be interested in furthering its rights in the area and purchasing Greenland from Denmark could make sound business sense. Of course, Denmark has a different viewpoint and Denmark's Prime Minister's rebuff of Donald Trump's suggestion made that very clear! It would appear that some things have not changed since President Truman expressed interest in buying Greenland back in 1946.

Then there are the scandals. Prior to the 2016 elections, Trump's history of inappropriate touching of women was widely advertised. During his presidential campaign footage emerged of Donald Trump claiming to demean women by what can only be termed sexual assault. The video shows him saying: 'I moved on her like a bitch, but I couldn't get there, and she was married. Then all of a sudden I see her, she's now got the big phony tits and everything.' (It's not clear who Trump was talking about.) 'I'm automatically attracted to beautiful [women] – I just start kissing them. It's like a magnet. Just kiss. I don't even wait. And when you're a star they let you do it. You can do anything ... Grab them by the pussy. You can do anything.'[19]

Clearly this did not negatively impact Trump's election campaign, but ongoing allegations and innuendo may yet cut through the President's Teflon coating. Since Trump's election, a number of women have accused him of violating their rights and there have been lawsuits issued against him. Of course, whether or not the things claimed by the plaintiffs actually occurred, is still subject to determination by the courts, but the very fact of these claims being made does raise legitimate questions about the way he observes the human rights of women and, probably, of other broader human rights' matters.

In 2019, further questions were raised in conjunction with the arrest and, before he could be brought to trial, the death in custody of the financier Jeffrey Epstein. In 2008, Epstein had been convicted of soliciting a prostitute and of procuring an underage girl for prostitution. He served almost 13 months in custody, with work release, as part of a plea deal; federal officials had identified 36 girls, some as young as 14 years old, whom Epstein had sexually abused. Following his release from custody, Epstein was able to resume his career in finance and, it is alleged, he was also able to resume his pursuit of underage girls for sexual purposes. His conviction appears to have very little, if any, negative impact on his circle of influential friends or business success and there is photographic evidence associating Prince Andrew, former President Bill Clinton, and President Trump with Epstein. All three deny being aware of inappropriate behaviour by Epstein, despite having been both in his home and with him on other occasions. Since a verdict of suicide was passed down, there have been repeated claims that the verdict was wrong and further investigation has been called for.[20] It is possible that Donald Trump could suffer some element of collateral damage: before he became President, Trump had called Epstein a 'terrific guy' and in 2002, told *New York* magazine that Epstein was 'a lot of fun to be with'. 'It is even said that he likes beautiful women as much as I do, and many of them are on the younger side. No doubt about it – Jeffrey enjoys his social life,' he was quoted as saying.[21] Of course, there is also the possibility that, among some elements in society, these allegations enhance Trump's image.

This issue of hubris also is indicated by Trump's promotion of his family. In September 2019, President Donald Trump's campaign manager, Brad Parscale, said that the president and his family are 'a dynasty that will last for decades,' prompting speculation about whether Trump's children might one day pursue their own bids for public office. 'The Trumps will be a dynasty that will last for decades, propelling the Republican Party into a new party,' Parscale said, according to Associated Press. 'One that will adapt to changing cultures. One must continue to adapt while keeping the conservative values that we believe in.'[22]

After taking office in 2017, Trump named his eldest daughter, Ivanka, and his son-in-law, Jared Kushner, senior White House advisers. From inviting her to the Group of 20 economic summit in Japan to including her in a small delegation that visited the demilitarised zone between North and South Korea, the president has repeatedly sought to promote Ivanka Trump on the world stage. Trump also used Kushner to lead his push to forge a Middle East peace plan. Additionally, the president's adult sons, Donald Trump Jr. and Eric Trump, have taken active roles in their father's re-election campaign, appearing frequently at 'Make America Great Again' rallies and denouncing Trump's political opponents on social media. Is it possible that he sees a Trump Dynasty as US Presidents in the not-too-distant future? Is it possible that his most ardent supporters would welcome such a move?

Another indication of hubris may be seen in Donald Trump's tweet of 28 November 2019 in which his head is photoshopped onto a poster of the super-buff, bare body of the fictional boxer Rocky Balboa – the character portrayed by actor Sylvester Stallone in the Rocky movie franchises. There was no caption or even any explanation given by Trump – just the photo. Given that Russian President Putin frequently posts photographs of himself as an action man, a possible explanation is that Trump wants to be seen as being equally athletic as Putin, but the response he drew was probably far more negative than desired. It certainly is a marked contrast from the photographs generally seen of Trump as he walks the golf course! Perhaps it is an attempt at humour.

Revolt from supporters

As already stated several times, the core supporters of Donald Trump are 'rusted on' and no matter what the evidence, their support is unwavering. Is it possible that this could change?

There is always a continuum between unwavering support and unwavering opposition no matter what the cause or person involved. The standard 'bell curve' is a well-known and widely used illustration of statistical truth. It is also understood that such a curve can be (and usually is) skewed in some direction so that, although the majority of the population fits under the highest point of the curve, that highest point tends to be located more towards one of the ends rather than exactly in the middle. As Vance Packard made clear in *The Hidden Persuaders* this is the audience to whom politicians address most of their messages because this is the portion of the population that may be prepared to change their votes.

No matter the rhetoric, Donald Trump knows that he lost the popular vote. He may, or may not, have been a stellar student at Wharton, but he knows at least, the basics of statistics. He is fully aware that there is a significant number of people who have provided support from a populist perspective rather than because they are committed to him personally and to his initiatives. This is why he continues with the denigration of those who dare to disagree or oppose him as well as why the emphasis on building 'the wall' remains front and centre. He is appealing, not to the majority of citizens who, according to the polls, oppose the wall, but to possible waverers in his support base. 'Look at me. Believe in me. I'm staying true to my promises and it's not my fault that there are delays. We are going to win because I'm a winner!' This is the message he sends.

This was evident in the Government shutdown over the December–January period of 2018–2019. It appeared as though Trump had been prepared to compromise on at least one occasion. However, under pressure from his most ardent supporters and from certain media, he doubled down and the shutdown continued. The damaging effect on the country or individuals was irrelevant to him. Remaining true to his follower base was imperative. However, there is now a new twist. In March 2019, the U.S. Federal Reserve stated that they expected growth of only 2.1 per cent in 2019 and 1.9 per cent in 2020, with chairman Jerome Powell saying the rate of growth had slowed more than anticipated from the strong growth experienced last year. That provided quite a contrast with the Trump Administration's forecasts of GDP growth of 3.2 per cent in 2019 and 3.1 per cent in 2020. This prediction will have impact on job growth, employment opportunities, and wages. It may also impact on employment statistics and, in terms of political impact, mean that some who were predisposed to support Trump could change their minds. Donald Trump once said his tax cuts, increased spending, trade policies and deregulation would deliver 'more jobs'. He predicted growth rates of four, five or six per cent GDP. Clearly that is now seen as being extremely unlikely. What will be the impact if these Trump promises prove to be ephemeral?

Which begs the question as to how long this can last. How many of those negatively impacted by the shutdown and other Trump-related activities were wearing 'Make America Great Again'-branded clothes and caps when not at work? How many of these were registered voters or who could now become registered voters? No matter their purported support, how will these people vote when the 2020 elections are held? At what point will the messages of those seeking to replace President Trump actually resonate with waverers? These are significant unknowns.

Perhaps more relevant is the 'hip pocket' impact of Trump policies. The potential impact of the trade war with China could also become a factor. Until 31 August, most of the tariffs the Trump Administration had imposed on Chinese imports since the trade war began in in January 2019, were directed to business inputs rather than consumer goods. That changed on 1 September when the first of two tranches of new tariffs on a wide range of consumer products became effective. This put a 15 per cent tariff on about $US112 billion of consumer products which meant that goods ranging from clothing, footwear and textiles to some consumer technology products, lawnmowers and tools, now incur the tariff. A similar tax on another $US160 billion or so of products is scheduled to become effective on 15 December and will be imposed on smartphones, laptops, prams, consumer electronics, sports equipment, video game consoles, toys and clothing and footwear not caught by the initial tranche. At that point, all $US550 billion or so of China's exports to the US will be taxed at rates ranging from 15 per cent to 30 per cent.

Before Trump initiated the trade war, the average rate of tariffs on Chinese imports to the US was only about three per cent. These new tariffs cannot help but have an impact on consumer spending as importers are highly unlikely to absorb the extra costs. The effect that higher prices may have on Trump's popularity is a massive 'unknown', but common sense indicates that many people will not be happy with them as the information available as at September 2019 indicated the average cost to US households will be in the vicinity of $1,000–$1,795 (depending on which research study is used) per annum or, at the median, about $27.00 per week, at a time when wages are largely stagnant. Effectively, Trump's trade war is increasing taxes through the increased import costs that are passed on to consumers. Given that, in his 2016 campaign, Trump promised that nearly every American would see a tax cut, this could have serious repercussions. The Republicans are notorious for reducing taxes and this could impact not only on Trump's core supporters, but also on the greater Republican party and its decisions regarding the 2020 presidential candidate.

The other side of the coin is that China's retaliatory tariffs are also now coming into effect. About $US75 billion of China's new tariffs on US products also commenced on 1 September 2019. Like China's earlier tariffs, they are directed at Trump's political heartland, mainly covering agricultural products and US-produced motor vehicles. A significant proportion of Trump's original supporters came from the areas where these tariffs will have maximum impact. And all this was before the corona virus pandemic exacerbated economic concerns across the world.

Notes

1 Dan Balz and Scott Clement, 'Poll: Majority of Americans say they endorse opening of House impeachment inquiry of Trump', 8 October 2019, Schar School of Policy and Government, George Mason University and the *Washington Post*. Available at https://www.washingtonpost.com/politics/poll-ma jority-of-americans-say-they-endorse-opening-of-house-impeachment-inquiry-of-trump/2019/10/07/be9e0af6-e936-11e9-85c0-85a098e47b37_story.html.
2 'Trump impeachment to go ahead says Nancy Pelosi', 5 December 2019. Available at https://www.bbc.co.uk/news/world-us-canada-50671570.
3 Martin Pengelly, 'Trump impeachment: Lindsey Graham will "not pretend to be a fair juror"', *the Guardian*, 14 December 2019. Available at https://www.theguardia n.com/us-news/2019/dec/14/trump-impeachment-lindsey-graham-will-not-pretend-to-be-a-fair-juror.
4 See, for example, Joseph Stiglitz (2014), *Creating a Learning Society: A New Approach to Growth, Development, and Social Progress*. New York: Columbia University Press.
5 Kate Raworth (2017), *Doughnut Economics: Seven Ways to Think Like a 21st-Century Economist*. London: Random House Business Books.
6 Jerome H. Black, 'Challenges for Monetary Policy', 23 August 2019. Available at https://www.federalreserve.gov/newsevents/speech/powell20190823a.htm.

7 Hong Kong Economy, latest developments, available at https://www.hkeconomy. gov.hk/en/situation/development/index.htm.
8 Tasha Wibawa, 'China's looming great wall of debt may have "major global implications"', 19 January 2019. Available at https://www.abc.net.au/news/2019-01-20/chinas-looming-great-wall-of-debt/10713614.
9 Katya Adler, 'Brexit: what to expect from UK–EU trade talks', 2 March 2020. Available at https://www.bbc.com/news/world-europe-51657084.
10 James Blitz, Jim Brunsden and Laura Hughes, 'Brexit timeline: key dates in the UK's divorce from the EU', 18 December 2019. Available at https://www.ft.com/content/64e7f218-4ad4-11e7-919a-1e14ce4af89b.
11 Kimberley Amadeo, 'US Economic outlook for 2020 and beyond', 3 March 2020. Available at https://www.thebalance.com/us-economic-outlook-3305669 and IMF, 'World Economic Outlook: Tentative stabilization, sluggish recovery', January 2020. Available at https://www.imf.org/en/Publications/WEO/Issues/2020/01/20/weo-update-january2020.
12 Jamie Seidel, 'A lot of suffering', 30 December 2019. Available at https://www.news.com.au/technology/environment/climate-change/a-lot-of-suffering-grim-3000yo-warning-about-to-come-true/news-story/84274e09f8cc1ae708bfb0b43947d297.
13 'Hillary Clinton's campaign chairman discusses hacking and how to beat Donald Trump in 2020', 20 March 2019. Available at https://www.abc.net.au/news/2019-03-20/hillary-clinton-campaign-chair-on-how-to-beat-donald-trump/10916326.
14 Byron Tau, 'Judge rejects White House claims of immunity for close aides', updated 25 November 2019. Available at https://www.wsj.com/articles/judge-rejects-white-house-claims-of-immunity-for-close-aides-11574722684.
15 'Joe Walsh becomes second Republican to challenge Trump for White House', 25 August 2019. Available at https://www.cnbc.com/2019/08/25/joe-walsh-becomes-second-republican-to-challenge-trump-for-white-house.html.
16 Geoff Earle, 'Donald Trump blasts Anthony Scaramucci as "unstable nut job"', 19 August 2019. Available at https://www.dailymail.co.uk/news/article-7371513/Now-Scaramucci-says-Donald-Trump-rocker-begs-Republicans-oppose-him.html.
17 Ishan Tharoor, 'The world is watching New Zealand's Jacinda Ardern', 19 March 2019. Available at https://www.washingtonpost.com/world/2019/03/19/world-is-watching-new-zealands-jacinda-ardern/?utm_term=.57c4ad2d7645.
18 Jeff Desjardins, 'This infographic shows how gigantic the Arctic's undiscovered oil reserves might be', 7 April 2016. Available at https://www.businessinsider.com/how-gigantic-arctics-undiscovered-oil-reserves-might-be-2016-4?r=US&IR=T.
19 Ben Mathis Lilley, 'Trump was recorded in 2005 bragging about grabbing women 'by the pussy'. 7 October 2016. Available at http://www.slate.com/blogs/the_slatest/2016/10/07/donald_trump_2005_tape_i_grab_women_by_the_pussy.html.
20 See entry at https://www.biography.com/crime-figure/jeffrey-epstein.
21 Lia Timson, 'Who was Jeffrey Epstein', 23 November 2019. Available at https://www.smh.com.au/world/north-america/a-terrific-guy-who-is-jeffrey-epstein-and-what-is-he-accused-of-20190717-p52811.html.
22 'Brad Parscale: Trumps "a dynasty that will last for decades?"', 9 September 2019. Available at https://www.bbc.co.uk/news/world-us-canada-49637593.

7 The future for the US

December 2019 marked the 70th anniversary of the North Atlantic Treaty Organization (NATO), formed after the Second World War. It was a major event with the leaders of all the member countries at a function in London. The summit was marked by sharp disagreements over spending and future threats including Turkey's role in the alliance and China, as well as a clash of personalities. On 3 December, a video appeared showing world leaders mocking Trump. It shows Canadian Prime Minister Justin Trudeau, British Prime Minister Boris Johnson, the French president, Emmanuel Macron, the Dutch Prime Minister, Mark Rutte and Princess Anne at a Buckingham Palace gathering. In audio caught on a nearby microphone, Johnson asks Macron: 'Is that why he was late?' before Trudeau interjects: 'He was late because he takes a 40-minute press conference off the top.' He goes on to say to the group: 'You just watched his team's jaws drop to the floor.'

On 5 December 2019 this was followed by the former Polish Prime Minister and President of the European Council, Donald Tusk, tweeting a photo of himself pointing a pair of fingers in an apparent 'gun' gesture at the US President's back. Mr Tusk's caption was: 'Despite seasonal turbulences our transatlantic friendship must last #Trump #NATO.' Mr Tusk is the newly elected president of the European People's Party – a conservative political party committed to strengthening the EU. He served as Prime Minister of Poland from 2007–2014. Apparently, the photo was taken at the 2018 G7 meeting in Canada when Mr Tusk was President of the European Council.

Only a few years ago ,it would have been unimaginable that an American president would have been the object of such public ridicule among world leaders in any gathering, let alone one of such symbolic importance. It would have been equally unimaginable that one of those allies would tangle with him so visibly under a global spotlight. In the past, no matter what they might have thought privately or discussed behind closed doors, respect for the United States and its importance on the world's stage meant that, in any public arena, nothing was said or done that could be seen as being disrespectful of the US president. The consequence of this sad event was also unprecedented: Donald Trump cancelled a scheduled press conference and returned to Washington.

The NATO summit made something very clear: the leaders of countries that have stood with America for years see no reason to faithfully support Mr Trump, the way they once might have done for a US president. They feel no obligation to be polite about him among themselves. In the space of only three years, something significant has happened to the prestige of the US – it can hardly be coincidence that these years are those of Donald Trump's presidency.

In February 1941, the editorial of *Life* magazine was headed 'The American Century'. In this editorial, Henry Luce, an American magazine magnate who was called 'the most influential private citizen in the America of his day' argued that the entry of the US into the Second World War was the moment when the US reached its true position as the dominant world power. It was the turning point on the world stage whereby the US would fully supplant Great Britain as the leader in international influence and power.

Today, it is clear that the influence of the US is waning and, under Donald Trump, there has been a move to replace the international influence of the US with a nationalism akin to that which pertained across the world around 100 years ago. Into the developing void, other powers such as China, are making increasingly aggressive steps to become preeminent. Given Donald Trump's self-interest approach and domestic focus, it is possible that he does not fully appreciate this as a real possibility (let alone probability) or, if he does realise it, that he is out of his depth in combatting it.

Across the world, there is an increasing public awareness today that the promises we received on the benefits of neoliberal economics were actually 'smoke and mirrors'. Over the past 40 years our economies may have grown, but the benefits have been disproportionately given to the top one per cent of people. Economies have grown, the few have benefitted, but the wealth of the vast majority has either stagnated or declined. There are many people in every country who know it does not need to be like this.

Over the last 40 or so years, our world has moved away from a sense of society to a belief that we exist in an economy. This was stressed by the late Margaret Thatcher, past Prime Minister of Great Britain, when she said: 'There is no such thing as society. There are individuals and there are families.' This is a world dominated by shareholder theories of economics in which any service offered by governments should be 'contestable' by private industry and in which spending anything more than is absolutely essential on employees, suppliers, taxes, etc. is 'theft from the shareholders'. Maximising profit is the only game in town.

Democratic hopefuls such as Bernie Sanders are challenging this approach and arguing for a more societal approach. This is being decried by Trump and strong supporters of the status quo as a radical agenda of making America a socialist country. However, such a simplification of the issue shows a total disregard for the concept of 'stakeholder theory'.

In 1984, Edward Freeman, a professor at the University of Virginia, challenged the shareholder theory of economics that had been advocated by Milton Friedman and others,[1] by arguing that in a robust economy more factors than just shareholders needed to be considered.[2] Freeman is in total accord with shareholder advocates in relation to the importance of profits – the differences lie both in the process by which such profits are generated and the way by which such profits are utilised. Shareholder theory argues that the only important factor for consideration is the organisation's ownership (the shareholders) while stakeholder theory argues for an element of social responsibility in which shareholders are but one of the important factors for consideration. This approach is a very long way from socialism.

For about 100 years, the world has had the opportunity to compare capitalism and socialism in its communist form. The evidence is clear. Capitalism, with its emphasis on open competition and reward for effort, has won hands-down. During the twentieth century, virtually all technological advancement and innovation came from capitalist countries. This is equally true for the arts and social interactions. Very few would dispute that the standard of living in capitalist countries was, overall, at a higher level than in communist countries over this same period. Since the fall of the Berlin Wall in 1989, and the subsequent collapse of the USSR, the once Soviet-bloc countries have been playing 'catch-up' with many seeking to re-align their philosophies and practices so as to become part of new blocs such as the EU. Even in countries remaining at least nominally communist – places like the People's Republic of China (PRC) and Vietnam – a new form of communism has emerged in which entrepreneurial activity is at least accepted, if not actively encouraged. Much of the recent rapid rise of the China as a world power can be directly attributed to this.

When people today such as the Republicans and/or Donald Trump and his supporters use the term 'socialism' it is generally meant to be a derogatory concept that equates with the worst excesses and failures of communist states. It is intended to back into a corner those who seek a more inclusive practice of capitalist activity. The result is that, as seen in many of the Democratic hopefuls for the 2020 election, any distinction between Republican and Democratic philosophies becomes, at best, blurred or, more frequently, lost. In this scenario the issue of 'shareholder theory' versus 'stakeholder theory' degenerates into a 'capitalist' versus 'socialist' (aka 'communism') debate that would have done Senator Joseph McCarthy proud.

Today's dominant view of capitalism arises from neoliberal thinking based on the shareholder theory of economics. This has permeated politics and business for at least the last 40 plus years. Ultimately, it lies behind the activities that have led to many of the 'booms and busts' of the late twentieth and early twenty-first centuries – including the Global Financial Crisis of 2007–8. The only thing that really matters is profit and wealth for the few even though such possibilities as 'the trickle-down effect' (in which benefits at the top eventually make their way to those at the bottom) may be outwardly espoused. The overwhelming evidence of today is that this approach exacerbates the problems that arise through an increasing gulf between the 'haves' and 'have-nots' in every society.

Underlying this is the approach advocated by Friedrich Hayek (the 1974 Nobel Laureate in Economics) in his book *The Constitution of Liberty*.[3] In this work, Hayek posits that civilisation is made possible by the absence of arbitrary restraints such as government regulation or public ownership. He argues that removing such restraints is essential for national wealth and growth. One of those who were also strongly influenced by Hayek was Milton Friedman, the 1976 Nobel Laureate in Economics, to whom President Ronald Reagan turned for advice. Under the patronage of Reagan, Friedman came to see implemented much of what he advocated in his book *Capitalism and Freedom*.[4] The result was that the neoliberal approach in which government plays minimal, if any, role in regulating business and in which public assets are sold into private enterprise is now widely accepted. It has become the economic orthodoxy of the Western world. Today it is the default approach taught by almost every course on economics across the world. Under this approach the cult of the individual reigns.

Milton Friedman believed that competitive forces would ensure the best results for everyone – lower prices through competition, coupled with better returns to investors, through lower operating costs. In Friedman's view, the central, if not the only emphasis of business is to make money for its shareholders. As stated earlier, this can easily lead into today's situation where many corporations and individuals believe that an 'end justifies the means' approach is both correct and desirable.[5] This fosters an extreme form of capitalism that can lead to an unhealthy emphasis on short-term results without serious consideration of organisational sustainability. Profit maximisation rules. It seems to assume that growth is limitless even if perpetual growth is as much a chimera as perpetual motion.

In contrast, stakeholder theory argues that the means is just as important as the end. Stakeholder theory, as propounded by Edward Freeman, argues that there is a variety of parties that impact on the profitability and success of any organisation. These include suppliers, employees, customers, society, governments *and* shareholders. He points out that executives, including those at the very top are still employees, even if they often speak of themselves as being different from *hoi polloi*. There is an interdependent relationship between these parties and, for a sustainable, profitable organisation, boards and management need to ensure all are treated equitably. This directly leads to the view that the operations of an organisation should not only occur within the bounds of the law, but also within a strong ethical framework.

Freeman is no less an advocate of capitalism and profits than is Friedman. The difference relates to 'how' the profit is obtained. For Freeman, the emphasis is on profit optimisation over time so as to increase the probability of long-term, sustainable success. Stakeholder theory accepts the truth of a research project from an international team of researchers at the Massachusetts Institute of Technology (published in 1972 by The Club of Rome as *The Limits to Growth*[6]) which argued that the earth's interlocking resources – the global system of nature in which we all live – probably cannot support present rates of economic and population growth much beyond the year 2100, if that long, even with advanced technology. Of course, this was not a popular message at the time and is even less so today, despite all the evidence available both then and now.

In his 17 January 1961 farewell address to the nation, President Eisenhower expressed his concerns about the dangers of massive military spending, particularly deficit spending and government contracts to private military manufacturers. He coined the term 'military–industrial complex'. Today there is not just a 'military-industrial complex' (although much of the US budget goes on military-related expenditure), but there is a comprehensive complex of business interests (military, pharmaceutical, health care, education, banking, transport, and others) that exercise excessive influence on government policies and practice at every level and across all political parties. These can and do ensure that, under the present approach, there is no narrowing of the economic gap. They use the chimera of 'socialism' (aka, a communistic approach) to ensure there is no change to the status quo – an approach criticised over the years by such capitalist luminaries as Jack Welch of General Electric, Kenneth Mason of Quaker Oats, and management guru, Peter Drucker. All these have argued that many of the problems faced today have been caused by this myopic emphasis on shareholder returns rather than long-term organisational viability coming from an emphasis on all stakeholders.

The 2020 Presidential Elections could prove pivotal to the future of the US. If Donald Trump is not re-elected (something that I consider possible, but unlikely) then I believe his supporters will seek to undermine whoever replaces him and will blame his loss on the House of Representatives, the Mueller enquiry, portions of the Judiciary, unfair or illegal voting behaviour, and, of course, the 'fake news' promulgated by 'fake media'. We could also see significant civil unrest and ensuing violence. This view was reinforced in March 2019 when, in an interview with Breitbart, Trump said:

> I actually think that the people on the right are tougher, but they don't play it tougher. Okay? I can tell you I have the support of the police, the support of the military, the support of the Bikers for Trump – I have the tough people, but they don't play it tough – until they go to a certain point, and then it would be very bad, very bad.[7]

If he wins (something that I consider has a far higher probability), then both the US and the world at large knows what to expect. We will see more of the same egotistical behaviour that panders to those who support his image as a 'winner'. He will continue to pursue the same zero-sum game of confrontation and manipulation and will continue to downgrade environmental and socially responsible activities. This will ensure that, no matter the reality of the impact on the US or the world at large, Trump's power and self-image is at the very least maintained.

I believe that either option (being re-elected or not being re-elected) will result in one of three possible scenarios. First, we could see a global reversion to nationalism. This scenario presumes that the disruptive approach advocated by President Trump is continued even though the outcome will be different from what is actually needed. His emphasis of 'America First' and actions of placing tariffs and penalties on products and services sourced from outside the US, has high impact and, as a direct result, the global marketplace changes forever with a move away from globalisation and a strong reversion to nationalism around the world. World peace and prosperity could be in serious danger.

Second, we revert to a continuation of the status quo from the pre-Trump era. This scenario can be illustrated by the metaphor of driving along a smooth, well-constructed highway when you are alerted to roadworks up ahead. Soon, the road conditions force you to slow down and it is no longer possible to utilise the cruise control on your car. For a while, the road deteriorates with various potholes and totally different and unfamiliar surfaces and conditions to be navigated. However, eventually, you reach the end of the roadworks; conditions revert to those that previously pertained; and you resume your comfortable journey. In this scenario, the power and influence of lobbyists and large corporations continues unabashed; the gap between rich and poor continues to widen; and we move ever further from a fair and equitable society in both the US and across the world.

Third, a world that has been shaken up by current events enables a new world order to emerge. This third scenario presumes that President Trump ultimately proves to be a catalyst towards the development of a new, positive world order. The traditional approach to change management argues that there needs to be an 'unfreezing' from the current state before real change can occur. In this scenario, President Trump will have 'unfrozen' the political, diplomatic, and economic worlds so that something significantly different can emerge and develop. The Trump presidency will have created an environment in which urgently needed systemic change can occur.

Of course, it must be noted that, if this third option eventuates, it may develop in ways totally different from what is expected. Is it possible that the Trump presidency could actually hasten the demise of Henry Luce's 'American Century'? Rather than a single power dominating in the next century, is it possible that a broadly 'Asian Century' could emerge? Trump's tactics have disrupted the rules-based global trading system. China is not the only Asian giant in Trump's sights. He picked a smaller trade fight with India when his administration removed it from a special programme which allows lower tariffs on some products made in low-income countries. The US said India no longer met the 'eligibility criteria'. Understandably, New Delhi responded with retaliatory tariffs of its own. Hopes of a quick return to the old trading norms now look increasingly unlikely.

Since 2012, China's share of world GDP has grown from around 15 per cent to 20 per cent, based on purchasing power parity. India's share of the global economy has doubled from four per cent to eight per cent since the turn of this century. It is clear that businesses and individuals from these countries have extensive investments across the western world and a wide range of western organisations outsource call centres and backroom operations to Asian nations. For well over 40 years there have been increasing numbers of Asian students studying at every level in schools and universities across the western world, so there is a very sound understanding across Asia of western business and political processes and practices as well as high levels of English language competency. However, some believe the politics of the Asian Century are far more tumultuous and complicated. Despite this, the economic transformation of the Asian region is unstoppable and gathering pace.

Given what must be considered a very high probability that Trump will be returned in 2020, to a very large extent the decision as to which of these scenarios actually eventuates post the Donald Trump era depends on what happens in the years between now and the 2024 Presidential Elections.

Whether or not Donald Trump is re-elected in 2020, unless the laws change, he cannot be re-elected to a third term. This means that those who want to replace him – whether Republican, Democrat, some other party, or independent – have a window of about five years in which to reposition themselves. Currently, the opposition to Trump is reactionary. Trump actually controls the narrative whether it is the various enquiries, the media, or the calls for impeachment. Those who want to replace Trump have now got the opportunity to take control of their narrative.

I suggest the third scenario is optimal. There is much to be done, however, if this third scenario is to emerge as a positive factor. There are global considerations, as well as nationalistic ones, that need serious attention. The concept of an Asian Century in any form is an abomination to those with racist tendencies. For those who believe that only Caucasians have the 'right' to world domination, the thought that countries that were once our colonial outposts with resources to be plundered is horrific. We can be sure that such people will present every negative stereotype and prejudice in order to denigrate Asians and to create a fear as to what might happen should they be in control. It is this concern about the unknown, especially should China become the dominant power in tomorrow's world, that drives much of the rhetoric and fear mongering that we find extensively at the end of 2019. Opposition and overt resistance are a far easier path than dealing with 'why' this change is occurring and 'how' it can be handled in a functional manner.

Elliott Jaques, a well-known academic researcher and author, argued that a key component of effective leadership is the ability to deal with ambiguity and complexity.[8] He notes that none of us can predict the future with any certainty because so many variables impact in the present, and will continue to impact (and perhaps intensify), as we move into the unknown. He suggests that those who are responsible for major organisations (and the US can certainly be described in such a term) need to be considering possible scenarios for a 50-year period. In other words, the focus of the President should be on the world as it could be in 50 or so years. When this is done, minor irritants such as perceived personal slights, inability to pass short-term legislation, and the like can be seen in perspective. The focus needs to be on the long term and in creating an environment by which a new, positive world could emerge. Such an environment does not come about by advocating a confrontational, winner-loser, zero-sum game at either national or international level. It can only come about if we are prepared to harness the best minds from across the world in a collaborative and co-operative endeavour to ensure everyone benefits. This immediately requires that all forms of discrimination, extremism, and hate are rejected and opposed. It also requires that issues such as the future of planet earth are front and centre to our considerations and actions.

Right now, there is little evidence that any current presidential contender has the requisite level of ability to deal with complexity and ambiguity. Looking at world leaders outside the US it is no better. Perhaps the time is ripe for a new, young, idealist (Republican, Democrat or independent) candidate, regardless of any discriminatory factor such as colour, gender, sexual orientation etc., whose feet are firmly set in reality, to emerge in the US. If that happens and she or he can garner sufficient support, then America could be 'great again'.

Robert Sapolsky, an American neuroendocrinologist, professor of biology and professor of neurology and neurological sciences at Stanford University, suggests that although we are encountering resurgent nationalism and many other varieties of human divisiveness, our emphasis should be to harness these dynamics rather than fight or condemn them. His plea is for leaders to appeal to people's innate in-group tendencies in ways that incentivise cooperation, accountability, and care for one's fellow humans. He says:

> Imagine a nationalist pride rooted not in a country's military power or ethnic homogeneity but in the ability to take care of its elderly, raise children who score high on tests of empathy, or ensure a high degree of social mobility. Such a progressive nationalism would surely be preferable to one built on myths of victimhood and dreams of revenge. But with the temptation of mistaking the familiar for the superior still etched into the mind, it is not beyond the human species to go to war over which country's people carry out the most noble acts of random kindness. The worst of nationalism, then, is unlikely to be overcome anytime soon.[9]

Across the world, large numbers of people are seeking a fairer, more equitable living environment. Stakeholder theory provides a capitalistic model by which this could actually evolve. This approach could lead to a situation in which the negative power of lobbyists and big business was curtailed, governments actually governed for the real benefit of everyone, and in which an equitable society came about. We could have a *pro utilitate hominum* approach. Yes, we would probably pay more tax – or at least the wealthy (whether individuals or corporations) would pay more because tax minimisation was more difficult – but we could provide the help needed by those more disadvantaged. Heck, we might even find that we started to live in a society again! Now there's a thought! It is also possible that the future of the US as a positive world force and as leader of the free world depends on it.

Notes

1 Milton Friedman (1962), *Capitalism and Freedom*. Chicago, IL: University of Chicago Press.
2 This was first proposed by R. Edward Freeman in his 1984 work, *Strategic Management: A Stakeholder Approach*. Boston, MA: Pitman. Later works by Freeman expounding on this concept include R. Edward Freeman (2010), 'Managing for Stakeholders: Trade-offs or Value Creation', *Journal of Business Ethics, 96(S.1)*: 7–9; R. Edward Freeman and Ellen R. Auster (2011), 'Values, Authenticity, and Responsible Leadership', *Journal of Business Ethics, 98(S.1)*: 15–23; Lauren Purnell and R. Edward Freeman (2012), 'Stakeholder Theory, Fact/Value Dichotomy, and the Normative Core: How Wall Street Stops the Ethics Conversation', *Journal of Business Ethics, 109(1)*: 109–16; R. Edward Freeman (2017), 'The New Story of Business: Towards a More Responsible Capitalism', *Business and Society Review, 122(3)*: 449–65.
3 Friedrich Hayek (1960) *The Constitution of Liberty*, Chicago, IL: University of Chicago Press.
4 Friedman, *Capitalism and Freedom*.
5 This is explored more fully in Douglas G. Long and Zivit Inbar (2017), *The Ethical Kaleidoscope: Values, Ethics, and Corporate Governance*. Abingdon: Routledge.
6 Donella H. Meadows, Dennis L. Meadows, Jorgen Randers, William W. Behrens, III (1972), *The Limits to Growth*. New York: Universe Books.
7 Alexander Marlow, Matthew Boyle, Amanda House and Charlie Spiering, 'President Trump: Paul Ryan blocked subpoenas of Democrats', 13 March 2019. Available at https://www.breitbart.com/politics/2019/03/13/exclusive-president-donald-trump-paul-ryan-blocked-subpoenas-of-democrats/.
8 Elliott Jaques (1998), *Requisite Organisation*, Arlington, VA: Cason Hall & Co.
9 Robert Sapolsky, 'This is your brain on nationalism: the biology of us and them', March/April 2019. Available at https://www.foreignaffairs.com/articles/2019-02-12/your-brain-in-nationalism?utm_medium=newsletters&utm_source=special_send&utm_campaign=summer_reads_2019_newsletters&utm_content=20190901&utm_term=newsletter-summer-popup-2019.

8   The global implications

The question we must now consider relates to the global implications around Donald Trump's re-election. Are we watching the death throes of 'the American Century' or are we witnessing the rebirth of the US as a powerful global force for good? (A very unpalatable alternative, of course, is that we are witnessing a rebirth as a global power for ill. It can only be hoped that this is only a theoretical rather than an actual possibility)

The first point that needs to be made here is that, whether Trump is re-elected or not, much of any moral high ground that was once held by the US has now been lost. What the Trump presidency has made clear is that the US will only ever act in its own interests (or at least those of its major lobby groups), despite any agreement that may have been signed and approved. Although, deep down, this has been implicitly understood by everyone, until the last few years it was seldom verbalised and, for most people, there was always the hope that they were wrong.

The evidence for blatant self-interest is clear. Here are some examples:

In April 2016, the US signed the Paris Climate Agreement with the long-term goal of keeping the increase in global average temperatures to well below 2°C above pre-industrial levels; and to limit the increase to 1.5°C, since this would substantially reduce the risks and effects of climate change. Across the world, the producers of fossil fuels and other vested interests lobbied hard against this as it would impact on the use of coal and similar fuels. In the US, lobbying was particularly effective to the end that, in June 2017, Trump proclaimed his intent to withdraw the US from the Paris Agreement – a rejection of climate change that moves the country toward isolation on the global stage.

In 2015, Iran signed an agreement to redesign, convert, and reduce its nuclear facilities and accept the Additional Protocol (with provisional application), in order to lift all nuclear-related economic sanctions, releasing tens of billions of dollars in oil revenue and frozen assets. The agreement was signed by the US, the UK, Russia, France, and China plus Germany and the European Union. In January 2016, the International Atomic Energy Agency (IAEA) certified that Iran had met the nuclear agreement's preliminary requirements, including taking thousands of centrifuges offline, rendering the core of the Arak heavy-water reactor inoperable, and selling excess low-enriched uranium to Russia. In quarterly reports since then, the IAEA has certified Iran's ongoing compliance. On 8 May 2018, United States President Donald Trump announced the United States was withdrawing from the deal.

Trump objected to the agreement's failure to address Iran's ballistic missile programme or its proxy warfare in the region, and he claimed that the sunset provisions would enable Iran to pursue a bomb in the future. Following US withdrawal, several countries, US allies among them, continued to import Iranian oil under waivers granted by the Trump administration, and Iran continued to abide by its commitments. But a year later, the US ended the waivers. 'This decision is intended to bring Iran's oil exports to zero, denying the regime its principal source of revenue,' the White House said. Iran responded by stating it would no longer be bound to its commitments as long as the other parties to the Joint Comprehensive Plan Of Action (JCPOA) were in breach of theirs. In July 2019, Iran exceeded the agreed-upon limits to its stockpile of low-enriched uranium, and then began enriching uranium to the higher concentration used in medical isotopes, still far short of the 90 per cent purity required for weapons.

On 3 September 2019, it was widely reported that an Iranian delegation was in Paris to work out the details of a financial bailout package that French President Emmanuel Macron intended to use to compensate Iran for oil sales lost to US sanctions. Apparently, in return for the money, Iran would agree to return to compliance with a 2015 nuclear accord. Both Iranian press reports and a senior US official said that the core of the package is a $US15 billion letter of credit that would allow Iran to receive hard currency, at a time when most of the cash it makes from selling oil is frozen in banks around the world. That would account for about half the revenue Iran normally would expect to earn from oil exports in a year. The letter of credit proposed by Macron was part of a broader effort by the French, with help from Germany and other European powers, to save the agreement, even after Trump renounced it as 'a disaster'.

This French initiative was heavily criticised by the US Administration (although other European nations appeared to be in support of the French initiative) on the grounds that it undermined the US Administration's effort to exert what Trump calls 'maximum pressure' on Tehran. Without the Administration's support for the deal, it is not clear whether European banks will risk US sanctions by extending credit to Tehran or whether the credit might be extended by the European Central Bank, or France's central bank, which would be more difficult for Washington to sanction. Accordingly, the path forward if agreement is reached with Iran, is still strewn with many rocks of uncertainty as to what the US response will be. Increasingly, however, the US appears to be relatively isolated on this issue and there are grounds for suspecting that part of the US insistence that Iran carried out the September 2019 attack on Saudi oilfields may be linked to undermining the French initiative.

Over the past two years, Donald Trump has repeatedly complained that Europe's NATO members are not contributing enough to the Alliance. He believes the US should not have to bear the burden of funding the defence of Europe. Donald Trump has repeatedly threatened to withdraw from the North Atlantic Treaty Organization. Current and former Trump officials who support the alliance, said they feared Mr Trump could return to his threat as allied military spending continued to fall behind the goals he had set. Russia and President Putin will be delighted if this happens.

The present Trump-initiated trade war with China is impacting on far more countries than just the US, but it is only one more step by Trump in his move towards protectionist policies. He has abrogated trade treaties such as the North American Free Trade Agreement (NAFTA) and withdrawn from discussions on a Trans-Pacific Trade Agreement as well as imposing tariffs on products from many other countries apart from China. He appears to be totally unconcerned about the collateral damage experienced by any other country.

The decision by Donald Trump to withdraw the US from the World Trade Organization (WTO) in 2020 will effectively emasculate a body that has been promoting free trade and the peaceful resolution of trade disputes. It now appears as though, by the end of 2020, the WTO board will not have sufficient members to even constitute a quorum for any meetings.

Now the stark truth must be acknowledged and accepted. An agreement with the US is not necessarily worth anything if the president decrees it fails to meet with his agenda. It is also clear that the US will seek to disrupt any agreement between other countries with which it disagrees. Despite this, the US still seeks to be the arbiter of what is acceptable across the globe. Can a 'US First' approach really help the US maintain any moral high ground?

Which brings us back to the global implications around Donald Trump's re-election. If the US is to retain any moral stature and be seen to be the arbiter of what is acceptable across the globe, then some significant changes are necessary. Such changes are extremely unlikely if Donald Trump is re-elected.

The US Constitution limits the tenure of any president to a maximum of two terms. This means that, unless there is a change to the US Constitution (something that is possible, but highly improbable) Trump will not have to pander to his supporters in order to be re-elected in 2024. He will have no motivation to change. He can be his usual, somewhat unpredictable self – following his urges and desires for power and control. This is unlikely to endear him either to many in the Republican Party (let alone the Democrats and the undecided), or to the world at large. The Republican Party may try to rein him in but, given their failure to do so in the past few years, it seems unlikely that any firm action will be taken. It is more likely that potential presidential candidates for 2024 will either seek to show their similarity to Trump in order to maintain Trump's momentum or that, if they feel there is sufficient opposition to 'the Trumpian way', they will seek to distinguish themselves from Trump. Either way, the Republican Party per se, is unlikely to strongly and publicly criticise one of their own – especially one who has enabled them to obtain their current level of power and influence.

If this happens then, worldwide, it is almost certain that we will continue to see a fracturing of the old (mainly) liberal democratic societies developed over the past 100 or so years. The last few years have seen a resurgence of nationalistic political parties who use the guise of patriotism to justify xenophobic and discriminatory behaviours to immigrants and, very often, tourists. Increasingly we hear a 'them' and 'us' commentary with 'them' always being seen as being the wrong people in the wrong place at the wrong time.

Consider the situation in Europe. It is less than 75 years since the end of the Second World War and most of those who experienced the extremely negative impact of the nationalism that arose between1918 and 1939, are dead. However, the underlying philosophies have never died – they simply been obscured while continuing to fester and morph into more socially acceptable forms. Since the mid-1970s, they have quietly become more visible and there has been a recent boom in voter support for right-wing and populist parties. One result of this has been the current moves by these parties to organise into a pan-European power bloc. While this can be seen as a back-lash against the political establishment, the truth is more likely to be a wave of discontent that taps into concerns about globalisation, immigration, a dilution of national identity and the EU itself. People are disillusioned because the promises made by the advocates of neoliberalism have been proven to be largely illusionary with the major gains going to the few and only crumbs for the many. In the US, people in Europe are looking for a saviour and, when desperate, will find a scapegoat on which to blame their ills. Nationalism has always been able to nominate scapegoats and to ensure that these are, at the very least, marginalised. We lack the stomach to admit that we were duped by neoliberal promises, so blaming our present situation on third parties enables us to avoid accountability.

With the UK having made Brexit a reality and, according to the BBC in May 2019[1]), a rise in nationalistic parties in: Sweden (17.6 per cent support), Finland (17.7 per cent support), Denmark (21 per cent support), Estonia (17.8 per cent support), the Netherlands (13 per cent support), Germany (12.6 per cent support), France (13 per cent support), Switzerland (29 per cent support), Austria (26 per cent support), Czech Republic (11 per cent support), Slovakia (8 per cent support), Hungary (68 per cent support), Italy (17.4 per cent support), Bulgaria (9 per cent support), Greece (7 per cent support), Cyprus (3.7 per cent support), and Spain (10.3 per cent support), this is no passing fad.

As mentioned in the previous chapter, Robert Sapolsky argues that the rise of nationalistic forces is totally understandable. He makes the point that,

> ... our brains distinguish between in-group members and outsiders in a
> fraction of a second, and they encourage us to be kind to the former but

hostile to the latter. These biases are automatic and unconscious and emerge at astonishingly young ages. ... Humans can rein in their instincts and build societies that divert group competition to arenas less destructive than warfare, yet the psychological bases for tribalism persist, even when people understand that their loyalty to their nation, skin color, god, or sports team is as random as the toss of a coin. At the level of the human mind, little prevents new teammates from once again becoming tomorrow's enemies.[2]

Sapolsky considers this issue from the perspective of neuroscience to illustrate that all of us make automatic, value-loaded judgements about individuals and groups and points out that some of these arise from learned behaviours while others seem to be present from birth. He uses the example of infants who, from earliest cognition, tend to respond more easily and to have an easier time remembering faces of people from the same race as their parents. He points out that this does not mean the parents actively or implicitly teach their children racism or gender bias but that the baby relates to what is familiar rather than to that which is different. As we grow and develop, we still tend to have a fundamental allegiance to the familiar.

This then can be manipulated to have an impact from a broader social perspective. We all belong to mutual, overlapping in-groups simultaneously. We may be members of a particular faith group, a sporting club, a local community, workplace, and the like. In each of these there will be a different set of 'us and them'. When these clash, such as people within the same faith community being of different racial groups, supporting different sporting clubs, coming from a different residential community, working for a different organisation etc., we are able to make explicit adjustments and the 'them' may be tempered by the 'us' experience but the specific features that humans focus on to make this determination vary depending on the social context and can be easily manipulated – such as, for example, by the wearing of particular uniforms or symbols. This explains the importance various communities attach to flags, dress, or facial hair. He argues 'The hipster beard, the turban, and the "Make America Great Again" hat all fulfil this role by sending strong signals of tribal belonging'.

Nationalism is not necessarily a negative. At its best it can prompt people to pay their taxes and welfare for their nation's 'have-nots', including people they have never met and will never meet. But it is easily destabilised, and the forces of globalisation can make people feel irrelevant and bring them into contact with very different sorts of people. When this happens, Sapolsky writes, '... nationalism can quickly devolve into something much darker: a dehumanizing hatred that turns Jews into "vermin," Tutsis into "cockroaches," or Muslims into "terrorists." Today, this toxic brand of nationalism is making a comeback across the globe, spurred on by political leaders eager to exploit it for electoral advantage.' Fears relating to the corona virus pandemic are further exacerbating this move to nationalism.

Notes

1 'Europe and right-wing nationalism: a country-by-country guide', 13 November 2019. Available at https://www.bbc.com/news/world-europe-36130006.
2 Robert Sapolsky, 'This is your brain on nationalism: the biology of us and them', March/April 2019. Available at https://www.foreignaffairs.com/articles/2019-02-12/your-brain-nationalism?utm_medium=newsletters&utm_source=special_send&utm_campaign=summer_reads_2019_newsletters&utm_content=20190901&utm_term=newsletter-summer-popup-2019.

Part Two

Lessons from 'the Trump event'

Part Two moves from what could be considered the 'cubic zirconia leadership'[1] of Donald Trump – a leadership that is dominated by egotistical behaviour and personal agendas – to consider the concept of 'diamond leadership'. This is a position where the entire leadership team eschews any personal agendas in order to focus on the higher organisational agenda. They do this to create an environment in which every person is treated equitably and is enabled to succeed. This optimises the probability that the organisation itself can be sustainably successful.

Note

1 Douglas G. Long (1998), *Leaders: Diamonds or Cubic Zirconia? Asia Pacific Leaders on Leadership.* Sydney: CLS.

9 What executives and leaders can learn from the Trump event

The term 'Trump event' is used as shorthand for the behaviour demonstrated by President Trump in the period from when he first became the Republican candidate for the 2016 US presidential elections through to the present. To understand it we need first to consider the concept of leadership and how this is practised by Donald J. Trump. This will lead us to similarities and differences between 'the US' as an organisation and the more commonly encountered organisations (for-profit and not-for-profit, public and private sectors), of our everyday experience.

What is leadership?

Any quick check of dictionaries will provide definitions of 'leadership'. They can probably be summarised as 'the art of motivating a group of people to act towards achieving a common goal … He or she is the person in the group that possesses the combination of personality and leadership skills that makes others want to follow his or her direction.' The problem is that these tend to conflate 'leader' with 'leadership'.

Elsewhere, it has been suggested that there is a difference between the 'leader' per se and 'leadership'.[1] It is argued that '… a "leader" carries out particular individual activities or demonstrates particular individual behaviours while "leadership" is the cumulative effect of the individual activities from all the organisation's leaders.' In other words, sometimes it can be the difference between focus on an individual or focus on a team or group of 'leaders' that enables us to assess the overall effectiveness of those who accept responsibility for achieving results – the real 'leaders'. There are occasions when results are achieved *despite* the formal leader rather than *because of* the formal leader. By this, it is suggested that a nominal or formal *leader* may be ineffective, yet the organisation still thrives, at least in the short term, because those without formal roles take it upon themselves to facilitate success.

It is a truism that today's environment is so complex and requires so much ability to deal with ambiguity, that no one person is able to deal appropriately with every challenge and issue on their own. There is so much information with varying levels of truth available from so many sources that fully comprehending them, analysing them, and deciding on appropriate action in an appropriate time frame is largely beyond the capability of any one person. The result is, when this happens, we tend to succumb to the bias of immediacy, where the most recent information becomes the basis for decision, avoid decisions until a crisis erupts, or abdicate accountability and responsibility in a manner which enables us to blame others when something does not go as planned. The situation is exacerbated when the leader is surrounded by 'yes men' and those who are caught in the throes of groupthink.

Attempts to avoid accountability and responsibility can extend to the very top of an organisation – the Board. In interviews with the chairperson of 130 organisations across Australia, New Zealand, and the US,[2] feedback from interviewees included the following:

- 'Why do I care about ethics? I don't know if I have any values, I am interested in risk. I have an atheist view of ethics. It is all about the risk management'.
- 'I joined an NFP (Not-for-Profit) board and had an intuition that there was something going on with the Chairman's behaviour. You are trying to convince yourself that they are not being unethical. Sometimes, nobody has the guts to say something, because you don't want to be offensive to anyone.'
- 'The new CEO of XX Corp was a yes-man to the board. The whole OHS (Occupational Health and Safety) went down – they cut head count and training. Thereafter the big issue happened due to H&S.'
- 'When I brought unethical behaviours to the board, the board stopped working with me.'

In the research interviews, it was also made clear that, in many cases, it could take years rather than weeks or months for issues involving ethics to reach Board level and, when they did, the focus was primarily on limiting damage rather than on addressing the underlying issues. Of course, when crises in relation to ethical behaviour did occur, there was plausible deniability from 'the leaders' on the grounds that they had policies in place, but others chose not to adhere to them!

In Australia, two Royal Commissions during 2018–19 that examined abuses in the financial sector and in the aged care sector, regularly encountered this refusal to accept responsibility – to be 'real' leaders – from those to whom the care of the various organisations had been entrusted. Examples in the US include such controversies as Ford's 'Pinto' car, the Enron scandal, the conduct of banks leading to the 2007 Financial Crisis, and, most recently, the ability of convicted sex offender, the late Jeffrey Edward Epstein, to avoid scrutiny by police and other authorities as he resumed his predatory practices after serving a prison sentence for sexual offences against underage girls.

The secret to an engaged and high-performing organisation is leadership – not just from the top-down, but from the whole team. By encouraging employees to cultivate leadership skills, it is possible to create a winning organisation that is proactive, productive, and stronger together. Being a leader does not necessarily mean being the boss. Every person has the potential to take a leadership role in some area of organisational life even if it is as simple as modelling the values that the organisation has espoused in contrast to the values they see demonstrated by their peers.

Distinguishing between 'the leader' and 'leadership' makes it impossible to avoid accountability and responsibility across an organisation. If 'leadership' is the hub around which everything in the organisation rotates then, to some extent, every person in the organisation becomes responsible and accountable for the quality and quantity of performance. This is the realisation and message that lies behind the Leadership for Performance Model originally developed in the 1990s.

In this model, the quality and quantity of leadership across the entire organisation becomes the focus and 'leadership' is the cumulative impact of what is said and done by all leaders no matter their position in the organisation. Individualism and egocentricity are actively discouraged and a co-operative, organisational outcomes-focused approach is encouraged from everyone.

Those factors which directly impact on performance are the 'ability' and 'willingness' or 'readiness' (or, if you prefer, the 'competence' and 'confidence/ motivation' or the 'capability') of the individual or group involved. It is important to note that these two factors of ability and willingness are related but totally independent. There are many people who are competent to do certain things – they have the ability – but they are not prepared to do them:

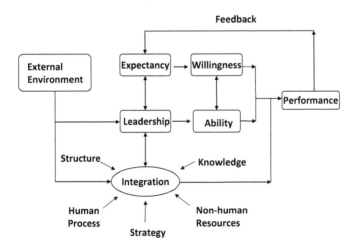

Figure 9.1 The leadership for performance model

they lack the willingness, confidence or motivation to do them – for some reason or another they lack the 'readiness' to perform. Again, this is not necessarily good or bad – for example, all of us can do things that are unlawful: fortunately, most of us are not motivated in that direction and so we can lead relatively quiet, law-abiding lives. On the other hand, there are many people who will enthusiastically declare themselves willing to undertake any task even when they have no idea of how the task should be done or what the task involves. Such enthusiasm without skill has either the potential to be very good as some innate competence comes to the fore and they learn quickly or the potential for disaster if what they do proves to endanger themselves and/or other people. It is well known that the effective leader does not confuse willingness with ability.

An important aspect here is the direct relationship between ability and willingness. Generally (but not always), the more capable a person is – the greater their ability – the more likely they are to be willing to demonstrate this ability. Similarly, even if a person has very little ability for a task or activity, if they are willing or motivated to learn, there is a high probability that they can develop the requisite ability in a relatively short time. Of course, the reverse is also true. People who have been 'turned off' from education or learning or who are frustrated in their work environment are far less willing to develop new abilities or to demonstrate the abilities they already have.

It is this area of willingness-ability-performance that is the focus of most leadership approaches and leadership development programmes. The emphasis of many programmes is on the immediate leader–follower interaction and how the leader encourages a person (or people) towards achieving what needs to be done. There can be no doubt that these factors are crucial to performance and that they warrant the considerable attention they have received. This is a totally appropriate focus for one-on-one or one-on-small-group interactions in environments of low complexity. But the issue of 'willingness' and 'ability' is not sufficient in most situations, such as when a larger group is involved or where the leadership is being exercised in more complex situations. For these we need a more inclusive model.

The additional factors that impact less directly on performance are found in two areas – those in the organisation and those in the more distant area of the environment in which the organisation operates. Consider first those factors within the organisation – knowledge, strategy, non-human resources, structure and human process – that impact on performance.

'**Knowledge**' refers to the aggregation of data and information available – it includes the history of the organisation in a micro and macro sense, as well as all the information that is necessary for the organisation to function effectively. Accordingly, an essential part of the knowledge component is a high-quality induction programme that links every aspect of every position with the vision, values and strategic orientation of the organisation. But this must be complemented with additional. relevant information.

Traditionally the organisational elders – the leadership team – have been the guardians of this additional knowledge and the ability to impart or withhold information has given these more senior people a significant power base – a power base that is often abused.

'Strategy' refers to the long-term approaches that are in place to help us achieve goals. It considers such things as our visions of the future and the goals that we set in order to get there. In commercial organisations (whether for-profit or not-for-profit), the issue of strategy is well known and usually well documented (even if 'strategy' is often confused with 'tactics'), but in small organisations and families there may have been no real discussion or planning in this regard, which can lead to 'policy on the run' and decisions being made that are immediately convenient yet which create longer term problems. It has been said that many of today's problems arise from yesterday's solutions!

'Non-human resources' refer to the assets we have available in both the short term and longer term. These may include things like time, cash flow (in a family, monthly wages), buildings, vehicles, machinery and the like. The availability of these for the right people, at the right time, in the right place and for the right use, has a very real impact on whether people are able to perform as required.

'Structure' refers to who does what and where everyone fits into the overall need to get things done. This is the aspect that draws together information, strategy and non-human resources. As has often been stated, 'structure should follow strategy' for effective operations. A key aspect of designing the structure relates to ensuring the non-human resources are available when and where required by those who need them. But it also deals with critical people issues such as discrimination. For most of our history there were clear-cut delineations between 'man's work' and 'woman's work', between 'young person's work' and 'old person's work', etc., and such delineations have led to many of the stereotypes and discrimination problems we still encounter today.

It must be noted that, in most organisations, there are two quite distinct structures – the formal one to which assent is given by everyone involved and the informal one which is the network of personal interactions and power alliances that has very significant influence over whether (and how) desired goals are achieved. Both structures are important, and attention is needed to both if desired performance is to be obtained. Structure should fit strategy – and sometimes that might mean that neither the existing formal nor the informal structures are appropriate.

'Human process' refers to recruitment, development, and the way in which people interact with each other. If the structure is appropriate then this sets up an organisation in which good, highly productive interpersonal relationships are far more likely to exist – of course, the opposite is also true. All people interactions are impacted by the value sets, attitudes, degrees of commitment, willingness to cooperate, and other 'behind the eyes' factors that affect how we behave. The human process factor is not only a key source of high productivity, but it is also an area of potential conflict and can be the source of much that makes an organisation dysfunctional.

Each of these factors (knowledge, strategy, non-human resources, structure and human process) on its own has a significant impact on whether desired performance is attained. Together, they have a multiplier impact on whether desired performance is attained. Accordingly, it is critical that they are adequately integrated to ensure compatibility and harmony. It is the extent to which these factors are appropriately integrated that determines whether an organisation has a positive or less than positive organisational culture.

Failure to adequately integrate these factors may well mean that no matter how willing and able a person or group is, they are unable to achieve desired performance because the system is working against them – the culture of the organisation is non-supportive. Leaders who have relatively low conceptual ability generally do not understand this. Invariably, such leaders have difficulty in bringing about the appropriate degree of integration and, thus, changing the organisation's culture to one that has a high probability of achieving desired results through a committed and engaged workforce.

But apart from factors inside the organisation, there are additional factors outside the organisation – the greater environment. The environment, from a leadership perspective, includes such things as the competition, suppliers, legislation impacting on personal, family and business organisation behaviours, and a range of other factors that are 'outside' the organisation itself. These could include such things as building regulations, occupational health and safety legislation, anti-discrimination legislation, minimum wage and employee entitlements, the overall job market, international and national economics, and myriad other issues that tell us *what* we may or may not do and *how* we may or may not do it. The Global Financial Crisis of 2008–2009 focused attention on these outside factors in a way that had not been seen since the time of the Great Depression 80 years earlier. Trump's presidency is calling us to revisit them once again.

In other words, whether desired performance is achieved depends on the individual, the organisation, *and* factors totally outside the organisation. The factors impacting on the individual and the organisational factors can be largely controlled from within the organisation: the environmental factors cannot.

But even the issue of 'willingness' and 'ability' is a little more complex than is often acknowledged. Over the past 50 or so years the motivation industry has emerged. Today it is worth millions of dollars throughout the world. The motivation industry is largely based on the premise that people will be inspired to greater performance through stories of hardship being overcome and success attained. The argument is that people receive a psychological boost through hearing of what others have achieved and how they have done it; that this will inspire them to become similarly successful.

There is an element of truth in this proposition – but it is also open to serious abuse. There are people who become as reliant upon or addicted to 'motivational seminars' as are other people to adrenaline, gambling, alcohol, nicotine and other legal and illegal drugs and activities. These people require a regular 'fix' – generally in frequently increasing doses (as can sometimes be seen in relation to sales teams where most of the remuneration is from commission on sales) – if they are to perform even close to the standards that are desired. To change the metaphor, some people are like campers around a campfire who vary their distance from the flames depending on whether they are comfortably warm, too hot, or too cold. Without the external stimulus they would be uncomfortable, possibly miserable, and unable to function effectively.

Most people want to do a good job. Most people want to put their very best in for their organisation. Preventing them are such factors as the quality and quantity of feedback and the stumbling blocks caused by inadequate or inappropriate integration of knowledge, strategy, non-human resources, structure and human process.

Research conducted during the 1990s[3] indicated people seek eight characteristics in their leaders:

- Self-confidence
- Values
- Integrity
- People
- Change
- Creativity
- Communication
- Environment

Looking at these characteristics in more detail:

Leadership requires self-confidence

The media promulgate the concept of *charisma* as essential for leadership. Trump is a very clear example of this. Accordingly, people, particularly in the political arena, are assessed on their *public appeal factor*. This has the damaging effect of encouraging misuse of the media as a means for attracting attention and the enacting of flamboyant behaviour (either positive or negative), in order to demonstrate one has the requisite amount of charisma.

Charisma is also an attribute that all too often fades into oblivion long before the leader moves out of the limelight. Rather than advocating and seeking charisma, true leadership builds and exhibits self-confidence and trust. Being seen as having charisma is not an indicator that the person actually has self-confidence.[4] The non-partisan American think (or 'fact') tank, The Pew Research Center, highlighted some of these issues in their report of 28 June 2017 on how the image of the US has been affected by President Trump.[5] They showed that, even though people often spoke of President Trump as having charisma, the overall image and reputation of the US has suffered significant decline since he became President.

From the evidence publicly available, there may be grounds for considering that Trump lacks true self-confidence. This is indicated in such matters as his well-documented and almost constant use of Twitter to rebuff any real or imagined slight from individuals or organisations; his claims of 'fake news' in relation to any item that is different from that which he would portray; the infamous film of his Cabinet meeting where each person present praised him in grandiose terms;[6] and on 28 June 2017 the online article revealing that *Time* magazine had requested that the Trump organisation take down framed copies of a fake cover featuring Donald Trump. The fake cover had been prominently displayed in at least five of the US President's golf clubs.[7]

Self-confidence does not mean being brash and constantly letting others know how good you are. Neither does it mean being aggressive or offensive. Rather it means having a realistic sense of one's strengths and weaknesses coupled with a determination to make a positive contribution to one's world wherever possible. Research across the world shows that those leaders who genuinely listen to others and acknowledge their own limitations are shown to produce better organisational results for longer periods.

In relation to self-confidence, it can also be useful to consider one's motivation. As previously discussed, some years ago David McClelland, a Harvard professor, identified three motivators that he believed we all have: a need for achievement (or 'inhibition'), a need for affiliation, and a need for power. People will have different characteristics depending on their dominant motivator.

People who have a need for affiliation prefer to spend time creating and maintaining social relationships, enjoy being a part of groups, and have a desire to feel loved and accepted. People in this group tend to adhere to the norms of the culture in that workplace and typically do not change or even challenge the norms of the workplace for fear of rejection. This person favours collaboration over competition and does not like situations with high risk or high uncertainty. Some of these people may seek affiliation because they need external affirmation as to their personal worth.

People who have a need for achievement prefer working on tasks of moderate difficulty, prefer work in which the results are based on their effort rather than on anything else, and prefer to receive feedback on their work. Achievement-based individuals tend to avoid both high-risk and low-risk situations. Low-risk situations are seen as too easy to be valid and the high-risk situations are seen as based more on the luck of the situation rather than the achievements of the individual. These people tend to achieve results because of the trust, respect, and rapport they have with those among whom they work. They are able to inhibit negative drives and exhibit high self-control in order to focus on what is to be achieved (hence the alternate term of 'inhibition'). For these people, positions in a hierarchy, titles, and the trappings of power are of secondary importance. People with this approach seem more likely to be able to adapt to changes in organisational structure and to concentrate more on enabling people to perform than on controlling people. It is not that they eschew positional power. When required, they are ready and able to use it. Rather, the difference is that this is an ultimate fall-back position, instead of being the normal mode of operating. Their authority tends to come not from the organisation or job per se. Instead, it comes from within because of their expertise, their communicative ability and the overall trust they both engender and demonstrate. These people tend to demonstrate considerable amounts of self-confidence and that enables them to focus on what is to be achieved rather than on what others may say or whether or not they are compliant.

The need for power is the desire within a person to hold control and authority over another person and to influence and change another's decision in accordance with his or her own needs or desires. The need to enhance their self-esteem and reputation drives these people and they desire to have their views and ideas accepted and implemented over the views and ideas over others. People who have a need for power enjoy work and place a high value on discipline. While the positive side of the need for power is that these people can be very good organisers who will refocus and restructure an organisation, the downside to this motivational type is that group goals can become zero-sum in nature. For one person to win, another must lose. Competition motivates them and they enjoy winning arguments. Status and recognition are what they aspire to and they do not like being on the losing side. They are self-disciplined and expect the same self-discipline from their peers and teams. The need for power is accompanied by needs for personal prestige and a higher personal status. It is a hallmark of egocentric behaviour which may indicate a lack of emotional growth. Compliance with 'my' wishes is essential for the power-motivated person.

McClelland recognised that the balance between these three can vary with life circumstances and also discussed the possibility that, overall, an equitable balance between all three would be attained in a well-rounded personality. Such a balance does not seem evident in President Trump. Based on these, it would appear that he is motivated primarily by power to the extent that relationships are welcomed only if they recognise and heed his power and authority. This power motivation for Donald Trump is consistent with McClelland's 1976 *Harvard Business Review* article where he argued that power is the great motivator and concluded from their research,

> that the top manager of a company must possess a high need for power—that is, a concern for influencing people. However, this need must be disciplined and controlled so that it is directed toward the benefit of the institution as a whole and not toward the manager's personal aggrandizement. Moreover, the top manager's need for power ought to be greater than his or her need to be liked.[8]

McClelland argues that in organisations there is a need for power, but not necessarily a desire for power except where it enables them to exercise leadership and vision. This is different from Trump's demonstrated desire for power; the President of the US requires power to enact the requirements of his role whereas Trump desires power to satisfy his ego. President Trump clearly has a great need for power but whether or not that is then directed to the benefit of the US as a whole is somewhat questionable. One strongly suspects also that his need for power vastly outweighs his need to be liked. McClelland and Burnham (2008), argue that effective and positive use of power motivation requires a person to have high self-control or 'inhibition' (closely related to 'achievement') so that responses are not primarily reactive to emotional stimuli. The point is made that '... In our earlier study, we found ample evidence that [persons lacking in self-control] exercise their power impulsively. They are more often rude to other people, they drink much, they try to exploit others sexually, and they collect symbols of personal prestige such as fancy cars or big offices.' They make the point that the very best power-motivated managers are mature. They say: 'Mature people can be most simply described as less egotistic. Somehow their positive self-image is not at stake in their jobs. They are less defensive, more willing to seek advice from experts, and have a longer-range view. They accumulate fewer personal possessions and seem older and wiser. It is as if they have awakened to the fact that they are not going to live forever and have lost some of the feeling that their own personal future is all that important.' It may also be possible that President Trump is impacted by a serious imbalance between the three motivators of power, achievement (or 'inhibition') and affiliation: that he lacks maturity?

From the perspective of a national leader, self-confidence involves recognising that neither they, nor their party, are omnipotent. There is no simple answer to the complex issues facing every government in every country. There is a constant tension between the need for revenue from direct and indirect taxes and the willingness and ability of people and corporations to pay those taxes. At the same time, it is recognised that people should provide for their own future. This need to, on the one hand, pay taxes while on the other hand look after oneself, needs to be balanced with a socially responsible government in which those in need are appropriately supported and/or assisted as and when necessary. Simplistic answers such as are often propounded by various pressure groups tend to be short term and single issue specific. They fail to deal with the degree of complexity involved in national leadership.

This, of course, begs the question of how do we develop self-confidence (a balanced sense of self-worth and a positive personal image)? This is one of the greatest challenges facing society. Until we get back to facilitating the development of self-confidence in people, we will continue to have significant proportions of the population of every country, across every socio-economic stream, acting in a dysfunctional manner.

Organisational psychologist Tasha Eurich believes that becoming more self-aware can lead to greater success, personally and professionally.[9] Her research shows that self-awareness is made up of two types of knowledge. One is introspective awareness: seeing ourselves clearly and knowing both what we value and what we aspire to do. But equally importantly, and frequently neglected, is the idea that we should also know how other people see us. She found that there are a considerable number of individuals who possess one of those types of knowledge, but not the other. Her research showed that 95 per cent of people think that they are self-aware, but the real number is closer to between 10 and 15 per cent, and this makes our society more delusional today than in the past. There are some people who are so focused on how other people see them that they are actually not acting in their own best interests. They don't even know what they want out of life, for example, which may indicate that they are unclear as to their personal values. She shows that self-awareness helps us make smarter decisions; helps us form better relationships; and helps us be more successful in our careers. Her data shows that people who are self-aware are much better leaders and also lead more profitable companies. To aid in self-awareness, Eurich suggests we need to ensure that the act of analysing or reflecting on ourselves does actually result in insight about ourselves. An important aspect of this is to obtain accurate feedback even when others are reluctant to tell us what they really think.

This must call us to reconsider the values on which our societies and our leadership are based. For self-confidence can be developed provided we are prepared to accept our need for development and are prepared to put in the time and effort of self-disclosure and reception of feedback. Sometimes others consciously assist us in developing it: in other instances, we develop it despite our circumstances. Leaders do not leave such things to chance – for either themselves or for others. They recognise the importance of self-confidence and they create a positive, healthy environment in which people can grow and develop.

Leadership is centred in our values

One of the mistakes often made is to talk of leadership in global or generalist terms. This is based on the assumption that the concepts and practices of leadership that are advocated in the US or Europe will be equally valid, for example, in Australia, New Zealand, South-East Asia. It also assumes that there is little, if any real difference between business, political, social, sporting, and other areas in which leadership is exercised. It fails to acknowledge that what is seen as acceptable and effective leadership in one country, may be quite different from what is advocated elsewhere. It also fails to recognise that different areas of human endeavour require different approaches to leadership in order to optimise the probability of success. For example, an acceptable and effective leadership approach in a strongly hierarchical society ,may be vastly different from what works in a more egalitarian society.

There appears to be some consensus in the literature that values are emotionally loaded attitudes or beliefs. They are those things to which we are so committed that we allow them to influence how we behave. Experience indicates that values are culturally specific. We learn our values from the environment in which we grew up. In most societies our values are influenced by family and the dominant religious or philosophical movement existing in our country or society. A direct result of this is that we experience constant conflict in relation to our values. Having been brought up in one environment, we later live and work in another. We can also become torn between the different messages we receive and the change in expression of societal values from one decade to another. We are continually faced with the challenge of deciding between what should be retained and what should be changed. A direct result of this is that, for many people, values are seen as items that can be selected from a shopping list of desirables. For others, the core values remain the same – the way in which they are expressed – their manifestation – changes as society evolves.

Unfortunately, many people fail to deal adequately with this issue of values change. When their beliefs are challenged, some people will recklessly disregard all they have been taught and previously believed. Rather than considering new and improved expression of the same core values, they discard one and embrace another in order to be relevant or politically correct. Others cling to the past expressions of their core values and refuse to consider the fact a new manifestation of these may be beneficial. Yet others, when faced with the new, seek to retreat even further into the past by advocating manifestations that were extant in previous periods.

There is an important caveat here relating to whether or not our values are 'right'. While there will always be some disagreement as to what is 'right' and what is 'wrong', there are clearly some areas of overlap. We can, for example, generally agree that 'respect' is an important value even if we have disagreement on whether that should be conditional or unconditional respect. Similarly, we can generally agree that values leading to indiscriminate violence and harm to others, are ones to be avoided.

Tasha Eurich suggests there is a solution to fully understanding our real values. She ties this in with developing self-confidence. Instead of going deep, go wide. Look at the themes and patterns between the events in your life. To understand your values, think about your last three or four jobs and what you liked about them, what you didn't. This enables a person to get feedback by looking for behaviour patterns which can be much more informative than long sessions of deep introspection.

Effective leaders know that values both can, and must, change with changing circumstances and that the manifestation of these values will change with them. They seek to ensure that the emerging values are always positive and are orientated to the betterment of our world in the broadest possible sense. They recognise that their own illustration of values will change as they personally grow and develop. They are prepared to grapple with the conflict in their own lives and to admit when they are unsure of what their demonstration of values ought to be. It is a sign of maturity that a person is prepared to constantly assess their current values framework against the reality of the circumstances within which they are operating then make the psychological and behavioural changes that are now necessary for real, on-going success not only for themselves but for everyone. Values such as this provide a bulwark against assessing values by only considering the current framework and pragmatism.

Donald Trump seems to be holding on to values that have worked for him in the past. He is used to operating within a privately-owned company that is relatively free from outside checks and balances. As such, he has had significant freedom in being as authoritarian as he wished and to replace at will any person who might disagree with him. He attained power and wealth in the business arena both by inheritance and through an aggressive pattern of behaviour in which he could intimidate˙ with impunity. It was of little consequence to him if he insulted or damaged others – everything was about 'the deal' and its benefits to Donald Trump. But now he holds what is arguably the most powerful position in the world. People pay attention to his every word and many adjust their opinions of the US based on what they hear. The circumstances have changed but he has not. He seems totally unaware of the adage of 'whatever behaviour got me to the position I am in today, is the behaviour that probably will make me unsuccessful in the future.'

Donald Trump is unused to the worldwide scrutiny attracted by the role of US' President and resents any suggestion that any way but his could be appropriate. His is a classic example of refusal to change – his behaviour in 2019 seems basically identical to what it was in 2016, this indicates little personal growth with no alteration in values.

Leadership is about integrity

Shakespeare's comments about integrity ring as true today as when first written for the character, Polonius:

> This above all: to thine own self be true,
> And it must follow, as the night the day,
> Thou canst not then be false to any man.
> *Hamlet*, Act I, Scene 3

Leaders must be people of integrity – their words and actions must be consistent, they must be people who can be trusted. Closely linked with this is the issue of *courage* – the willingness to do the right thing even when it conflicts with what others want you to do. Clear examples of this can be found in people such as William Wilberforce, Abraham Lincoln, Mahatma Gandhi, Martin Luther King Jr, and Nelson Mandela.

The *Oxford English Dictionary* defines 'integrity' as 'entirety, soundness, honesty'. When explored during research leading to the 'Leadership Diamond',[10] participants made it clear that they understood 'integrity' to mean that a person was true to their values; that they kept their word. This was encapsulated in interviews where participants said: 'Leaders are people who have the courage to show consistency between what they espouse and how they behave. They can be trusted'; 'They are people who keep their word', and 'integrity means "walking the talk" – showing consistency between words and behaviour.'

Integrity evolves from values rather than the reverse. In order to demonstrate that one is worthy of trust, one first needs the assumption that being trustworthy is a worthwhile characteristic – a function of one's values. If there is any apparent discrepancy between espoused values and actual behaviour, the issue of integrity is raised by the very fact of this dissonance. This raises another issue in relation to integrity. Can a person be effective if there is dissonance between their values and those of their organisation? Any such dissonance will be demonstrated by the leader's behaviour – and followers will believe what they see in preference to what they are told.

As already discussed, Donald Trump has never led an organisation in which he was answerable to an independent body. His business experience is with a family-owned organisation where none of the legislated regulations of checks and balances found in a public corporation have been instituted. In a family business he was able to be as despotic as he wished – the golden rule applied: he who owns the gold makes the rules. He has tried to take that same approach into the presidency – appointing family members to senior positions in his administration and blatantly using his position to market the Trump empire. He has also made it clear that he prioritises personal loyalty rather than commitment first to the US per se, and to him as a consequence of that – those who fail to show total allegiance have relatively short tenure. The result is a dissonance between his personal values and the constitution of the US. It is this that has brought about his current problems in relation to the investigations into his behaviour as President. If history is to remember him as one of the great presidents, then almost certainly something will need to change.

Normally, of course, we tend to assume that the values espoused by our leaders have a degree of congruence with our own. So it is that we hear those things with which we agree while either not hearing or else ignoring that which differs. Many of Trump's supporters heard him speak of 'cleaning out the swamp of Washington', of developing new employment opportunities in such places as mines and manufacturing, and so on, without considering his track record of business dealings or his comments on minorities and women. Confirmation bias and selective hearing are intertwined. Alternatively, of course, it is possible that there is a high degree of congruence between the values of those who voted for him and of those demonstrated in Trump's past business dealings and his comments on minorities and women. Either way, there is a question as to how history will eventually view the presidency of Donald Trump.

Leadership is about people

Management is about systems and procedures. Management seeks to bring in appropriate controls and to ensure that everything is done in the right way. Leadership is concerned about people – how they are affected by the nature of their work and the environment in which they work; what are the barriers impacting on their performance; what are their socio-emotional needs, and so on.

A characteristic of leaders is that they are 'people people'. They are interested in the welfare and betterment of others and they seek to ensure others are treated as individuals of real worth. The implication of this is that leaders are totally non-discriminatory. Any decision using characteristics such as male or female, heterosexual or homosexual, married or single, coloured or white, old or young, religious or non-religious, religious affiliation, nationality, or any other negative discriminatory criteria is anathema to those who are genuine leaders.[11] The criteria leaders use for assessing others relate to knowledge and competence – things that can be learned and developed – rather than matters over which an individual has little if any control.

There can be no leadership unless other people are involved. Sometimes it seems as though this is forgotten by the populist approaches. Leadership means much more than simply influencing people by charisma. It means truly relating to people. A 'leader' is not a leader unless he or she is actively involved in the process of leading – of interacting with people. Leadership is an interactive process that, by definition, implies that there will be followers – people who are being influenced by the leader while, in turn, they are influencing the leader. To a leader, people are more than important! To a leader, people are the very reason for their existence. Working with people, inspiring people, empathising with people, helping people grow and develop: these are the very core of the leadership ethos of effective leaders.

In the business arena (if you like, as a business 'leader') Donald Trump could be abrupt and abrasive, show little real concern for his employees or contractors, and concentrate on doing deals that would be ultimately to his personal benefit. Perhaps he was even able to confuse fear with respect – people doing what he asked because they feared dismissal rather than people doing their jobs because of their commitment to him and his organisation. Trump measured his success by increase in personal wealth, power and influence rather than in how these impacted on the organisation overall. But now he is playing in a totally different arena – far larger than any within which he has previously played – and with vastly different rules and requirements. Now 'success' is measured not only by 'what' and 'when' but also by 'how' rather than by 'how much more'. 'Success' in the first arena does not necessarily equate with 'success' in the second. Donald Trump owned (and owns) his corporations and could largely do what he liked. However, there is a very real sense in which the whole world owns the US and he is operating in a totally different milieu. A lack of inhibition and affiliation in the first arena may have been tolerable because of ultimate ownership, but a lack of inhibition and affiliation in the second may prove a tragedy.

A further issue around the 'people orientation' demonstrated by Donald Trump was found in September 2019 in remarks about the homeless in California. According to California's Department of Housing and Urban Development, an estimated 130,000 people are homeless in California on any given day, more than in any other state. The Los Angeles Homeless Service Authority stated in 2019 that the population of homeless in the nation's second-largest city had increased 16 per cent in the past year. In response, California's Governor, Gavin Newsom, has made housing affordability a priority, committing $US1.75 billion to the creation of new housing and encouraging or forcing cities to approve new home construction because low housing vacancy is a major contributor to the problem of homelessness. The state recognises that it has a serious problem and it is trying to deal with it in positive ways, including opening refuges for homeless people. However, instead of helping California address the problem, Donald Trump's response was to state that San Francisco's homeless are damaging the environment and to say he would ask the Environmental Protection Agency to issue a notice to the city demanding change in less than a week. He said the issue was an environmental one because 'tremendous pollution', including syringes used by homeless addicts to inject drugs, was flowing into the Pacific Ocean from Bay Area cities. 'They have to clean it up. We can't have our cities going to hell.' There was little, if any, concern shown for either the homeless or the broader population of California.

Positive attention to people issues is critical for sustainable success. Practical ways of showing people that you care, such as wage increases and better working conditions, have consistently been shown to help the economy through enhancing employee engagement and positively impacting on organisational results.

But the same principles apply to the broader community. Political leaders, especially in first world countries, who concentrate on financial results along with associated systems and processes rather than on people are also failing the leadership test. When it is claimed that refugees and migrants should be subject to strict restrictions such as being unqualified to receive free medical care or any benefits in order to reduce government expenditure and to 'save local jobs', it ignores the reality that these same people create new demand for products and services as well as, once they are in stable employment, adding to the national wealth through the payment of taxes. If we fear terrorism (and most sensible people do) in relation to this, then it makes more sense to engender commitment to our country and its values rather than to alienate those who are most vulnerable to terrorist influence. Managers seek to perpetuate the status quo. Leaders seek to bring about a new tomorrow. An implication of this is that leaders recognise the cyclic nature of organisations: there are periods of growth, periods of stability, and periods of decline. They recognise that each of these phases requires a different sort of leadership and those who are the most effective either ensure that they have the flexibility to adapt or that they have the maturity to pass the leadership role to another when appropriate.

In many ways it is this strong orientation towards people that distinguishes a leader from a manager. Managers primarily deal with assets – money, materials, equipment. People are valued only as long as they are providing an adequate return on investment: people are simply another asset. Leaders, however, move beyond this paradigm. Leaders work with people in such a way that everyone can become committed to achieving desired results. On the way, they help these people in their personal and professional development so that they can better achieve results not only today and for today's tasks, but also for tomorrow and its demands.

Leadership is about change

Leaders recognise that whatever is being done today is generally being done by the most up-to-date and efficient means as possible, but that obsolescence is never far away. Consequently, they are constantly challenging the process and seeking new ways of doing things. Leaders are not afraid of change but rather welcome it as the way to personal and organisational growth and development.

In 2013, *Harvard Business Review* explored the rate of adoption of technology. They showed that:

> It took 30 years for electricity and 25 years for telephones to reach 10 per cent adoption but less than five years for tablet devices to achieve the 10 per cent rate. It took an additional 39 years for telephones to reach 40 per cent penetration and another 15 before they became ubiquitous. Smart phones, on the other hand, accomplished a 40 per cent penetration rate in just 10 years, if we time the first smart phone's introduction from the 2002 shipment of the first BlackBerry that could make phone calls and the first Palm-OS-powered Treo model.[12]

In other words, we accept that changes in technology are ongoing, increasingly complex and adopted at an ever-increasing pace so why should we expect things to be different in other areas? After all, adapting to changing technology requires changes in both our mental models and our behaviour. Is it unreasonable to argue that such changes will impact on not only *how* we think and act, but also on *what* we think, believe, and do – in other words on our values and their consequent behaviour? As a person develops from baby to infant to adolescent and into adulthood, we expect to see change in mental models and behaviour – in fact, we usually become very concerned when such changes fail to occur. Why should we expect this change process to suddenly stop somewhere between the ages of around 18 to 30 years? Where are we failing as individuals and societies, that we perpetuate an expectancy that a change in personal values and behaviour will suddenly become the exception, rather than the rule?

This factor of a lifetime acceptance of the need for change is explored by Lynda Gratton and Andrew Scott from the London School of Economics in their book *The 100-Year Life*[13] in which they show that life expectancy is increasing such that a child born in the west in 2016 has a more than 50 per cent chance of living to be over 105 years old whereas a century ago, the expectancy of living to that age was less than one per cent. The implications of this increasing life expectancy are enormous and in most First World societies today we can see in the demographics of an ageing population and longer working lives. We have become used to a three-stage life – education, career, and retirement – encompassing somewhere around 70 years. Of these 70 years, about 35–40 are dedicated to an income-generating career and 5 to 10 years are those of retirement. But we may now have to adjust to a world in which our income-generating period extends to 50 plus years and our retirement extends for some 20 to 25 years. How can we adjust to this in a positive manner so that the quality of life can match the quantity of our life? An inability to accept and adapt to change will be disastrous. And that adaptation starts with encompassing the reality that in this new, exciting world, our existing values frameworks whatever they are, and our behaviours will face serious challenges. The future belongs to those who understand this and who make the necessary adaptations.

There is another very important point here when we consider change. That is the recognition of getting rid of what we don't want is quite different from getting what we do want. Donald Trump has emphasised what he does not want in the US. He talked of 'our jobs being taken by migrants' or 'or jobs being shipped overseas' and fuelled discontent among those without jobs or those otherwise affected by today's reality but has shown no ability to replace that with what he (and the US at large) really need. The trade wars are an example of this difficulty. His 'getting rid of what we don't want' has created an unstable macro-economic environment in which everyone but Trump can be blamed for domestic and international issues.

When working on any change programme, it can be helpful to start with an important set of questions.

Answering these questions helps ensure an individual or organisation is not simply 'getting rid of what they don't want' but that they are becoming focused on 'what they do want'. It enables evaluation of the change initiative by comparison of what is attained with what was desired. It also enables the scope of the change to be determined. In other words, is the change to be one of something within basically the same existing parameters or is it to be a change that requires a new values framework with associated cultural and behavioural implications. Change for the sake of change, in other words primarily a cosmetic or political exercise, is a dysfunctional activity that will reduce confidence in a leader and the organisation.

Leaders who are worthy of the term need to understand both the reality and the implications of what is involved when they advocate change so that it can be a positive experience for everyone – not just the few with power and authority.

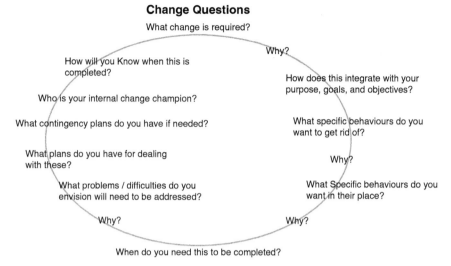

Figure 9.2 Change questions

Leadership is about creativity

It is very easy for leaders to become risk averse. Results are demanded and rewards tangible and/or intangible, depend in part on this. The temptation is to stick to what is tried and true or to do what is 'safe' rather than to introduce new ideas.

Change requires new ways of thinking about the present and the future. It requires us to take a new look at what we do and how we do it. This, in turn, brings about a need for creativity and innovation – very difficult to find in a world that encourages conformity to rules, regulations, and the whims and wiles of the dominant leaders and managers.

In the First World, we live in what has been described as a 'throwaway society'. It is easier and less costly to replace things that stop working or get damaged than it is to repair them. Unfortunately, all too often this includes people – the 'human resources' in organisations. Coupled with this is the constant release of 'new and improved' versions of whatever it is we use. This then leads to the earlier quoted scenario described by the *Harvard Business Review* article on the pace of adoption of change – we have both more frequent changes and faster take-ups than ever before, and things are only getting faster. An obvious implication of this is that we do not, and cannot, rely on what existed yesterday in order to move into tomorrow – innovation and creativity need to be our constant bywords.

Change starts by developing a clear understanding of where you are going and what you will look like when you get there – the concept of vision and/or goals. If this is so, then the path to successful change lies in leaders being creative. After all, if you are trying to bring about something that does not yet exist, then there are really no tried and true ways for getting there. In such a scenario, innovation is critical. Of course, it is not necessary always for the creativity to be found in the leader, per se. What is important is for the leader to tap into sources of creativity or innovation and be prepared to incorporate it into his or her approach. Many leaders give lip service to harnessing the energies of others while insisting that followers do things only in a manner which is acceptable to the leader. Under such circumstances innovation and creativity soon disappear or are seriously limited in their impact.

In a world that is screaming out for creative solutions to established problems in all areas, including business, we are failing to respond. The majority of us seem to be caught between the rock of needing new solutions and the hard place of not wanting our comfort zones to be disturbed. When innovative solutions are suggested to, for example, the problems of drug abuse, domestic violence, sexual abuse, prison overcrowding and tax reform, we find reasons why the solutions will not work – very often without ever putting them to the test. Part of the reason is that we keep trying to get rid of what we don't want rather than trying to bring about what we do want. Far too often we try to do both together without distinguishing between them.

If ever there has been a time in which we need creativity, it is now. Perhaps the lack of creative solutions is a sad indictment of the quality and quantity of real leadership on all sides of politics, business, and society at large. It is reflected in political point-scoring and promotion of core ideology rather than in the genuine desire to find solutions and bring about a better society. The reality is that, almost without exception, the idealism with which most people enter political life gets seduced by the realities around obtaining or retaining the power of government.

A genuine desire to find creative solutions and to bring about a better society is not really what we see when we look at Donald Trump – or indeed, in almost every national leader today. At a time when we should be focusing on new technologies and different approaches to meet all of our needs, we find many countries more influenced by pressure groups than they are by science. The result is, on one hand, a resurgence of old technologies such as the use of fossil fuels and, on the other hand, a continuation of practices such as punishment rather than rehabilitation for those guilty of crimes and an emphasis on force rather than on de-escalation of domestic and international conflict of all sorts.

Creativity requires courage. And that is a commodity that seems sadly lacking in far too many of our leaders – including politicians. Part of this seduction is the recognition that all organisations (including political) need money and there can be times when this facilitates an 'end justifies the means' approach of questionably ethical behaviour. It takes courage to stand against this pressure and to remain true to one's ideals because opposition will arise. We may talk innovation and creativity; we may welcome innovation and technology in such fields as communications and engineering; but, underlying all of this, we want to ensure that, in Mrs Patrick Campbell's words, we 'don't frighten the horses'.[14]

There are areas where Donald Trump has been prepared to challenge the status quo and to take a totally different approach (arguably 'creative'), from that of his predecessors and to what is deemed 'right' according to conventional wisdom. Prime among these has been his decision to engage directly with Kim Jong-un of North Korea, eventually crossing into North Korea for an historic meeting. Whether, this has had the desired outcome, that is, North Korea abandoning its nuclear weapons, remains to be seen, but certainly, tensions with North Korea seem to have diminished in the last two years although this may be only that the problems are masked because Kim Jong-un has attained the recognition he has sought for so long.

In other areas, Trump's different ('creative'?) approaches have exacerbated existing tensions. His reneging on the international agreement with Iran and his increasing use of rhetoric and sanctions against Iran is a clear example here. Can threats of violence really be called a 'creative' approach?

Iran has a long history of conflict with its neighbours and it has been highly vocal in its threats to other countries including the US. But Trump has exacerbated the threat by ending the Iran nuclear deal and provoking Iran. With the September 2019 attack on Saudi oilfields – an attack that Saudi Arabia and the US blame on Iran, even though parties in Yemen have claimed responsibility, there is now the very real risk of war. Donald Trump is threatening war but the questions asked around the world: Will he or won't he strike? Will he or won't he risk the lives of American soldiers in an unnecessary war? Or will he try to manufacture another photo-op summit that does nothing but mask the real problems? It can be argued that Trump has turned America's Iran policy into a farce, while increasing the likelihood of tragedy. Trump has vetoed every congressional attempt to end support for the war in Yemen and every time tensions spike, too many voices on both sides of the aisle respond with the kneejerk reaction of considering military action against Iran. Even if the drones used against the Saudi oilfields did originate in Iran (and there are few grounds for doubting that is the case), is Iran providing weaponry to Yemen's Houthi forces any different in principle from the US providing weaponry to Saudi Arabia, or Russia providing arms to the Syrians?

For optimum value, leadership creativity needs to be directly linked to an organisation's vision and strategy in such a way that all parties benefit. Doing something different – being 'creative' – just because 'one can' or because it sets you apart from your predecessor can easily become dysfunctional because it is done out of a power motivation, rather than from an achievement motivation. In other words, it is done to enhance one's own self-image rather than to benefit everyone through the achievement of organisational objectives.

Leadership requires good communication

Good leaders communicate with others in such a way as to bring about commitment to goals and objectives. Good leadership is not primarily about coercion or conscription. Good leadership is about getting people to buy into what needs to be achieved.

A key word for over 20 years has been that of 'communication'. Parents and children do not 'communicate'. Employers and employees have 'communication' breakdowns. Relationships end because of a failure to 'communicate'. Almost every organisation will willingly talk of their 'communication' problems. 'Communication' has become a word that is used by everybody as a catch-all concept for failing to talk; failing to write; failing to listen; failing to hear; failing to understand. It is a word widely used yet often not understood.

Leaders know communication is the key to all human activity and they seek to ensure the right communication is made. They know that means of communication are as varied as are people – and they ensure they do not limit themselves to only a very few of these: that often the means by which a message is transmitted – the 'communication medium' is of equal or even greater import than the message itself.

However, communication is quite different from dictating how others should behave, then bullying them into submission. Leaders ask questions because they are genuinely interested in their answers. Leaders listen; leaders are prepared to show their emotions. Leaders do not manipulate others. Leaders adapt their speech and actions to better suit their followers' willingness and ability to understand. Leaders can make the complex simple without being simplistic. Leaders build – they don't destroy. Leaders develop other leaders. Leaders accentuate the positive without ignoring the negative. Leaders are role models – not critics.

An all too commonly encountered fact of life is that one person thinks he or she has communicated simply because they have said something, issued a memorandum, or sent a letter or e-mail. The recipients may well have seen the video, heard or read the words – but the message may not have registered or have been understood. Even if it has registered and been understood, the past may have intruded to such an extent that the message is not believed, or the message's application is seen as being for someone else.

For all leaders, the competing demands of position are such that certain things are done almost perfunctorily. A memo is sent, or a telephone call is made; a meeting is addressed, or a presentation made, and we then move on to the next urgent item. Under such circumstances it is easy for us to think we are communicating when our intended recipient is still saying 'huh?' It takes time to communicate. It was Sir Winston Churchill who is reputed to have apologised to the recipient of one letter in words that went something like 'I apologise for the length of this letter. I didn't have enough time to write a short one'.

We live in an age of 'infotainment'. There are people who want all their information dressed up in the same guise as is found in the television programmes they watch. We are constantly under pressure to assimilate large amounts of information covering a wide variety of topics and issues – and that is just to survive on a daily basis! In such an environment it is easy to miss important messages simply because they are not presented with sufficient force and clarity to attract our attention.

As leaders, we need to be aware of this and to ensure that we are truly communicating. This means that we need to take the time first to ascertain the best medium for communicating with each person or group of people. Second, it means that we must check carefully to ascertain that the message has been heard, understood, and will be applied. Third, we need to follow up to ensure that the action we need is being implemented. Yes, this is time consuming. Yes, this can be very frustrating and can involve us in changing priorities so that communication is done properly. But surely, as leaders, our priority ought to be one of communicating the vision? After all, shouldn't we be doing what is important – rather than just those things that are urgent?

Whether or not others like it, President Trump has ascertained the best medium for communicating with his target audience. According to Pew Research, only 24 per cent of Americans use Twitter and the majority of those are younger Americans.[15] It is highly possible that the majority of Americans get Trump's Twitter feeds from media personalities and commentators such as Rush Limbaugh and his contemporaries. This may have led to a situation in which, while the old media is possibly still more influential, the new media has become a shortcut for those in the old media who cannot or do not do their research. It is necessary in the old media to be the first with the news. Thirty years ago that meant a headline on a story that had been verified, written, proofed and edited before publication. Now there is no time to undertake the process and so a tweet by the President is reported immediately. By the time it is fact-checked it is old news.

Of course, this begs the question as to the responsibility of leaders to ensure they are communicating what is accurate and factual, rather than being an exercise in manipulation to further their own personal agenda. And that, quite clearly, raises again the issue of values.

Leadership creates an environment in which people can be successful

This should be the ultimate purpose of all leadership activity – creating an environment in which people can be successful. Effective leaders do not seek to control other people and they do not seek to manipulate them in the negative sense with which that word is usually used.

All leadership takes place in a particular context and so, to really understand leadership we must consider it in relation to that context. For example, parenting, a key, yet often undervalued leadership role, takes place in the context of the family. Politics takes place in the context of national, state, or local government and must be considered in relation to that context. Business, sport, the military, religious activity, education and others take place in their particular contexts and must be considered in relation to them. Success in one context does not necessarily guarantee success in a different context – there are myriad successful business leaders who experience abject failure in the family context, and there are many successful politicians who would be absolute disasters at running a business. It is possible, too, that we could see an apparently successful businessperson evidencing him or herself as a disaster in politics.

With this in mind, the environment of leadership takes on an increasing importance. If a leader is to be successful, they must clearly understand the environment in which they are operating and they must accept responsibility for ensuring that they create an ambience in which people are set up for success and in which they can experience personal growth. In organisations, the environment we support reflects the values we espouse. Leaders are constantly involved with the conditions under which, and in which, people live and work. They are concerned about this and realise they have a responsibility to their followers.

What this says is that leaders need to ensure they are not removed from the people they are leading – and polling or focus groups may not necessarily aid this. Good leadership is not about abdicating responsibility whether under the guise of *delegation, empowerment*, or any other buzz words. Rather, the leader is very deeply involved in the work of followers – not to replicate or check, but to ascertain those issues or processes that are creating performance difficulties. Once these are found, leaders seek to remove the problems or, at least, to minimise their negative impact on the followers.

In 2014, The Center for Creative Leadership released a White Paper on Agile Learning[16] in which they stated: 'In times of change, leaders need to be more agile than ever. Adapting to new business strategies, working across cultures, dealing with temporary virtual teams, and taking on new assignments all demand that leaders be flexible and agile.' The paper argues that there are five behaviours that characterise leaders who are 'agile learners' and so are better able to take their organisations into the future:

> Innovating: They are not afraid to challenge the status quo.
> Performing: They remain calm in the face of difficulty.
> Reflecting: They take time to reflect on their experiences.
> Risking: They purposefully put themselves in challenging situations.
> Defending: They are simply open to learning and resist the temptation to become defensive in the face of adversity. ... High learning-agile individuals seek feedback, process it, and adapt themselves based on their newfound understanding of themselves, situations, and problems

The first four are positive indicators of learning agility while the fifth (being defensive) is a sign that agility is absent. Mitchinson and Morris say: 'learning-agile individuals understand that experience alone does not guarantee learning; they take time to reflect, seeking to understand why things happen, in addition to what happened.' They argue that there is one behaviour (being defensive) that characterises leaders who are low in 'agile learning' and so will have difficulty taking their organisations positively into the future. These are leaders 'who remain closed or defensive when challenged or given critical feedback tend to be lower in learning agility.'

If a leader is going to create the environment in which everyone is set up for success – in other words, where success is deliberately facilitated for everyone rather than being a random end-result variable – he or she needs to develop as 'agile learners'. Given all the evidence available since Donald Trump first entered the presidential electoral race back in 2014, it would appear that he lacks the characteristics deemed necessary by The Center for Creative Leadership. While he may appear to challenge the status quo, in fact Trump is a strong supporter of the status quo so long as it benefits him. He also seems incapable of receiving feedback with which he disagrees. He comes across as being very closed or defensive when challenged. Observation of politicians, corporate CEOs and other such people deemed 'leaders' across the world, indicates that a great number of these similarly seem to be lacking in 'agile learning' behaviours. Perhaps this helps explain why we have so many apparently insurmountable problems in the world today.

How does this compare to the Trump experience?

Chapter 1 referred to Vance Packard's book *The Hidden Persuaders* and how the insights of psychology lead to image and brand becoming vital to the election of candidates and parties. The emphasis in democracies today has become one of focus on the individual, rather than on the political party and its policies. This has increasingly encouraged egocentric behaviour by leaders across the world. Nowhere is this more obvious that with Donald J. Trump. (Although it is possible Boris Johnson might come close in the UK.) Previous presidents have all stamped their personality on the White House and on the image portrayed by the US, but Donald Trump has taken this to a new level. Whether one supports or opposes Trump, his political abilities (as is true for all populists), lie in making, rather than responding to, the political agenda and subsequent discussions. The result is that everything centres on what is good for Donald Trump rather than what is best for the US and the world at large.

Donald Trump does not appear to demonstrate the characteristics of the 'Leadership Diamond' are set out above. Since he became the Republican Presidential Candidate for the 2016 elections, Donald Trump (whether as candidate or as president) has exhibited:

- An authoritarian leadership approach that brooks no denial. As has been shown, he does not like to be contradicted and insists on doing things his way despite any negative impact his tweets and general pronouncements may have. Donald Trump appears to operate as an individual leader rather than as a key member of a comprehensive leadership group. He has alienated both the Democrats and significant numbers of his own Republicans. This is evidenced by his current difficulties in getting both Congress and the Senate to pass some of his desired legislation.

- A strong desire to get what he wants despite any impact on other people. As has been shown, he openly admits to using bankruptcy laws to his own advantage.
- A high need for power and control. As has been shown, if people do not conform to his demands, he dismisses them from their job.
- A high need to for people to be loyal to him personally. This appears to have been one of the key factors behind his dismissal of the FBI Director, James Comey as well as his dismissal of other White House advisors.
- A need for others to praise him. The 2017 video of orchestrated praise by his Cabinet highlights this.
- A high level of willingness to confront and fight those with whom he has differences rather than seek conciliation and consensus. He has a track record of litigious behaviour.
- A low ability to develop strong interpersonal relationships and trust across both political and socio-economic divides. The revolving doors around appointments to White House positions are evidence of this.
- A low regard for the checks and balances of executive power that are found in the US Constitution. He has called the Constitution into question when unable to immediately get his own way and, several times, has expressed a desire for the two-term limit of presidency to be changed.
- A low regard for diplomatic niceties and general politeness. The 2017 leak from the White House of his telephone conversations with the President of Mexico and the Prime Minister of Australia shows this. It is also seen in his general denigration of national leaders who have the temerity to question his judgement and/or to disagree with him. Perhaps the most recent example of this was found in his comments about the Prime Minister of Denmark after she rejected his comment about 'buying Greenland' and his subsequent withdrawal from a planned visit to Denmark.
- An unwillingness to accept any personal criticism or other feedback that contradicts his self-image or that might dent the façade of power and success that he projects in the public arena. Anything that does not conform to President Trump's perceptions and utterances is denigrated as 'fake news'.
- An inability to look beyond the short-term impacts of his decisions and actions. This is shown by the need for various members of his Cabinet to later make statements explaining how what Donald Trump has said is different from what he really means.
- A lack of ability to empathise and perceive things from the perspective of others.
- Denial of statements made by him even in the face of recordings of those statements.

In 2014, The Center for Creative Leadership at Columbia University added a further overlay to this concept of creating the environment for success.[17] Their research showed that 'adapting to new business strategies, working across cultures, dealing with temporary virtual teams, and taking on new assignments all demand that leaders be flexible and agile.' In other words, a fixed mindset in which a person is slow to make meaning from their various experiences and to use this learning in order to better interact with people and to create the right environment, is a recipe for career stagnation and/or derailment. They point out that successful leaders recognise different levels in an organisation require different skills and approaches which necessitates willingness and ability to learn throughout their careers. An approach which creates the right environment for performance success at one level, may be quite different from what is required at another level. This means that trying to predict an individual's potential for future success based exclusively on past performance and demonstrated skills and abilities is fraught with danger. Rather any prediction of leadership success needs to be based on the recognition that fundamentally different behaviours are required across organisational levels and that the behaviours that are effective at one level do not necessarily lead to success at the next: an individual's current skill-set is of secondary importance to their ability to learn new knowledge, skills, and behaviours that will equip them to respond to future challenges. The paper argues that 'our focus must shift to finding and developing individuals who are continually able to give up skills, perspectives, and ideas that are no longer relevant, and learn new ones that are'.

Perhaps this should be compulsory reading for those who will vote in the 2020 presidential elections. (It should certainly be compulsory reading for all who aspire to any form of leadership!) Donald Trump does not appear to demonstrate this ability to learn new knowledge, skills, and behaviours. He exhibits a fixed mindset in which, no matter the issue, his intuition and/or understanding/knowledge is always totally adequate, and any undesirable results are the fault of others and their intransigence. He seems to believe that, in terms of leadership, 'one size fits all'. Which, of course, begs the question as to whether any of Trump's challengers would really be any different.

Similarities and differences in the everyday world

The Columbia University White Paper[18] reported research that was based on perceived problems with the way in which leaders are selected in the US business world. In 2011, participants on a leadership development programme responded to questions as to how they typically responded to challenging situations at work. This led to considering a range of workplace predictors of performance. While the paper does not list the behaviours set out below, it does highlight that failure to have a growth mindset impedes rather than promotes the development of the right performance environment. This understanding can help understand and correct some specific factors that are all too often encountered in all performance environments.

First, the issue of disruption and change

Since the1960s, computer technology has been increasing its influence over every part of life. From very cumbersome and complicated machines that required specialists for every part of their operation it has evolved to the point where virtually every person has access to highly sophisticated information technology on their personal telephone, watch, or spectacles. Along with this, technology has evolved to the point where it is possible to track the movements and activities of people every moment of every day. Privacy and secrecy as once was known are all but a distant memory. We may denigrate the widespread use of facial recognition technology in countries such as China, but, across the world, the universality of CCTV, the use of 'plastic' rather than cash for commercial transactions, and the requirement to provide photographic evidence of identity for things such as opening a bank account or interact with government departments means that identification and tracking is possible (and almost certainly probable) despite any privacy laws.

The libertarian concepts that maximise political freedom and autonomy, emphasising freedom of choice, voluntary association and individual judgement have influenced (although not necessarily driven) the situation in which we find ourselves today. As discussed in Chapter 7, it would appear the major drive has come from the libertarian-inspired concept of shareholder value as espoused by Hayek, Friedman, and the like. Under this approach, the only thing that really matters is the accumulation of wealth and power for the elite and any attempt to limit my autonomy so that you (unless you are one of 'us') can have your autonomy must be resisted. The more I know about you, the easier it is for me to gain my ends and for me to control you.

This is where the issue of disruption comes in.

Throughout the 1970s and into the 1990s, we were increasingly told that any activity of government could be performed more effectively and efficiently by private industry and that any public assets could be better managed if they were sold to private investors. Those who opposed or even cautioned against this approach were castigated and sidelined until the quest for shareholder value dominated all sides of politics in almost every country. That this quest caused major disruption to individuals and society cannot be denied. The gap between the 'haves' and the 'have-nots' rapidly increased and the probability to acquire significant wealth by personal effort in a trade or profession decreased until, today, in most countries, unless you own assets such as real estate or stocks in public corporations, or are a successful entrepreneur who can develop and start a high potential start-up, you will remain a 'have not' despite any education, training and/or personal competence. Of course, if, in addition to being devoid of assets, you are 'low skilled' and in primarily manual work, you are unemployed, you suffer any debilitating illness or injury, you are old, or are otherwise unable to work, or are in any other marginalised group, then you have a high probability of being pilloried (at least metaphorically) and charged with being an economic liability rather than being assisted to develop as a productive asset to society. Forget the concept of governments and business having social responsibility. As Margaret Thatcher said, 'There is no such thing as society. There are individuals and there are families'! Only the economy matters.

At this point, we should be very clear. Disruption is nothing new and it is essential for progress. Throughout time, technology has been an immense help in this disruptive process but its role is that of an aid in the disruptive process rather than being an end in itself. Technology is not inherently good or inherently bad. Technology, per se, is neutral. There is really no room for Luddites[19] today whether we believe we live in a society or an economy.

To live is to experience change and disruption is an essential ingredient of this. Considering the experience of change across life stages, Shakespeare may well say,

All the world's a stage,
And all the men and women merely players.
They have their exits and their entrances,
And one man in his time plays many parts,
His acts being seven ages. At first the infant,
Mewling and puking in the nurse's arms.
Then, the whining school-boy with his satchel
And shining morning face, creeping like a snail
Unwillingly to school. And then the lover,
Sighing like furnace, with a woeful ballad
Made to his mistress' eyebrow. Then, a soldier,
Full of strange oaths, and bearded like the pard,
Jealous in honour, sudden, and quick in quarrel,
Seeking the bubble reputation
Even in the cannon's mouth. And then, the justice,
In fair round belly, with a good capon lin'd,
With eyes severe, and beard of formal cut,
Full of wise saws, and modern instances,
And so he plays his part. The sixth age shifts
Into the lean and slipper'd pantaloon,
With spectacles on nose and pouch on side,
His youthful hose, well sav'd, a world too wide
For his shrunk shank, and his big manly voice,
Turning again toward childish treble, pipes
And whistles in his sound. Last scene of all,
That ends this strange eventful history,
Is second childishness and mere oblivion,
Sans teeth, sans eyes, sans taste, sans everything.
As You Like It, Act II, Scene vii

But Shakespeare lived and wrote at a time when obvious change was primarily seen in the individual. Corporations as understood today were unknown, governments were relatively stable, national and international communications of any sort were relatively difficult and one largely remained in the social stratum within which one was born. In the main, change was slow and largely capable of easy management. Succeeding years have brought new technologies and a new reality. This is especially the case in the twenty-first century when the sharing of information is instantaneous (no matter its accuracy), and 'instant' change is demanded. The old line that, back in the 1960s, was often on a poster in printing premises, 'Of course I want it today. If I wanted it tomorrow, I would have come tomorrow', is now the harsh reality.

As is understood by every person involved in change processes today, if change is to occur, there needs to be an 'unfreezing' from the current default modus operandi. This is the role of disruption and the importance of 'disruptive technologies' as an enabling tool must be recognised here.

In their day, the axe, the horse, the cart, the bicycle, the steam engine, electricity, the car, the typewriter, radio, and the like were all examples of disruptive technologies and (at least for the more recent of these) most took considerable time to be widely adopted. The resistance came because of cost, scarcity, and fear of the impact if there was change to the status quo.

Today's disruptive technology is different mainly only in its form and in the time taken for its widespread adoption. Very often, rather than being tangible it consists of computer code or 'software' that can be applied to a range of tangible items. For example, Mechatronics is an interdisciplinary engineering field encompassing electrical engineering, mechanical engineering, computer engineering, telecommunications engineering, and a few other forms of engineering. Essential in this is the software that controls the end product – and that can be produced without recourse to major physical assets such as plant and equipment.

The purpose of disruption today is no different from its purpose in the past – to enable things to be done more efficaciously. This was part of the appeal of Donald Trump as he campaigned in 2016. It was no secret that many people believed there were problems with the status quo in Washington. Along with other populist emphases, Donald Trump, in promising to 'drain the swamp' appealed to such people. They believed the perceived self-interest and sense of entitlement considered to exist in the Capitol would be weeded out and that a new, better government would evolve. This, of course, has not happened but, like any mediocre CEO who values his or her job, Trump has created an environment where he can blame others for any of his failures to deliver. 'Don't blame me. Look over there,' is the cry, 'It's parties outside of my control that are to blame.' The message is: 'When things go as planned, I am responsible so I should get my bonus. If things don't go as planned, it's not my fault, so I should still get my bonus!' A cynic might comment that this is what they call a 'win-win' situation!

In looking at Donald Trump's performance as President, cynics may claim that Trump had a strategy and that he has achieved everything he intended, but that seems somewhat unfair. If, as has been claimed, he never actually expected to become President, then his lack of a comprehensive strategy is understandable. Of course, if his real purpose was to use the campaign only as a marketing exercise for his business interests, then the cynics' claims may be true.

However, Donald Trump's apparent lack of foresight in developing a comprehensive strategy as part of 'Plan B' is a different issue. It would appear that one of the key reasons why Trump has not met the expectations of many supporters, is that while he could talk of what he wanted to change, there was no enunciation of what the new situation would look like and, consequently, no carefully mapped out strategy to bring this about. The result has been a focus on short-term immediacy and personal agendas rather than a long-term cohesive approach that focuses on the organisation (that is, the US overall). Of course, the message from Trump is that what is good for him is also good for the US – a view not dissimilar from those who advocate the trickle-down effect of tax cuts that benefit the 'haves' will, at some indeterminate future time, also be of real benefit to the 'have-nots'.

Good leaders always prepare not only for what they want to achieve, but also have a clear understanding of the alternatives should they be needed. They also ensure that their focus is on the organisation before themselves – even if that means they need to sacrifice some personal ambitions and agendas.

Donald Trump tends to operate in an immediately reactive mode to stimuli. When this happens, he has no time to consider his response or even to ensure consistency with past comments. He seems to share his first thoughts with little or no consideration as to their overall impact. While this approach may mean he is actually 'thinking out loud', it creates uncertainty and concern in his audience.

The Myers Briggs Type Indicator (MBTI)[20] is a frequently used tool in the workplace for helping people understand more about themselves and in the development of self-confidence. The concept uses four pairs of continua and provides a possible 16 profiles with which a person can identify. One of these pairs is the continuum of extroversion versus introversion. These terms refer basically to the way by which a person processes information – a person towards the extroversion end of the continuum will tend to process information aloud while a person towards the introversion end of the continuum will tend to process information quietly and internally.

This may help us understand the frequency and tone of tweets from President Trump. An extrovert's response may well send a barrage of tweets with little or no thought as to any implications. A case of what, in the military, is sometimes called 'ready, fire, aim'! However, if President Trump tends towards the introvert end of the continuum, then what is tweeted would be his final opinion formed after some rapid internal processing of the same stimuli. There appears to be very little evidence supportive of any argument that

Donald J. Trump could be an introvert! Introverts tend to be slower to voca-lise even when they are being reactive. Internal processing limits immediacy in response to stimuli. Their approach is far more one of 'ready, aim, fire'!

Over the years there has been much research arguing that extroversion is an important characteristic for a leader. Perhaps the best-known research sup-porting this is that behind the Big Five personality traits[21] (also known as the five-factor model (FFM) and the OCEAN[22] model). This looks at personality traits and, inter alia, argues that being outgoing and energetic is a key char-acteristic for leadership success. When considering this, it is tempting to ignore the difference between personality and behaviour because of an underlying suspicion by some that leaders are born not made – in other words, leadership is not an acquired skill.

Personality tends to be relatively fixed – it is highly unlikely that a person can make significant changes to their overall personality even if they can 'tweak' it around the edges. However, as we all know from our own experi-ence, behaviour can be learned. This is the message that underlies all leader-ship training initiatives. The vast majority of us are not qualified to assess personality, but we are all qualified to make judgements on behaviour. We know whether the behaviour we observe is, according to our personal value system, appropriate behaviour or inappropriate behaviour. If an organisation clearly defines the behaviour they want demonstrated across their operations then, despite a person's location on any introvert-extrovert personality con-tinuum, these desired behaviours can be demonstrated, encouraged, and developed. They can be learned.

Beware of the 'ready, fire, aim' approach of immediacy – especially when reacting to undesired stimuli. Immediacy can be problematic. It also legislates against considering and preparing for any negative variables and undesirable consequences that may emerge. The immediate solution of today may well become the problem we need to confront tomorrow.

A major reason why leaders fail to consider the long-term implications of their decisions is that they have a short-term focus. They may talk the long-term, but the reality is that short-term dominates. In the political arena, elected persons need to face their constituents on a regular basis. A direct consequence of this is that at least part of their behaviour between elections is focused on re-election. Organisations that are listed on the various stock exchanges of the world need to report their financial position on a quarterly basis and to maintain continuous disclosure of information that could impact on their financial viability and success. A direct consequence of this is that CEOs are consequently monitoring their stock price and, as was seen in, for example, Enron,[23] ensuring that the information available to the market fits their desired image. The problem arises when this focus on the short-term leads us to lose sight of (or at least seriously blurs) the long-term. From a public relations exercise of highlighting positive factors and down-playing negative ones, the step to the fraudulent stage of stock manipulation can be quite small. This is even more of a problem when executive bonuses are directly linked to the reported results on a quarterly and annual basis – the desire to obtain the bonus can overcome all other considerations. The less there is any attention paid to the desired state of the organisation in, say, 15–20 years, the easier it is for this crossing of the boundary to occur.

While it is almost always impossible to predict all the variables that will impact as any decision is implemented, this is not a ground for ignoring them. An essential component of all project planning is to identify factors that could impact on the project's success as well as identifying possible unwanted consequences resulting from the project's activities. When this is done it becomes possible to include approaches that optimise positive variables while ameliorating those that are undesirable. Sometimes organisational leaders seem to forget this.

When this forgetfulness occurs, there is an emphasis on achieving goals set by the leader regardless of whether it is best for the organisation and despite any emergent factors that may impact. A 'crash or crash through' approach is taken and any undesirable consequences are blamed on a variety of scapegoats in order to maintain the leader's personal myth. Ideology becomes far more important than facts or negative impacts on innocent parties. A myopic (or short-term) vision dominates, potentially to the detriment of all.

Certainly there are times when a short-term vision is required. Crisis management is an example of this. If an organisation is facing an existential crisis, then a focus on survival must take precedence over everything else. In these cases, often it is necessary to make very hard decisions even though they have undesirable consequences for some. Every first responder emergency worker well understands that if a patient is not breathing then resuscitating the patient takes precedence over any other injury. Worrying about a potential fracture or other injury in this resuscitation process is immaterial and only heightens the prospect of failure.

The more senior a person is in any organisation, the more their focus needs to be on the long term while also handling the immediate situation. It is like driving a racing car. A racing driver needs to be making extremely fast decisions relating to braking, speed, and the like while simultaneously focusing on the most distant visible portion of the track so as to maintain direction; being aware of what is around the next corner; preparing for this corner, and yet, simultaneously handling the variables of vehicle performance, instructions from pit crew, track conditions, weather, the actions of fellow competitors, and the like. A high level of ability to deal with ambiguity and complexity is essential.

People who lack the requisite level of ability to deal with ambiguity and complexity, tend to seek an immediate (or almost immediate) answer to every problem. However, as H.L. Mencken, a twentieth-century American journalist, essayist, satirist, cultural critic and scholar of American English is reputed to have said, '*For every* complex *problem there* is an *answer* that is clear, *simple, and wrong*' and '*There* is always an easy *solution to every* human *problem* – neat, plausible, and *wrong.*' Some might argue that decisions such as Donald Trump's initiation of a trade war with China is but one example of this.

While many people, when considering issues around decision making, focus on the alternatives of fast or slow decision making, this is the wrong emphasis. The critical issue relates to the timeliness of the decision. Only in instances where an immediate response is vital, should fast decision making be utilised – usually this means seeking the simple answer. The reality, especially in organisational life, is there are very few occasions when this is appropriate. This means that good leadership will ensure the longer term and wider implications are considered and strategies developed for dealing with these. They will be focusing on the quality rather than the quantity of decisions with a view to what is best for the organisation overall rather on the impact a decision may have on the leader's image. This is a key reason why shared leadership models can prove so effective.

As the pace of change and disruption quickens across the world, leaders face an onslaught of new and complex questions. An effective leader can process vast amounts of data and complexity, often very rapidly. They show a high level of ability in dealing with ambiguity. Truly standout executives, however, do more than live comfortably with chaos: they take ownership of complexity by creating simple, operational narratives around it that can be readily understood and embraced by those who work for them. This combination of simplifying and operationalising complexity provides a critical foundation. Such leaders strive to create clarity on the problems their business strategy seeks to solve but ensure they are not being simplistic. They emphasise the reasons the organisation is uniquely positioned to address those challenges and offer a simple strategy for winning that has just three or four priorities. They then seek to operationalise complexity by creating a simple plan and driving clarity on the solutions solved by the company's strategy. Their emphasis is on developing simple, but not simplistic, solutions to all issues.

When an appropriate level of ability to deal with ambiguity and complexity is absent, PHOG management emerges as the dominant approach. As discussed in Chapter 1, PHOG Management is where decisions and subsequent actions are made on Perception, Hearsay, Opinion and Guess rather than on facts and analysis. It is a prime cause of the all-too-often encountered reality where today's solutions become tomorrow's problems. The result is that we wind up in a vicious spiral of reacting to the undesirable impacts of inadequately considered decisions and activities. Unfortunately, this is an all-too-often encountered phenomenon where people believe and act on what they want to believe rather than on the facts.

For some 50 or 60 years Donald Trump has been consciously building his personal myth. For a lifetime this has featured showcasing glamour, surrounding himself with apparently adoring beautiful women, and maintaining the appearance of vast influence. He built on this with his reality TV show *The Apprentice* and furthered it in 2016 at the Republican Party's 2016 convention, where he first suggested the US was a declining power before declaring 'I alone can fix it.' Since becoming President, he has ensured that no-one of independent stature remains part of his administration. He has established a new form of arbitrariness in US government – the Trump whim – which now affects the entire world.

This developing of a favourable myth is not new. Every politician – especially those that move into positions such as President or Prime Minister – does this and, through it, persuades his or her constituency. Many then continue the myth to the extent that facts are not allowed to intrude. The myth is promoted as reality. Donald Trump demonstrates this characteristic. Perhaps, eventually, some such people even come to believe the myth is reality.

It is the difference between the myth of him being the ultra-wealthy successful businessman who can use these same talents to 'Make America Great Again' and the reality of global financial clouds that have been generated, in part, by his own actions that prompt his personal attacks on the Chairman of the Federal Reserve. Trump lacks the willingness (and perhaps the ability) to acknowledge his own contribution and therefore seeks to ensure there is a third party to blame if economic downturn occurs. Nowhere was this more obviously seen than in Trump's August 2019 tweet that Jerome H. Powell, Chair of the Federal Reserve, might be a bigger enemy of the United States than the President of China because the Federal Reserve refused Trump's demand to lower interest rates significantly. The President said that the high cost of borrowing hurts the US economy.

Business leaders are not immune to myth-developing and myth-promulgating behaviour. Any time a business leader is seen as epitomising their organisation, there is a danger that the myth may prevent, or at least limit, facts taking precedence over PHOG in business decisions. The demise of the earlier mentioned Enron is but one example.[24]

Unfortunately, some or all the above issues are sometimes forgotten in change initiatives whether these are undertaken by governments, business operations (whether for-profit or not-for-profit), societies of all sorts, and individuals. When this happens, initial enthusiasm for the leader's cause can quickly degenerate into scepticism about the reason for the change and disillusionment regarding the leader's competence and value. If this is then accompanied by the leader's tenure being terminated, or some other factor intervening to ensure that the desired end result of the change initiative cannot be realised, the willingness of those involved to again welcome any future change initiatives is severely tested. The well-known phenomenon of resistance to change then quickly becomes apparent. Change fatigue commences and a climate develops where the status quo will be defended no matter how inappropriate or ineffective that status quo may be.

Second, legal and ethical

From the outset of Donald Trump's original campaign for the US Presidency, the issue of ethics has been an area of concern. There has been consistent criticism around his refusal to release his tax returns, the potential conflict of interest because he has failed to put ownership of his companies into a trust over which he has no influence, and the use of Trump-owned premises for a wide range of meetings. In August–September 2019 these issues flared again, both in relation to Trump-owned facilities in Ireland and also after he suggested that the 2020 Group of Seven summit of world leaders, which will be hosted by the US, should be held at the Trump National Doral Miami golf resort.

This, possibly 'tongue-in-cheek' comment about hosting a major international conference at one of his own resorts, was preceded by an incident in Ireland. Vice-President Mike Pence had visited Ireland for a formal meeting with the Irish President in Dublin. However, instead of staying in a hotel in Dublin, Pence chose to stay two nights at Trump International Golf Links and Hotel in Doonbeg, more than 140 miles away necessitating costly and logistically complex travel. The Vice-President's Chief of Staff said that this was because Trump suggested the Vice-President stay there – something that appears to have become commonplace with Republicans who, according to a Center for Responsive Politics study, have spent at least $20m at Trump-family hotels since 2015. This claim was refuted by President Trump who later said he never spoke to Pence about staying at the golf resort, contradicting the comment from the Vice-President's chief of staff.

In the US, presidents are prohibited from accepting any payment from the federal or state government, beyond their salary. Trump appears to have found a way around this inconvenient law. By government officials staying at his hotels, he is not receiving any additional money directly from federal or state sources. Prominent in those condemning this practice is Democratic presidential hopeful, Senator Elizabeth Warren. She said the incident was 'another example of what appears to be open corruption in this administration' and asked about the costs associated with Pence's trip, whether the State Department reviewed his plans, and whether it was aware of a 'suggestion' by the President for Pence to stay at the Trump International Golf Links and Hotel Doonbeg.

This event occurred despite reports that Congress is investigating Donald Trump over a potential conflict of interest involving increased US military spending at Prestwick airport near Glasgow and visits to his Trump Turnberry golf resort. It follows reports of the airport offering 'cut-price rooms for select passengers and crew', along with free rounds of golf at Turnberry for US military staff and civilian air crews. The air force confirmed that seven crew from a C-17 aircraft stayed at Turnberry in March. The U.S. Department of Defense said that a stopover of a U.S. Air Force C-17 and its crew at Trump Turnberry in March 2019 had not been unusual, and they had 'used the closest available and least expensive accommodations to the airfield within the crew's allowable hotel rates'.

A comment in *The Ethical Kaleidoscope*, is pertinent here:

> In February 2016, Knowledge@Wharton released the first of a series of special reports on business ethics. This report concentrated on business

ethics as a means of enhancing corporate governance and drew a clear distinction between the purpose of an organisation – its raison d'être – and its mission (what an organisation actually does). It argued that, until the directors of an organisation actually understand why the organisation exists, why it needs to exist, why would it be missed if it didn't exist and what would be missing in the world were it not for the organisation, then actually deciding what an organisation should do and how it should act is futile. When the board has clear answers to these questions, then proper corporate governance – the phenomenon of action-guiding – becomes possible and true corporate governance can be achieved.[25]

Does Donald Trump actually understand that 'why the organisation exists, why it needs to exist, why would it be missed if it didn't exist and what would be missing in the world were it not for the organisation' is different for the Presidency of the United States of America from what it is for the Trump empire?

Ethics is a complex subject but, although there are many different ethical approaches, there seems to be a consensus that ethics is all about what one *ought* to do as opposed to what one actually does. And herein lies the rub. Is 'what I *ought* to do' based on my own judgements or on those of other people? In turn this leads to the issue of 'absolutism' versus 'relativism' in terms of ethical behaviour. The absolutist argues that 'what I *ought* to do' is a constant across all variables while the relativist argues that it depends on the situation – in other words, the variables impact on 'what I *ought* to do'. *The Ethical Kaleidoscope* argues that underlying either of these approaches is found in the values (or 'world views') a person holds (see Figure 9.3).

These world views arise from the interaction of our personal values and the shared value system within which we live. If my immediate societal environment is a highly competitive, individualistic one in which my primary concerns are for myself then that will impact to the end that there is a strong probability I will demonstrate such in my own behaviour – my values will be 'me' orientated. If, however, my immediate societal environment is a collaborative one in which the needs of others are either as important or more important than my own, then that will impact to the end that this will be demonstrated in my own behaviour. My values will be 'us' orientated.

But, in turn, these approaches based on the immediacy of our environment will be impacted by the greater environment – the culture in which we live.

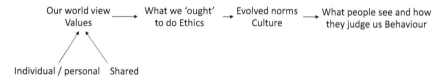

Figure 9.3 The relationship between values and ethics

Questions as to what is 'right' or 'wrong' only arise when the values we espouse and practice are different from those of other people. The dominant culture tends to be determined by the value sets broadly espoused by the greatest number of people. Various sub-groups such as clubs, associations, communes and societies then develop around people with common value sets with each group having its own view of 'what I *ought* to do'.

Donald Trump has a 'me' world view. Therefore, 'what I *ought* to do' is simple. I can and should do anything I wish in order to further my own ends. I may dress this up and present it in a form that is sociably acceptable to my support base, but, no matter the rhetoric, my eyes will be firmly set on what is best for me. Because this world view is not too dissimilar from that of many others (both in the US and across the world), a dilemma is then created for observers and commentators. So it is, that the extremes of the neoliberal approach and its long-term negative impact on business and society can emerge and continue, despite any negative impacts on the world at large. And thus it is, that the Republican Party (and many in the Democrats) remains largely supportive of Trump despite his violations of, for example, traditionally accepted norms around business divestiture and the release of tax returns.

In the lead up to the 2020 presidential elections, some of these ethical issues are being raised. Trump was very strong on 'drain-the-swamp' rhetoric in his 2016 campaign, but this seems to have been largely lost in practice. The excesses he condemned in 2016 still exist and may well have increased. So long as strident opposition came primarily only from a relatively small number among his Democrat opponents, he was content to let the status quo remain among the others. He has invited business executives and lobbyists into his administration. Additionally, a number of Cabinet departments and agencies have drawn close scrutiny for potential conflicts of interest, including the Environmental Protection Agency and the Department of the Interior. A widely held view seems to be that Trump has flouted convention so why should others see any reason as to why they should change – 'what is sauce for the goose has become sauce for the gander'.

As the 2020 election looms, some Democratic nominees are attacking concentrated wealth and economic power and its influence over government. Prominent among these are Elizabeth Warren and Bernie Sanders who are raising themes of economic inequality and promises of sweeping political and social reform. Both describe the country's political institutions as rotten and vow to make vast changes to the economy. They sound vaguely reminiscent of Trump in 2016! Warren, however, at least says she has a plan for making these changes although, at the time of writing, details as to this plan are somewhat sparse. Trump, in contrast, has now cast himself as a bulwark against the power not of corporations but of a 'failed liberal establishment'. He nominates this as an enemy attacking the country's sovereignty and cultural heritage. He has moved to combine the long-standing grievances of the white working class with a newer, darker angst about immigration and cultural change.

The big question to be answered in 2020 relates to any evolved norms that, since 2017, have become the dominant current US culture. The Democrats are struggling to determine if they would be better off appealing to voters with a soothing promise of returning to normalcy or presenting a more activist message about economic and social injustice. Trump is hoping the morph from 'draining the swamp' to conflating the legitimate concerns of many in the lower socio-economic groups with concerns about immigration and culture change will work for him.

In this, Trump's approach is not significantly different from that of leaders in many other organisations regardless of the sector within which they are found. A sense of 'me and my desires are untouchable because of my position' can be found in every organisation in which there is abuse of public trust and/ or any form of unethical (even if legal) behaviour at the top. It is always true that when unethical and/or inappropriate behaviour is found in the lower echelons of an organisation, the fault has started at the top through either active modelling of such behaviour or a failure to address such behaviour in a timely fashion.

Third, emotional intelligence

A concept that is widely recognised today as being very important is that of emotional intelligence. Often associated with Daniel Goleman, emotional intelligence is the ability to identify and manage your own emotions and the emotions of others.[26] It is generally said to include three skills: emotional awareness; the ability to harness emotions and apply them to tasks like thinking and problem solving; and the ability to handle interpersonal relationships judiciously and empathetically, which includes regulating your own emotions and cheering up or calming down other people. The evidence to date indicates that Donald Trump may, at the very least, experience some difficulty in regulating his own emotions. He also appears to have difficulty in focusing constructively on others: his focus seems always to be on himself.

When people have the self-confidence to work with others rather than seeking to control others, this is always apparent. Such people find common ground and create a desire to achieve a shared vision. They are also the people whose opinions seem to carry the most weight in group discussions and problem solving and they are the people with whom others want to work. No matter whether they have formal leadership roles, they are perceived as leaders by those around and are respected as such. Others generally consider them as having empathy because they are responsive to the legitimate needs and concerns of those with whom they interact. Because they can understand others' perspectives, they are able to explain themselves in meaningful ways and this, of course, is an essential skill in getting the best out of those with whom one works. These people think about others' feelings and respond to these in a manner that demonstrates unconditional respect.

Unfortunately, research suggests that the more senior a person becomes in any organisation (including political positions), the less they retain these skills for any apart from their closest associates. It is not uncommon to hear a senior executive speak of 'my people' yet, when challenged about different treatments for those at different organisational levels, for the executive to admit that 'my people' are primarily only those who are my direct reports or, at most, one level removed.

This is an understandable situation. In any large organisation, people become increasingly isolated from its day-to-day activities. Level one managers are generally in direct contact with non-management personnel and activities but, from level two management up, contact with non-management personnel and activities is increasingly filtered. The result is that the more senior one becomes in an organisation, the more one is isolated from the day-by-day issues and concerns confronting those on whom the success of an organisation depends – the non-management personnel. Time constraints make filtering necessary. Having a layer of handlers who make their own decisions about what the leader should or shouldn't see is essential for smooth operations. Under these circumstances it is easy to forget that deference to authority is deeply engrained in most societies. It is natural for employees, even at the highest levels, to occasionally hold back opinions and feelings that they fear might contradict or irritate the boss.

To make this point is not to criticise organisational hierarchy. The more senior one is in any organisation, the greater the level of ambiguity and complexity with which one has to deal and, in dealing with it, one has to rely on information provided by others. Senior executives tend to be shielded from organisational problems and data. They are given limited and filtered information about their operations, employees, and customers. We rely on this information and advice because we have to trust those who answer to us. Accordingly we see these trusted people as 'our' people because, without them, our ability to function would be seriously impaired.

Unfortunately, this can lead to the organisation having dysfunctional management practices. This is especially the case if the boss is insecure or capricious – and power may make leaders less likely to listen to others' advice. These CEOs become supported by a team of 'yes-people,' people who don't push back on bad decisions or offer different opinions. Such 'yes-people' can create an echo chamber that amplifies the CEO's views rather than enriching them. Groupthink becomes dominant. This could become a very real problem should any president be so lacking in self-confidence that those in his or her cabinet were increasingly selected from the president's personal friends and vocal supporters rather than being the most qualified person for the job.

A dual focus (focusing both inwardly to understand oneself and focusing outwardly and constructively on others) is an essential component of emotional intelligence. The dual focus assists a person devise strategy, innovate, and lead. A primary component of leadership is to direct the attention of others in order to achieve desired results. To do this, a leader needs, first, to have the ability and willingness to focus their own attention on what is really important for the organisation rather than on what is important for the leader him or herself.

This dual focus is linked to the ability to recognise and accept intuition but to couple this with analysis and judgement of that same intuition. In other words, a good leader recognises their instinctive response to stimuli, allows their intuition to influence any potential response, but then seeks to explore likely biases that may be intruding, and any undesired consequences that could arise from the response. The resultant judgement then leads to the formal response. These leaders utilise an internal locus of control rather than allowing the external stimuli to control their reaction.

This approach leads to authenticity in leadership. When people can see that a leader is putting their key values into positive, practical behaviour, they are generally more willing to respect and trust the leader. In other words, they see the leader as being consistent both internally and externally. In part, this means that a leader needs to pay attention to what others think of him or herself – not for the purpose of furthering an external locus of control, but from the desire to receive feedback that can help in the leader's personal growth. Feedback such as this is especially valuable when it is sought and encouraged from those people who are respected by the leader and whose feedback will be candid. Seeking such feedback is not easy for people with relatively low levels of self-confidence. Such people are more comfortable giving instructions rather than creating an environment for success.

Seeking feedback to facilitate personal growth is a major aspect of self-control. A wide range of studies across the world indicate that a person's level of self-control is a more powerful predictor of financial success than is IQ, social class, or family circumstance. Cognitive control (self-control) is the act of putting one's attention where one wants it and keeping it there despite all distractions. For the self-confident person, this cognitive control is focused on what is best for the organisation rather than for oneself and feedback is sought to ensure one's focus remains where it should. Cognitive control is something that can be learned and the seeking, receiving, and acting on feedback from valued others is an important aspect of this learning process.

A leader with high emotional intelligence is not necessarily the one who is focused on achieving financial results or on understanding the organisational culture. Rather such a leader will recognise that achieving desired results and ensuring a positive organisational culture are the natural outcomes from accepting and understanding one's own feelings; controlling their own impulses; being very aware of how others see them; understanding what others need from them; and helping others focus on what is best for the organisation with the clear understanding that when the organisation prospers, all its people benefit. In other words, such leaders recognise that the *process* of leadership is a core component of the *concept* of leadership. These leaders create an environment in which others can be successful.

Fourth, internal or external locus of control.

To develop self-confidence, people need to be encouraged to ask a simple question when encountering new and potentially difficult circumstances: 'Can I change the situation or do I need to change my response to the situation?' It is the issue of locus of control – the extent to which people believe they have power over events in their lives.[27] A person with an *internal locus of control* believes that, no matter the situation, he or she can exercise at least some influence over events and their outcomes. Someone with an *external locus of control* blames outside forces for everything.

The probability of positive outcomes, regardless of the circumstances, is enhanced when an internal locus of control is encouraged. In such instances, the reality of any situation is accepted but it is recognised that I still have some control rather than being a victim of whatever has happened. In the case of fear of further change and/or of desire to return to the status quo, we see people who refuse to adapt to the new reality. Such people may be unhappy with Donald Trump as President yet view the possibility of Trump not being re-elected as something to be avoided as far as is possible. For these people, external factors have impacted but the individual lacks the internal control mechanisms necessary for a positive response. 'Better the devil you know than the devil you don't'!

Locus of control refers to the extent people believe they have control of their own destiny. A person with an internal locus of control believes they can control their fate through their own efforts. A person with an external locus of control believes that their destiny is controlled by outside forces. People with an internal locus of control tend to resist close managerial supervision – they see this as limiting initiative and creativity. A person with an internal locus of control will carefully consider a situation from both a macro and a micro perspective before responding. At the same time they will ensure that their decision making is timely. An emphasis on compliance 'because this is the right way' from these people can prove dysfunctional.

A person with an external locus of control, however, may be far more suited to highly structured activities. A person with an external locus of control may well prolong decision making (or abdicate from it) because of the fear that it may be 'wrong' and 'wrong' decisions could have unpleasant personal repercussions. To avoid the potential for such unpleasant consequences, people with an external locus of control may be more concerned about second-guessing 'the boss' than they are about the impact of the decision on the well-being of the organisation. Eventually, the organisations they run have the potential for negative rather than positive contributions to society. When such people dominate boards, groups, teams, societies, and the like the probability of groupthink and its likely negative consequences is heightened.

Fifth, growth mindset or fixed mindset.

Stanford University's Carol Dweck talks of two mindsets – a fixed mindset, the belief that intelligence and talents are fixed and cannot be changed or developed, and a growth mindset, a belief that instead, we start with a basic set of attributes and they can be developed through dedication and hard work.[28] Although she does not extend this to consider resistance to or acceptance of change, Dweck does consider the impact of a growth mindset on motivation, and productivity in business, education and sport. One cannot help but wonder whether there is also a possible link between one's personal growth and a mindset in relation to one's perspectives on politics, religion, and the like. Is it possible that a closed mind as to the possibility of developing things like one's own intelligence and talents also impacts on one's ability to consider the need for growth and development in such broader areas of life? Does a fixed mindset eventually lead to the situation described in a popular 'insult card' that was around many years ago: 'My mind's made up: don't confuse me with the facts'?

A growth mindset and an internal locus of control are closely linked. If I believe that I am in control of my destiny and that, even if I cannot control what happens to me, I can control how I respond, then a growth mindset is essential. After all, it is extremely unlikely that I will always encounter that same (or very similar) external stimuli. Accordingly, as I encounter new situations, I need to develop new thinking in order to deal effectively with these. When things go wrong (and they will) or when I make an incorrect decision (and I will) my emphasis needs to be on what I can learn from this rather than 'who' or 'what' can I blame. The learning question: 'If I encounter the same or a similar situation in the future, what could I do differently?' becomes paramount.

A growth mindset can be found in people whose approach to life and its issues is centred in the brain's prefrontal cortex rather in the amygdala.[29] The prefrontal cortex is the cerebral cortex covering the forward portion of the frontal lobe. This region of the brain has been implicated in planning complex cognitive behaviour, personality expression, decision making, and moderating social behaviour. It enables one to distinguish between real and imaginary danger and to respond appropriately to either. The prefrontal cortex enables a considered response that will lead to personal growth and learning. In contrast, the amygdala is an almond shape set of neurons located deep in the brain's medial temporal lobe. This is the source of the well-known 'fight, flight, or freeze' response that all animals have in the face of danger. It can be dominant in people with an external locus of control because it cannot distinguish between a real and an imaginary threat, but responds the same even when danger is assumed, rather than actual. The amygdala provides an emotional response to whatever stimuli are encountered. It tends to replicate responses that have proved effective in the past rather than developing new approaches to new situations.

This begs the question as to whether Donald Trump has an internal or an external locus of control. He certainly appears to have a fixed mindset in which he is always right. Yet there can be absolutely no doubt that he believes that he is in control of his destiny. The issue, however, centres on whether he believes he can control what happens to him. Trump appears to believe that he can. By overt belligerency towards those with whom he has disagreed in the past, he seeks to influence the behaviour of those who might dare to question in the future. He seeks to create fear so that at least instrumental compliance will pertain, and he will get what he wants. He appears petulant as he makes pre-emptive strikes against potential foes by making it clear that if he fails to get his way, he will escalate action to enforce his will. As a result he is constantly monitoring his environment so that he can, if you like, 'react in advance'. Accordingly, he does not deal with the complexity, ambiguity and reality of situations but tries to control external forces so that he does not have to change. He seeks to always reduce things to the lowest common denominator of the 'win-lose' dichotomy. In this approach there is really no complexity (and thus can often be very little actual reality!). Such an approach indicates an external locus of control and an unwillingness (and perhaps an inability) to experience personal learning growth.

While there is considerable debate as to whether a growth mindset can be taught, there is far less debate around the value of encouraging hard work, learning from failure, being committed and having grit and resilience. These attributes are capable of bringing out the best in everyone. Good leaders encourage these attributes in everyone secure in the knowledge that they are beneficial to both the individual and their organisation.

Sixth, bullying.

Like many others in leadership roles across the world and in every sector of human activity, Donald Trump operates under a 'win-lose' approach to issues. One of the dangers with a 'winner-loser' dichotomy is that it encourages bullying. If I see 'losing' as the only alternative to 'winning' and my goal is to be always seen as a 'winner' then it is a short step to using 'an end justifies the means' approach. Under these conditions, bullying can become a major factor. It can be argued that this is a hallmark of Donald Trump's approach and that of a great many other politicians and other people in power across the world. It is not limited to the political arena. One of the most commonly encountered problems in many organisations is that of psychological bullying.

Abusive supervision (psychological bullying) is one of the more dysfunctional types of leadership. Of recent years it is gaining more attention as a very real problem in the workplace. Workplace bullying is defined as 'subordinates' perceptions of the extent to which supervisors engage in the sustained display of hostile verbal and nonverbal behaviours, excluding physical contact.'

Psychological bullying often goes on much longer than physical abuse. It is less obvious but can be more insidious, leaving long-lasting deep-seated physical and mental damage. Abusive supervision doesn't just affect the person at whom it's directed – it can affect an entire workplace. Its presence can extend to others 'second hand,' as they hear about it or witness it occurring in co-workers and friends. And if it spreads to other people, it may affect employees' overall perception of the company they work for – and, in true domino effect, this can affect the productivity of the company itself. It is an insidious, destructive, and extremely active virus.

Achieving high performance requires having the confidence to take risks, especially in a knowledge-intensive world. In a workplace, psychological safety is the belief that the environment is safe for interpersonal risk taking. People feel able to speak up when needed – with relevant ideas, questions, or concerns – without being shut down in a gratuitous way. Psychological safety is present when colleagues trust and respect each other and feel able, even obligated, to be candid. When an organisation minimises the fear felt by people, performance at organisational, team, and individual level is maximised. Bullying actively encourages fear in whatever environment it occurs, and it is indisputable that this adversely impacts performance no matter the level or source from which it comes.

It's important to note that working in a psychologically safe environment does not mean that people always agree with one another for the sake of being nice. It also does not mean that people offer unequivocal praise or unconditional support for everything you have to say. Psychological safety is not an 'anything goes' environment where people are not expected to adhere to high standards or meet deadlines. It is not about becoming 'comfortable' at work. Psychological safety enables candour and openness and, therefore, thrives in an environment of mutual respect. That mutual respect starts with the leader or manager treating his or her reports with unconditional respect and ensuring that the addressing of inappropriate behaviour is done in a way that demonstrates this respect for the other.

When bullying of any sort exists in an organisation it indicates a leadership issue at the top. While toxic leaders may be found at any level in all organisations, when it is not addressed and removed it indicates that those at the top (right up to the Board) are either complicit or have abdicated much of their responsibility. This happens because leaders are failing to ensure the right environment for on-going organisational success. Indications of this failure at the top include functional incompetence, immorality, manipulation, fraud, abuse, tyranny, deviancy, illegality and unethical behaviour at any level of the organisation. In an organisation that has an inappropriate environment, many people might be working hard and trying their best to make it effective for everyone but you will find morale is low, customers/clients are losing faith and, eventually, the organisation loses business until the whole system breaks down and it becomes fractured. In the medium- to long-term, good people do not work for bad bosses.

Early action is the key to preventing destructive leadership and eliminating bullying. Everyone in authority has a responsibility to ensure inappropriate behaviour is dealt with immediately any indication is discovered. That action needs to be taken at all levels. Senior leaders need to take a stand, to be clear about their values, to have the courage of their convictions, and to ensure that the espoused values are also the practised values. Underlying this is the issue of respect.

There is a large amount of evidence that shows Donald Trump is disrespectful of people from a wide range of backgrounds. His comments about US politicians, judges, and public servants with whom he disagrees, together with his comments about migrants and leaders from many other countries are indicative of this.

There are two types of respect when it comes to interacting with others – conditional respect and unconditional respect. Donald Trump seems to exhibit only conditional respect.

Conditional respect – the 'normal' way in which most of us deal with others – says I will only show respect to you as a person when and if you do what I want you to. It is an 'us versus them' approach. In other words, I will respect you only if you perform in the manner I want you to.

With this mindset controlling our values and behaviour we find that people who fail to meet our conditions tend to be treated differently from those who do. It might be a matter of nationality, colour, ethnicity, sexual orientation, marital status, religious affiliation, or any other point of differentiation. Equally it might be a matter of language, behaviour, mode of dress or the like. If you conform to 'my' expectations and standards then I will treat you differently from how I treat those who are non-conforming. We see this in every aspect of life, in almost every society, from the very earliest years of life.

The principle of 'operant conditioning' developed by the psychologist B.F. Skinner[30] is based partly on this. Skinner coined the term operant conditioning which generally means changing of behaviour by the use of reinforcement which is given after the desired response. This is a basic and important tool used (sometimes inappropriately) by parents in their nurturing of children into adults, of teachers throughout the education process, and of those in authority in every area of our lives. Do as I want, and you will be rewarded. Fail to do what I want, and you will be punished. Although this was not exactly what Skinner argued, it is a small step for this to degenerate into the reality of 'do what I want, and I will show you respect. Fail to do what I want, and I will not show you respect until you change'. When this happens (and it certainly does) the scene is well and truly set for dysfunctional conflict and discrimination of all sorts.

The other side of the coin is unconditional respect. This is probably best seen in the way most parents interact with their newborn babies and infants. We understand that it is useless to complain to a baby about its crying so we try to ascertain the reason. Is the baby hungry? We feed it. Is the baby uncomfortable? We change its diaper. Is the baby experiencing discomfort from teething or some ailment? We try to alleviate the discomfort or seek medical help for the ailment. We know that the baby or infant is totally dependent upon us so we provide whatever is necessary without any attempt to get compliance in return. This unconditional respect says, 'no matter what you do, I will always love you and care for you'. Most parents have no difficulty in understanding and applying this. The situation changes as the infant starts to develop cognition. Once an infant can begin to understand something about what they are doing, we all too often move into the demonstration of conditional respect.

Now, it is necessary to be very clear about the difference between giving unconditional respect and dealing with inappropriate behaviour. There should never be any reluctance to deal with inappropriate behaviour. A civil, harmonious society is not possible unless there is a clear understanding of what is acceptable or unacceptable in our words and actions. We need to confront those who act inappropriately no matter the environment in which they do it. And, yes, that includes the international scene. It is the way by which we handle this confrontation that is critical. Our current way is to conflate the person and their behaviour. This is a serious mistake.

While an individual and their behaviour are obviously inter-related, they are also different. Like babies, some people act in inappropriate ways because they do not know any better. Some people act in inappropriate ways because somewhere along the way they have learned that such action gets them the goals they seek. Some people act in inappropriate ways because they are involved with an antisocial group or philosophy. To reiterate, this needs to be addressed.

However, addressing inappropriate behaviour has a far greater likelihood of long-term success – genuine behaviour change – if it is done in a manner that makes it clear the person, per se, is always acceptable even if the behaviour is not. When this distinction is made, it becomes possible to deal with the cause of the inappropriate behaviour rather than our more common approach of eliminating one symptom only to have the same issue recur, often even more vehemently, in a different guise. A failure to recognise this difference in children can lead to young people and adults developing serious problems in relation to their self-image and that, in turn, can lead to serious on-going psychological issues, including suicide. Is it any wonder that, in the broader world, failure to show unconditional respect to all people creates insurmountable international problems?

This need for unconditional respect of the individual includes terrorists. Imagine, for example, how different the world may have been if, after 9/11, President Bush and his supporters had not conflated terrorist acts with religious beliefs and geographical location. After all, terrorism is neither religion nor location specific – and, in September 2001, the US already had evidence to demonstrate it. Terrorist attacks, even in the US, were nothing new.[31] What was new in this attack, was the magnitude of the damage in such an iconic city as New York and in such proximity to the US capital, Washington, D.C.

What then developed was also new. In the past terrorist attacks had been treated as crimes to be investigated by police with perpetrators and their supporters duly arrested and prosecuted. This approach had proved very successful in the US and most other western countries. However, President Bush determined that a military response was necessary. He argued that the attack on US soil was an act of war and he responded with a 'war on terrorism' which has led directly to many of the problems around ISIS and other extremist groups today. We have confused 'what' people do with 'who' people are. When this happens, we lose our capacity to actually find out 'why' such actions occur (we assume we already know this) and so ensure that all who approximate our definition of 'bad' are punished regardless of reality. This is yet one more example of today's solutions creating tomorrow's problems.

As has been indicated earlier, the world today tends to have a vastly different opinion of the US under President Trump than it has had under most previous presidents. A key factor in this shift has been the lack of respect Donald Trump has shown to minorities, foreigners, and people with whom he disagrees. President Trump appears to be a strong exponent of conditional respect and, under those conditions, the leader him or herself finds the personal standings they have with others tends to diminish rather than grow.

A well-known axion in the military is the key message that respect is earned – it does not come simply because of one's position in the hierarchy or any other status symbol. The military also once taught that the earning of respect starts by showing unconditional respect to others. As was stated often, 'when it comes to the crunch and you need people to go far beyond normal standards of performance, it is not your rank that will get this. It is the trust and rapport, the respect, you have earned from your troops.' In other words, obtaining high performance is more likely to occur when your personal power equals or exceeds your positional power. Positional power will get compliance. Personal power will get commitment – and commitment is necessary for superlative performance. Commitment starts when respect exists.

Messages for executives and leaders

As a leader or aspiring leader at any level, one of the biggest challenges faced is to inspire and motivate other people so that they can take the right actions on behalf of themselves and the group – that is, to have impact. That's why it is necessary to be a leader with a strong presence in every interaction. As a leader, every aspect of your presence – including your physical self, your intellect, your voice, and your emotions – is intimately bound up with your message.

Many people in positions of authority struggle with their leadership presence. They adopt the kind of persona that they assume a leader is supposed to have such as cadence, authoritative body language, studied informality, and (when speaking publicly) a package of carefully curated slides. Most of the time, behaviours like these are immediately recognised as a performance. If you try to adopt them, people will know you aren't authentic, and they will assume your message isn't either. Being an authentic leader doesn't mean just 'winging it' or saying whatever you feel. It takes time, experience, and practice to learn to transform your impulses into insights – and to articulate them and act on them in a way that fulfils your purpose and builds the relationships you need.

All those in leadership roles are well aware of the simple organisational model represented in Figure 9.4.

And most leaders also know that this model fails to draw attention to the complexity within each element. To resolve this problem, good organisational leaders ensure they are considering organisational variables. These can be briefly summarised as including (see Figure 9.5).

Ranking and expansion of each variable heightens the probability that the optimum factors can be addressed in resolving organisational performance issues. Every sector (public, private, for-profit, not-for-profit etc.) and every organisation within each sector will have its own variables and comparison enables identification of common and different factors so that attention can be placed on those providing the greatest probability of success in any intervention. Once the desired end variables are determined and promulgated, effective leaders then focus on improving the quality of the initial causal variables and on improving the processes that comprise the intervening variables.

There is very little evidence to support the contention that Donald Trump's leadership approach shows any awareness of the complexity and ambiguity

Figure 9.4 Basic organisation model

Causal Variables   +
- Organisational structure
  - Forms of employment such as F/T, P/T, Contract, Casual across the organisation
  - Reporting structure
  - Accountability
- Organisational objectives
- Management and supervisory practices and behaviour
- Capital investments
- Needs and desires of members
- Regional demography and socio-economic environment

Intervening Variables
- Cognitive orientations
  - Information
    - Relevant
    - Appropriate
    - Comprehensive
    - Timely
  - Concept of my job or role
  - Concept of roles of others to whom I relate
- Work group traditions, values & goals
- Past experience
- Expectations
- Personal motivations

End Variables
- Organisational earnings
- Production cost
- Waste
- Employee commitment / engagement
  - Belief in equitable treatment across all levels and areas
  - Personal earnings
- Absenteeism
- Labour turnover
- Grievances

Figure 9.5 Variables impacting performance

arising from organisational variables whether in business or as President. He certainly demonstrates a low level of ability to deal with them in an appropriate and functional manner. His leadership presence does not inspire trust and engagement among many of his fellow US citizens. A great many of his people are uncommitted and disengaged with what Trump is seeking to achieve. In such a situation, sustainable high performance for the US is an extremely unlikely end variable.

Things need to be different in tomorrow's world.

Leadership

In the years since the Second World War, the study of leadership has become a major field across the world. The application of research findings has moved our understanding from a simple 'command and control' approach to the realisation that leadership is actually a very complex concept that needs constant attention.

Today's rate of change within organisations is greater than ever and leaders are constantly required to adapt. Adapting to new business strategies, working across cultures, dealing with temporary virtual teams and taking on new assignments requires flexibility and agility. Leaders at all levels need to create the environment in which their people can be successful. They need to consciously set their people up for success rather than letting success be a random end variable.

Traditionally, we have looked at past performance in order to predict future success. This can be problematic because fundamentally different behaviours are required across organisational levels. Behaviours that are successful at one level do not necessarily apply at the next. This can have a direct effect on performance in all areas. We need to be assessing prospective appointments based on their ability to deal with the level of ambiguity and complexity that the position will encounter. In other words, on ability to deal with future demands rather than on having dealt successfully with issues in the past – a totally different assessment process. While past performance is important and gives us some essential clues, the focus needs to be on what the person has learned from that experience and how they will apply that learning in the new role.

Elliott Jaques, an English researcher and consultant, made the point some years ago that leadership is not a generic concept. He argued that you can only really understand and/or develop leadership when you recognise the context within which leadership is being provided.[32] His point is that effective leadership is always dependent upon a range of factors and the way in which it is exercised can vary significantly across the levels, areas, and types of organisations in which people live and work. Accordingly, we need to ensure that our emphasis when appointing leaders is that they are able to adapt to the context and level within which they will be providing leadership.

Directors

If the leadership position for which a person is being considered is at Board level – a directorship – those responsible for the selection need to remember the board actually sets the moral and ethical tone for the organisation. If an organisation has moral or ethical lapses, then it is on the shoulders of the board that the ultimate blame should rest. This is especially important for the role of Chairman. The person in the most senior leadership role sets the standard for the organisation – a situation graphically demonstrated by Donald Trump.

As President, Donald Trump holds the most senior leadership position in the US. His behaviour sets the standard and, if that standard is below constitutional and/or community expectations, then this needs to be dealt with by the rest of the board. In the case of the President, the people with this responsibility comprise the other elected officials. In the case of the US, this role needs to be filled by Congress and the Senate because the President gets to appoint his/her Cabinet while Congress and the Senate comprise elected persons. It is because of the polarisation of party politics that such checks and balances are currently working poorly in the US.

The message here for corporations is to ensure that directors – the organisation's elected officials – have the conceptual skills to fulfil this role and that they are not partisan supporters of the Chairman or CEO. Although the primary reason for their appointment may have been their technical expertise (finance, marketing, engineering, etc.) a director needs to recognise this broader responsibility and to understand that their primary responsibility and loyalty must be to the organisation per se rather than to the chairman and/or any specific group or clique on the board. Where loyalty is primarily given to an individual or group rather than the organisation then the scene is set for unethical (and/or possibly illegal) behaviour such as has been all too often seen in corporate collapses or corporate misbehaviour across the world.

C-Suite and executive team

If it is the board that is responsible for setting the tone of the leadership throughout an organisation, it is the C-Suite[33] and executive team that operationalises and models this leadership. In terms of how the organisation functions on a day-by-day basis, it is the C-Suite and executive team who establish (or who fail to establish) an environment in which the organisation can be successful. These people are responsible for the operational aspects of an organisation. In other words, in terms of obtaining and maintaining a high-performing organisation, it is at the C-Suite and executive leadership level 'where the rubber meets the road'.

In most large organisations people will seldom if ever have direct contact or even exposure to the organisation's directors. In fact, in many cases, most people at the lower organisational levels may have absolutely no knowledge whatever as to who the directors are, let alone would be able to recognise them if encountered on the street. The situation is different with those at the C-suite level. Far more people in any large organisation are likely to be aware of members of their executive than they will be of directors. It is the executive team's names and faces to which they will be exposed most frequently when senior leadership are mentioned because it is about these people (rather than the board) that any media are more likely to be reporting and commenting.

Given the hierarchical nature of most organisations, it is unlikely that in the event of inappropriate leadership behaviour at this level, such behaviour will be directly addressed by other members of the C-Suite and executive team – especially if it is by someone at the same stratum. Accordingly, the key responsibility for ensuring appropriate behaviour from this level lies with the board. It is the board that appoints the CEO and which, generally, signs off on other C-Suite positions and it is the Board that determines remuneration elements such as performance bonuses. If the board fails to endorse the right person and/or if the remuneration elements fail to motivate for appropriate behaviour, then the board has failed in a key area of responsibility.

Managerial leadership

Managerial leadership is the level at which most leadership development interventions focus. The reason for this is that the more senior one is in an organisation, the more it seems to be assumed that leadership will have been learned on the way up. Such an assumption sometimes appears to presume that the type of leadership provided should remain virtually the same no matter at what level one works or the type of organisation for which one works. As has already been said, this assumption is now being seriously challenged because it is becoming increasingly apparent that the type of leadership required does change with one's progression through an organisation. At this managerial level, the leadership required is primarily one-with-one or one-with-small-group and it is focused on the short to medium term aspects of an organisation

Traditionally, managerial leadership is all about control. In part this is what has led to the much-discussed distinction between 'management' and 'leadership' that led at least one writer[34] some years ago to suggest that 'management is about doing things right: leadership is about doing the right thing'. What this means is that managerial leadership requires people to recognise that there can be occasions when, as is reputed to have been the case with Admiral Lord Nelson in the Battle of Trafalgar, a 'blind eye' is turned to infractions of policy and practice. These should be few and far between, but they can occur. It also means that managerial leaders should look for what they can positively reward – 'catching people doing something right' – rather than seeking out mistakes. Managerial leaders need to confront mistakes and errors from the perspective of 'given a similar situation, what could you do differently in order to obtain better results?' rather than facilitating an excuse-driven, risk-avoidance culture in which people spend as much (or more) time second-guessing 'the boss' or seeking to avoid unpleasant consequences, than they do on achieving desired results.

1 *What does this leadership look like?*

While the detail of what is involved in creating the right environment for sustainable high performance will vary across organisations, organisational levels, and the various areas within each organisation. As earlier indicated, The Center for Creative Leadership's White Paper on Agile Learning demonstrates that the leadership that provides this environment for success, has five key things in common:

- Question the status quo.

These people recognise that 'whatever we are doing today, we are doing in the most up-to-date obsolete way possible'. In other words, they recognise that there is always a better approach possible and they seek to find it.

- Overcome unfamiliar challenges.

The 'fight, flight, or freeze' syndrome can affect even the best people at times. Most people can experience short periods of feeling inadequate when unexpected problems and challenges arise. Leaders providing an environment for success acknowledge these feelings but move beyond them to remain present and engaged as they handle any stress caused by such issues.

- Spend time reflecting and learning from experience.

The more senior a person is in leadership roles, the greater the demands on their time as they confront an increasingly complex world with all its ambiguity. This can bring about the situation where pressure prevents reflecting on what has happened. Leaders providing an environment for success take time to reflect on 'given a similar situation again, what could I do differently?' so as to enhance their own learning.

- Try new things.

It is very easy for leaders to become risk averse. Results are demanded and rewards depend in part on how we manage risk. The temptation is to stick to what is tried and true or to do what is 'safe' rather than to introduce new ideas. Leaders providing an environment for success are willing to venture into unknown territory and to be pioneers. They evaluate new directions and assess potential risk prior to selecting their way forward.

- Are not defensive.

Especially when under pressure, it is easy to become defensive when challenged or when given unwanted feedback. This is demonstrated by the provision of excuses or 'reasons' so as to justify what has happened. Leaders providing an environment for success accept the reality of what has happened, actively seek feedback, then adapt their behaviour.

The matter of good managerial leadership cascading down from good board leadership through good executive leadership is vital in a high-performing organisation.

Whereas only a relatively few years ago, staying with an organisation longer than about five years was quite common and most employment was on a full-time basis, today employment on a casual basis is rapidly becoming the norm for a great many people. With this change in employment conditions comes no security of employment and, sometimes few, if any benefits other than money. Additionally, the rise of imports from across the world and the globalisation of almost all national economies mean that organisations want and need their people to be highly productive very quickly after commencing employment. If people are not highly productive very quickly, then, because of the nature of their employment, turning over staff is nowhere as onerous as it once was (although arguably it is more expensive than ever before!).

If the board and executive have failed or are failing in their leadership responsibility, accountability, and effectiveness then don't be surprised if your management's effectiveness is mediocre and/or confused. (Similarly, the corollary applies. If your management's effectiveness is mediocre and/or confused, then take a good hard look at the board and executive because the odds are that the source of the problem is found at the very top.)

When everything else is properly in place, it is on the shoulders of managers, across all organisational levels and areas, that the responsibility rests for facilitating the engagement of people with their job, their peers, and their organisation. When such engagement really exists then people accept responsibility for their own actions, and they see themselves as fully accountable for the quality and quantity of output. When this happens, an organisation is well on the way to high performance. But there will not and cannot be a high-performing organisation with highly effective managers unless the board, C-suite and executive team have created the right environment – and that needs both real leadership and also, in many cases, a very different form of leadership from that which currently pertains.

2 *Communication*

It matters not what organisation is considered. In virtually every organisation, if people are asked about problems and concerns, 'communication' will be nominated. All too often, 'communication' seems to be a catch-all word that covers everything from 'I'm unhappy and/or disengaged and don't really know why' through to 'no-one really talks to me and I don't know what's happening'.

The truth is that a leader is only as good as his or her communication. Effective leaders are good communicators – and that means being a good listener as well as being clear in what and how you say things whether verbally or in writing. Communication also means using a language that your listeners can understand – it's no use speaking English (or any other language) if your listeners can't understand that language and there are no good interpreters around! Similarly it's no use using technical language or jargon if your listeners can't understand it. Communication also means 'keeping your message simple' as well as checking to see that your listeners have heard and understand your message.

During the 1950s there was little emphasis on 'how' people communicated. However, as already discussed, in 1957 came Vance Packard's *The Hidden Persuaders*, and William Sargant's *Battle for the Mind*. In 1964 came Marshall McLuhan's *Understanding Media: The Extensions of Man* in which he introduced the phrase 'the medium is the message'. Much of the current emphasis on *how we* communicate rather than *how **and** what* we communicate can be dated back to works such as these. Looking at 'leaders' on television, hear them on the radio, or read of them in the written press it is often difficult to ascertain what they really believe and what, if any, is the goal they are trying to achieve other than massaging their own egos. This emphasis on *how* things are presented, rather than on *what* is presented, often results in very shallow, populist approaches that are designed for 'sound bites' rather than for edification. People seem to want to keep themselves in forefront of mind rather than to inform and to enter into dialogue.

Leaders who communicate well understand and are able to use three key components:

- Powerful questioning which is a process that shows respect for the other person.
- Observational listening which shows people that they are being listened to.
- Optimistic listening which shows belief in the other person.

These three attributes are those which create an environment in which both we and those with whom we interact are able to grow.

Powerful questions are those questions that trigger the right responses because they:

- Focus on the other person and their thinking, not the detail of the issue or problem.
- Are clear of any attitudes and beliefs of the questioner.
- Are easy to understand.
- Provide useful (rather than interesting) answers from the person with whom the discussion is taking place.

Powerful questions are not easy questions to ask because they are not our default way of questioning. In the past, society's approach to questioning has been so that the questioner can make the decision or a judgement, or that the questioner can resolve the issue or problem being faced. In a basically hierarchical society, predicated on obedience or conformity such approaches were possible (even if often unsuccessful), but that is no longer the case. Now those in authority (at least in most of the western world) face the very real probability of overt criticism and loss of respect and authority if their decisions or 'solutions' are wrong or inadequate. (Or even if they are *perceived* to be wrong or inadequate!)

Powerful questioning creates a totally different situation for the person to whom feedback is being given. It says to the other person something like: 'I may not have all or even many of the answers, but we can work through this together' or 'I may not be happy with what you have done, but I respect you as a person and therefore I want to work with you in order to resolve this issue.' This is the sort of questioning that elicits a totally different response from what is usually obtained. This different style of questioning can lead to real behaviour change and to significant growth in both parties. It can also lead to obtaining innovative and increasingly appropriate answers to otherwise apparently intractable problems and complex issues.

The very act of changing our default approach to questioning is a powerful tool in communication. When this shift commences, we are on the way to getting 'what we want' rather than simply getting rid of 'what we don't want'.

Observational listening has the purpose of reflecting back to the speaker what you see and hear. This shifts the leader's attention away from his or her own internal processing (e.g. analysis, judgement and assumptions) – i.e. away from the leader's own thinking – to what is actually happening within the other person's brain. Accordingly, observational listening harnesses power that may otherwise be unlikely to be readily available for problem resolution.

While powerful questioning may be a new skill for many people, observational listening has been around for many years under such guises as reflective listening, non-directive counselling, etc. It is listening that picks up both verbals and non-verbals then ensures the speaker understands that the full import of what they are saying and feeling is being heard.

It has been suggested that for the majority of people, listening is most often:

- For opportunities to sound intelligent.
- For a chance to say something funny.
- For how I could sound important.
- To information I want.
- To external distractions – other noise, music etc.
- For what's going on for the other person.
- For approval.
- To my own thoughts, not listening to the other person at all.

- To be able to understand the problem.
- For how I can benefit.
- For the opportunity to one-up the other person.
- For the details so that I can help solve the problem.
- For how I can undermine the other person's point of view or position.
- For how I can change or end the conversation[35]

When we consciously shift our default way of listening away from anything in this list, we concentrate on the real message that the speaker is seeking to give. The building up of 'what we do want' increases in pace. Now creativity and innovation can become realities.

Traditionally, a leader listens only when he or she chooses and, even then, only for their own benefit as they believe that they must make a decision or form a judgement. Much current leadership listens so that they can understand the problem in order to solve a problem or resolve an issue. We need leaders who listen so that he or she can engage the other person with the solution.

Optimistic listening makes it clear to the other person that there are probably a range of possible solutions to every issue and/or problem. For a whole raft of reasons, a solution that might be nominated by the leader may not be the best possible. Therefore engaging with the other party or parties enables better problem solving and decision making. When this is done properly the relationship between the parties involved moves to a collegial rather than a hierarchical one and all those involved have the opportunity to experience growth. Now everyone involved is engaged with each other *and* with that which needs to be done. Commitment is enhanced.

The combination of observational listening and optimistic listening enables the leader to engage the other party in developing and implementing any solution. It effectively removes hierarchical imbalance and creates an atmosphere in which multiple viewpoints can be provided and in which both issue/problem analysis and resolution are team based. The impact this has on others is immense. It is abundantly clear that authentic and strong attention on another and *for them* is the underlying social mechanism that triggers engagement. As all the research shows, when people are engaged both with activities and those people around them, productivity improves in all areas.

Moving to communicate in this way, however, challenges the dominant manner by which people interact today.

Today's younger people no longer fit any 'obey or conform' requirement. We see this shift in the general response by younger people to authority whether it is in school, work, or society at large. Today's youth are not interested in 'toeing the line' and they are prepared to openly rebel if this is demanded of them. While it is true that young people have always demonstrated a rebellious element that offended their elders and the powers that be, today the phenomenon is more widespread than ever before. Young people today demand to be fully engaged in what they are doing and with the people with whom they are doing it – and through such technology and media as mobile telephony, the internet, and social networking sites such as Twitter and Facebook they have available the means for making such demand on a scale as has never existed before. This universality of social media means that, today, people of all ages tend to rely on digital communication platforms for much of their interpersonal interactions.

But this does not mean that the importance of face-to-face interaction and actual verbal discussion has diminished. If anything, the importance of face-to-face interaction and dialogue has increased – even if we don't really want to acknowledge this. Organisations tend to be very good at using digital technology for passing on instructions, for disseminating information, and for gathering opinions through surveys, such as those for assessing employee satisfaction. In fact, the use of digital technology-based surveys has become so prevalent that the term 'survey fatigue' has become commonplace and because of this, far too often, those who respond do so in a cursory manner. They are encouraged in this somewhat perfunctory approach by the recognition that history in most organisations shows that their leaders will still do whatever they intended despite any feedback they receive. Accordingly, any changes are far more likely to be cosmetic than substantial. Anyone who doubts this only needs to look at the reaction of governments when they fail to get their own way (especially if this is through the legal system overturning some legislation or edict) or business leaders in their pursuit of organisational goals.

Just as Donald Trump challenged the status quo in terms of traditional media being the medium through which he communicated to his audience, so leaders in every other sphere of human endeavour also need to challenge the status quo in how they communicate to their audience. If 'engagement' is an issue in your organisation, then the problem most likely lies with the leadership and the medium by which they communicate with their people. As Donald Trump has found, when there is a disconnect between words and actions, other than among the most ardent supporters, people will believe what they see rather than what they hear. Although Trump's popularity rating appears to have remained stable throughout his presidency, today even some of his most ardent supporters have expressed a degree of dissatisfaction in terms of his behaviours. As has often been said: 'It's no use talking the talk unless you also walk the walk'. Although most leaders 'talk the talk' – usually by using digital media, far too few actually 'walk the talk' by face-to-face interaction. This is where many communication issues begin and how they are promulgated and exacerbated. Communicating primarily through digital forms is a significant problem in today's world.

Face-to-face communication makes perfunctory reading of messages, casual answering of surveys and the like, far less likely. When we are in face-to-face, one-with-one or one-with-small group dialogue (even if it is in some form of teleconferencing) it is possible to read non-verbals such as body language, tone, eye contact, etc. In other words, it is possible to engage fully with the other person. When this happens and real listening occurs, clarification emerges and commitment is enhanced. People always know whether conditional or unconditional respect exists. Unconditional respect leads to authentic communication. When this happens, an environment exists in which people:

- Contribute creative and innovative ideas.
- Help others develop a shared sense of what is really important.
- Spend time helping others with their personal learning issues.
- Show consistency between espoused values and personal behaviour.
- Seek out challenging opportunities for people to grow, innovate, and improve.
- Focus on a better future.
- Are able to communicate complicated ideas clearly.
- Show empathy and concern when dealing with others.
- Experiment with new concepts and procedures.
- Facilitate the building of collaborative approaches.
- Foster positive relationships with the broader community.
- Present others with a positive approach to change.
- Communicate excitement about future possibilities.
- Ensure that those who did the work get the credit.
- Deal with conflict in a positive and creative manner.
- Share information and knowledge widely and appropriately.

These behaviours are critical for a high-performing organisation no matter the sector in which it operates.

3 Vision

A 'vision' is a very broad, positive statement about what the organisation seeks to achieve over a period well in excess of any period for which it can effectively plan. It provides a sense of direction and is a light on which to focus during periods of uncertainty and turmoil. It should be couched in positive terms. In other words, rather than setting out what an organisation does not want to be (i.e. stating something negative), it should be clear about what the organisation can be (something positive). It is an inspirational 'big picture'. It will probably include such words and phrases as 'world class performer', 'the best', or some other idealistic terminology designed to position the organisation ahead of any competitor. Unfortunately, in many cases this vision may well degenerate into a generic statement that could be applied to any organisation. This occurs when any concept of 'vision' is a platitude rather than a key driver of performance. However, in the organisations that make optimum use of a vision, this provides an organisation-specific picture of an organisation's aspirations and the path it is taking to realise these.

Over the past 40 or 50 years it has become increasingly common for organisations to be seduced into 'short-termism'. With quarterly reports to the stock market and relatively short-term (3–5 year) incumbency of CEOs, coupled with significant monetary rewards for achieving desired annual results, the vision of organisation can (and, all too often does) focus primarily on the period of CEO incumbency. All too often, as perceived from outsiders, the attitude seems to be along the lines of 'I'll make sure I hit my targets and hope that things go well after I leave, but my responsibility ends when my incumbency ends.' This may be unfair to many hard-working members of the C-Suite, but it tends to be a widely held view in the broader community – especially when there seems to be a dearth of information as to what vision the organisation has in train for the following 30 or so years. This is particularly true in the political realm where elected persons face regular assessment through the electoral process.

A good vision has much in common with a rainbow. A rainbow attracts attention. It is colourful and appealing. At the same time, everyone understands that it is not a specific goal or location to which someone can go but rather indicates a general direction to something that is a long way away. It is, if you like, a metaphor of hope rather than something concrete or specific. If a person wants to head towards it, then the general approach needs to be determined (a strategy) and specific compass directions need to be set (objectives and goals).

The vision, however, should not be simply a collection of hard numbers and precise detail. Everyone can see a rainbow and admire it without being confused as to its fluidity and aspirational nature. A vision should, however, lead to specific objectives, strategies, goals and activities that, together, can facilitate making the vision a reality. It's not easy to ascertain Donald Trump's 'rainbow' – although it could be self-aggrandisement.

One of the best, relatively recent examples of this from a nation's perspective was found in Malaysia at the end of the twentieth century. In 1991, the Prime Minister of Malaysia, Mahathir Mohamad released Malaysia's Wawasan 2020.[36] The vision called for the nation to become a self-sufficient industrialised nation by the year 2020. It encompassed all aspects of life, from economic prosperity, social well-being, world-class education, and political stability, as well as psychological balance. Wawasan 2020 was widely publicised and every person was encouraged to buy into the vision and to help make it a reality. It gave people a sense of pride as to what their country could become and set a framework for action. This then set in train the complete set of processes that have brought Malaysia to the stage it is at today. In 2018, the then Prime Minister of Malaysia, Najib Razak, furthered the process by initiating the National Transformation 2050 or *Transformasi Nasional 2050* (TN50) initiative. In this new vision, by 2050, Malaysia would be 'a nation of calibre, with a new mindset'. However, following a change in Prime Minister and with Najib Razak under a corruption cloud and facing prosecution, this was officially cancelled later in 2018 although some elements of it have been retained. Rainbows are always ephemeral and move well ahead of where a person actually stands.

One of the tools used to ensure people understood Wawasan 2020 was music. Composed in accordance with Malaysia's PM, Tun Dr Mahathir's original Vision 2020, a musical rendition became one of Malaysia's most popular patriotic songs.[37] This filled the role of a 'vision trigger'. The song did not set out Wawasan 2020 in its entirety, but it reminded people of the vision's core messages.

Vision triggers are powerful symbols for reinforcing and perpetuating the vision in a shorthand form. Today's most obvious example of vision triggers is to be found with Donald Trump who has made very good use of a vision trigger through his 'make America great again' slogan. Unfortunately, today vision triggers are often abused with slogans being introduced and promulgated independently (or in lieu of) any vision of substance. Slogans supplant substance.

In every area of human endeavour, most people seek some form of an aspirational vision. No matter what their present situation, most people want to believe that tomorrow can be better than today – especially if today is fraught with problems and there seems no immediate prospect of improvement. Failure to ascertain some element of hope can easily lead to the negative spiral through anxiety, depression, hopelessness and, all too often, to illicit substance abuse, violence and/or suicide. Hope, even if initially in miniscule amounts, can lead to positive results and growth – especially when it is accompanied by or can be found in an environment in which personal growth and success is encouraged and fostered.

The starting point to building an organisation in which people are committed, are high achievers, and which has a high probability of a long life is to be found in a strong organisational vision. Such a vision will focus on the long-term aspirations for the organisation and will be expressed in a manner that inspires those on whom it will depend in order to be realised. It should also have a vision trigger that will help everyone recall and work towards achieving the future that the vision promotes.

4 Values

The values we practice are the values that drive our organisations. This raises the issue of 'espoused values' as opposed to 'actual values'. Where we do not 'walk' what we 'talk', as has already been made clear, it is the 'walk' that people believe. Many organisations speak about 'our people' in their value statements. Many of these same organisations then treat people at different levels in totally different ways. The issue of remuneration is a case in point. At the top level, Directors and Executives may receive significant increases based on 'performance' while those on or close to the basic wage will be told that any increase is out of the question. The abuse of this 'performance' component is all graphically illustrated when the executives who have overseen companies that have acted illegally and/or unethically are still deemed worthy recipients of millions of dollars of largesse even while those at the lower echelons are finding their remuneration frozen or that jobs have disappeared.

The problem arises because 'values statements' tend to be written in terms that allow for considerable interpretation. They are couched in such generic terms that they provide little or no real guidance as to behaviour. This results in an 'ambiguity of values'.

An understanding of the real values operating in an organisation is probably the most important critical consideration relating to the future of an organisation. As previously stated, the values we practise – rather than those that are in any values statement – are those that really drive the organisation. As stated above, if you want to know the values of an organisation, look at what is being done rather than at what is being said. In organisations that are really 'values driven', the values statements are presented in a behavioural form such as: 'We value our employees. This means that ...' or 'Safety is a key value in this organisation. This means that ...'

Such organisations don't have a huge list of 'values'. They distil their values to the most basic yet comprehensive form possible so that there are only around five (plus or minus two) value statements and each of these is supplemented by very clear behavioural implications. The result is everyone can quickly become aware both of the statements themselves and of what they mean in the day-to-day operations. In these cases, it ought to then follow that if any person, from the chairman down, contravenes any of these values their on-going employment in the organisation ought to be under serious threat. Perhaps this possibility of dismissal for failure to enact the espoused values is why so many 'values statements', if they exist at all, are wishy-washy motherhood statements that can be widely interpreted.

Another reason for the use of values statements that are couched in ambiguous terms may be related to the philosophy underlying an organisation's activities. If the underlying philosophy arises from shareholder theory (See Chapter 7) then the only important factor for consideration is the organisation's ownership and every other consideration must be viewed through the lens of 'could this negatively impact returns to shareholders?' If the answer is 'yes' then shareholder theory argues that this could be viewed as 'theft' from shareholders and so should be avoided. Depending on the organisational level at which 'could this negatively impact returns to shareholders?' is asked, different answers may be given and so what is deemed acceptable behaviour at one level may be viewed quite differently elsewhere.

Writing values statements in behavioural terms removes any such ambiguity. It enables congruity of decisions across all areas of an organisation and thus makes it far more obvious as to whether everyone is 'walking the talk'.

5 Strategy

Strategy is the art of positioning resources to achieve the organisation's overall objectives and purpose. It provides clarity of purpose across the organisation. Without clear strategy, leaders may be so pre-occupied with day-to-day activities that their organisation loses momentum. To be totally effective, an organisation's strategy must be understood by everyone and it must be the key driver of decisions whether the board and/or c-suite are dealing with macro organisational issues or lower level personnel are dealing with issues at the functional level.

Good strategy starts with understanding an organisation's purpose – its raison d'être! This is where link to the vision becomes important. The prime reason for any organisation should not be 'to make money'. The prime reason for an organisation should be that it seeks to provide a service or goods that others will find of value. If it does this provision of such goods or services well then profit ('making money') will be a natural consequence and the organisation will thrive because of the benefits provided to others. Focusing on 'making money' per se can easily lead to unethical and exploitive behaviour.

As President, Donald Trump does not seem to have any clear and coherent strategy for the US. We know that he believes the US is being exploited by those with whom it has a trading deficit and by those with whom it is in various defence alliances. We know that he believes immigrants and refugees can be portrayed as people who will take jobs from US citizens and pose a threat to their security. For these he has strategies such as withdrawing from trade agreements, NATO, initiating trade wars, and building a border wall. But as to any cohesive strategy for assisting the US retain its dominant role in world leadership, there appears to be a total vacuum.

For as long as most people can remember, the US has seen its purpose as being a guiding light for such things as democracy, free trade, and international decency. But, today, there is no real sense of the US having an overall purpose other than looking after its own interests no matter what the impact on others. From being globally concerned and active, it seems to have retreated to a very local focus. Donald Trump's stream of consciousness tweets are scoured unsuccessfully for a coherent US strategy. The result is a void in global leadership with pretenders to the throne simultaneously fighting among themselves while also seeking to further undermine the United States' global dominance.

Leaders of all organisations need to be clear about their organisation's purpose and to build their strategies around this. The best leaders can then ensure that these strategies are well-known and understood and are promulgated across the organisation as a driver for decision-making. People want to be part of an organisation with a purpose in which they can believe and clear indications of how that purpose can be realised. When these are lacking the organisation suffers and runs the risk of losing market share and eventually becoming irrelevant.

It is well-known that strategy is all about the direction in which an organisation intends to move and creation of a path by which it intends to get there. Unless a clear strategy is in place, managers may just focus on obvious problems and engage in 'putting out fires'. Managers may be so preoccupied with day-to-day pressures that their organisation can lose momentum. Accordingly, a clear strategy can lead to higher organisational performance as it helps coordinate diverse organisational units, helping them focus on organisational goals. In order to do this, strategy development requires an examination of internal organisational characteristics and external environment changes. As all managers know, a high-performing organisation then uses this information to decide:

- Where to compete? (In what market or markets (industries, products etc.) will we compete?)
- How to compete? (On what criterion or differentiating characteristic(s)) will we compete? Cost? Quality? Innovation?
- With what will we compete? (What resources will allow us to beat our competition?) and,
- How will we acquire, develop and deploy those resources to compete?

This information is then promulgated across the organisation through:

- Corporate-level strategies (top management's overall plan for the entire organisation and its strategic business units).
- Business-level strategy (a document that seeks to determine how an organisation should compete in each of its strategic business units (SBUs).) and,
- Functional-level strategy (a document that seeks to determine how to support the business-level strategy.)

Most major organisations do this well. Their leaders recall that, many years ago, the Chinese General, Sun Tzu is reputed to have said: 'All men can see the tactics whereby I conquer, but what none can see is the strategy out of which victory is evolved. Do not repeat the tactics which have gained you one victory, but let your methods be regulated by the infinite variety of circumstances.'

However, it is the stage of strategy implementation where major problems occur.

In developing and seeking to implement strategy, it is essential to remember the impact of culture. When culture and strategy are not in a symbiotic relationship then the probability of effective strategy implementation is low. Far too frequently the importance of culture as an enabler (or otherwise) of strategy implementation is forgotten or overlooked. Yet, as shown in Figure 9.6, it is strategy that bridges the gap between the past and the future – and culture is the sum of accretion of those things that have worked in the past less those things that have not worked in the past. Culture is a very significant force for good or for bad.

6 Culture

A high-performing organisation knows what it is doing, where it is going, and how it will get there. It achieves planned growth and profitability. Its people are engaged and empowered. When you walk into a high-performing

Figure 9.6   Leadership and strategy

organisation there is a positive 'buzz' that comes from people wanting to be there and being fully engaged with both their work and the organisation. There tends to be plenty of healthy discussion and argument, but this is totally focused on the best way of achieving desired results and personalities are not attacked. There is no sense that disagreeing with 'the boss' as to the best way of achieving results, or making a mistake, will result in any form of punishment or censure. There is a strong sense of openness, caring and support so that everyone can succeed.

A culture in which loyalty to the leader takes precedence over loyalty to the organisation and in which disagreeing with the leader is seen to be rewarded by censure, denigration, and/or other negative consequences, will never result in a high-performing organisation. The dominant culture will be one of fear and, in this environment, instrumental compliance will pervade, and group-think become paramount. Such a culture removes rather than enhances the ingredients for high performance: cooperation, innovation, creativity and functional conflict where the emphasis is on finding the best way we can all bring about the organisation's success.

In organisations where leaders are focused on the future of the organisation first and foremost and see their role as creating the environment in which people can achieve results, lie the ingredients for high performance. At every level, such leaders consciously set up their people for success by ensuring that the right people are available to do the right thing at the right time, in the right place, by the right methods, and with the right resources. These leaders focus on empowering their people with minimal controls required because everyone is clear about the parameters within which they can act and decide with any mistakes being used as an opportunity for learning. ('If you encountered a similar situation again, what could you do differently?') Everyone is told the truth, the whole truth, and nothing but the truth. 'Spin' is eschewed so that facts can be dealt with. Problem solving takes precedence over recrimination.

Such organisations foster relationships that are based on unconditional respect. The emphasis is on what people have in common rather than on what makes us different. There is no discrimination of any kind at any level to any individual or group. Differences are respected and valued as key components of a vibrant working society. Bullying, sarcasm, 'put-downs', power games and manipulation are totally absent. The 'grapevine' comprises significantly more positive news and support than unsubstantiated rumours and negativity. Everyone is willing to share their knowledge, skills, and expertise to help others develop because the focus is on where the organisation is going, how it is going to get there, and what each person can do to facilitate this process. People focus on 'us' rather than on 'me'.

Unfortunately this positive one is not the dominant culture we see today in the US or in most countries across the world. We certainly see it in some corporations and similar organisations, but the 'us culture' is very much the exception rather than the rule.

Vision (purpose), strategy, and culture go hand in hand. Once there is a clear sense of purpose then strategies can be formulated and promulgated. However, unless the issue of culture is also addressed, any strategy that is counter to the prevailing culture has only a low probability of successful implementation.

For most people, a sense of 'me-first' is the reality even if we seek to portray a different image. Our personal survival and that of those who are closest to us is an underlying driving force and motivation in most of what we do. Abraham Maslow made that very clear – survival and belonging are our most basic motivational drives.[38] This is part of the reason why capitalism dominated over communism. It is also why neoliberalism has become our dominant world-wide economic model over the past 40 or so years. It is a 'me-first' approach in which, despite rhetoric to the contrary, at least in the 'shareholder theory' approach, the end is more important than the means. It taps into our most primitive urges for personal survival and belonging. This, in turn, in the US, brought about a culture in which Donald Trump could thrive and prepared the ground for his successful presidential aspirations. Since 2017 Donald Trump has further developed this culture through his emphasis on difference and on nationalistic behaviours. 'America First'. This is fast becoming the new dominant culture of the US.

Organisational culture does not suddenly appear. Nor does it change 'overnight'. It emerges over time as the accretion of things that have been tried and work or are rewarded and those things that have been tried and have not worked or which have incurred punishment. As Donald Trump has shown, it is relatively easy to deepen an existing underlying culture. It is a vastly more difficult task to bring about change from an undesirable culture to a desirable one.

In any organisation, the most senior leaders influence the culture for better or for worse. During the incumbency of any CEO, what that CEO says and does, together with any inconsistencies between these, impacts on the organisation's culture. What 'the boss' touches is seen to be important. In other words, what the boss says will be listened to. What the boss does will be watched. What the boss emphasises will be seen as important. Eventually what the boss is believed to want will become 'the way we do it around here' – the culture. There is a very real sense in which 'the boss' eventually creates an organisation in his or her own image. When the incumbency of 'the boss' ends, the new boss will find it very hard to drive any new strategies unless he or she is also prepared to deal with the issue of the associated culture change that will be necessary.

Developing an appropriate culture has two distinct phases. The first phase is to understand and document the existing culture. The second phase is to ascertain the cultural aspects that should be retained and those that should be changed. There are always some positive aspects to any culture and it is on this foundation that any new culture can be built.

While it is important to understand and document the existing culture, it must be recognised that there will be elements of the culture about which people are reluctant to speak. This is especially the case if there is a history of 'shooting the messenger' by actively discouraging honest feedback and the expression of personal views. It is also a difficult task if the new 'boss' is an internal promotion because research makes clear that the longer a person has been in any organisation, the more their personal values adapt to fit the organisation's standards for career success. Observation and discussion will reveal much about the general cultural milieu but, for optimum success moving forward, specific detail is needed so that appropriate tweaking is possible rather than trying to introduce 'culture change' in some generic fashion.

The second stage in this process is a 'strategy-culture match'. This is the process of considering the extent to which each element of the strategies is supported by the existing organisational culture. Any cultural elements that show a negative relationship are those that need attention: almost certainly they will be working against successful strategy implementation. Once identified, they can be prioritised and a process developed to bring about the necessary change.

Methods for identifying cultural specifics can include:

- Walking the floor and asking for people's informal opinions about the organisation, its culture and ethics. Use your intuition to determine if there is a need for empirical data.
- Conduct regular internal cultural audits using external consultants.
- Look at voluntary turnover across the organisation and the reasons for it. Also, be aware of areas in which there is frequent and/or regular involuntary turnover.
- Look at the leave balances. Consider the utilisation of personal (sick) leave and compare it to the national average. When higher than the benchmark, it can be a sign of management and ethical issues (such as bullying, stress, etc.). High annual leave balances could potentially show the following:

a   Employees are not encouraged or are afraid to take leave (indicating a management problem that could be connected to planning, productivity and ethics).
b   Employees are not reporting their leave – meaning that the management is turning a blind eye to employees failing to follow the rules.
c   Employees are afraid that, in their absence, some form of illegal or otherwise inappropriate behaviour might be inadvertently uncovered.
d   Employees are concerned that taking leave will highlight the capacity of others to fill the role and lead to their redundancy.
e   Employees 'don't have a life' and are married to their jobs and need to be at work to feel valued and to prop up their self-esteem.

- Conduct employee opinion surveys to measure whether the leaders (according to the different levels) are perceived as fair and trustworthy. Such surveys should be conducted by an independent third-party organisation that, apart from a contract to conduct the survey, has no other direct or indirect link to the organisation or to any person employed by or associated in any other way with the organisation.
- Look carefully to ascertain what are the true company values that guide decision making at all the organisational levels? What is their relationship to the organisation's espoused values?
- Review the whistleblowing policy and its implementation. What are the consequences or ramifications of exposing unethical behaviours in the organisation? This could be asked in a periodically conducted anonymous ethics survey for the team or a random sample of the team (in large organisations).
- Ask management across the organisation as to how their decisions benefit other business areas within the organisation.
- Enquire whether celebration of success takes place at the lower levels of the organisation rather than being found only at the top levels.

Experience indicates that any areas requiring change are seldom 'global' across the organisation. This means that bringing about cultural change can usually be focused on what is working elsewhere in the same organisation and focusing on 'what we do want' rather than emphasising 'what we don't want'. Achieving the positive is always an easier message than is removing the negative! This is especially the case when you have positive examples available from within the same organisation.

7 Accountability

When people seek to avoid personal responsibility and accountability or, by any other means, put their personal psychological or material gain ahead of doing the right thing by the organisation and this behaviour is tolerated, it can easily become part of the organisational culture. The longer such behaviour goes on, the deeper it penetrates into internal organisational processes. Both personal and shared accountability is essential.

Donald Trump is a prime example of a person who seeks to avoid personal accountability. He commits so many small transgressions that no big one ever sticks to him. He has become adept at dodging criminal charges while simultaneously claiming they are part of a Democrat witch-hunt. As already indicated, almost certainly, he will avoid impeachment or even serious censure because those responsible for ensuring accountability to the US Constitution are unwilling to move beyond partisan politics – power is a very addictive drug and, like it or not, for the foreseeable future, the Republicans have the ultimate power.

In 1938, the philosopher Bertrand Russell delineated various kinds of power: economic power, priestly power, hereditary power, power over opinion, naked power, and so on.[39] He argued that institutions and cultures must keep each one of these forms of power in check and stop them being converted easily from one to the other. He warned that if economic power turned into political power, the likely result would be abuse of power. He made the point very strongly that, at every level, there is a need for personal and societal responsibility and accountability – failure to hold people accountable leads to dysfunctional activity.

The need to hold people accountable is true in all organisations. All too often, the people with ultimate power have a vested interest in allowing the status quo to continue. This may because of laziness; because they were largely responsible for the hiring or promotion of an individual; because of some social connection, or any other reason or excuse. Whatever the cause, in far too many cases people are able to avoid accepting personal responsibility and the organisation suffers. In many cases, those who abdicate from demanding personal responsibility and accountability from those closest to them, will happily and vehemently demand responsibility and accountability from those with little or no power to object, or who respond in anything other than a 'yes, sir' manner. Society's treatment of people with mental illness, disability, addiction, the unemployed, the poor and disadvantaged, etc., is far too frequently found to be evidence of this.

Accountability in an organisation starts with the Board and then cascades down. This was made very clear by Sir John Harvey-Jones who is quoted as saying: 'If a company is successful it is due to the efforts of everyone in it, but if it fails it is because of the failure of the board. If the board fails it is the responsibility of the chairman, notwithstanding the collective responsibility of everyone. Despite this collective responsibility, it is on the chairman's shoulders that the competition and the performance of that supreme directing body depends.'[40]

A properly constructed performance programme will create an environment in which this accountability is facilitated because it will ensure that the results critical for organisational success are properly aligned and supported. The process for doing this is shown below:

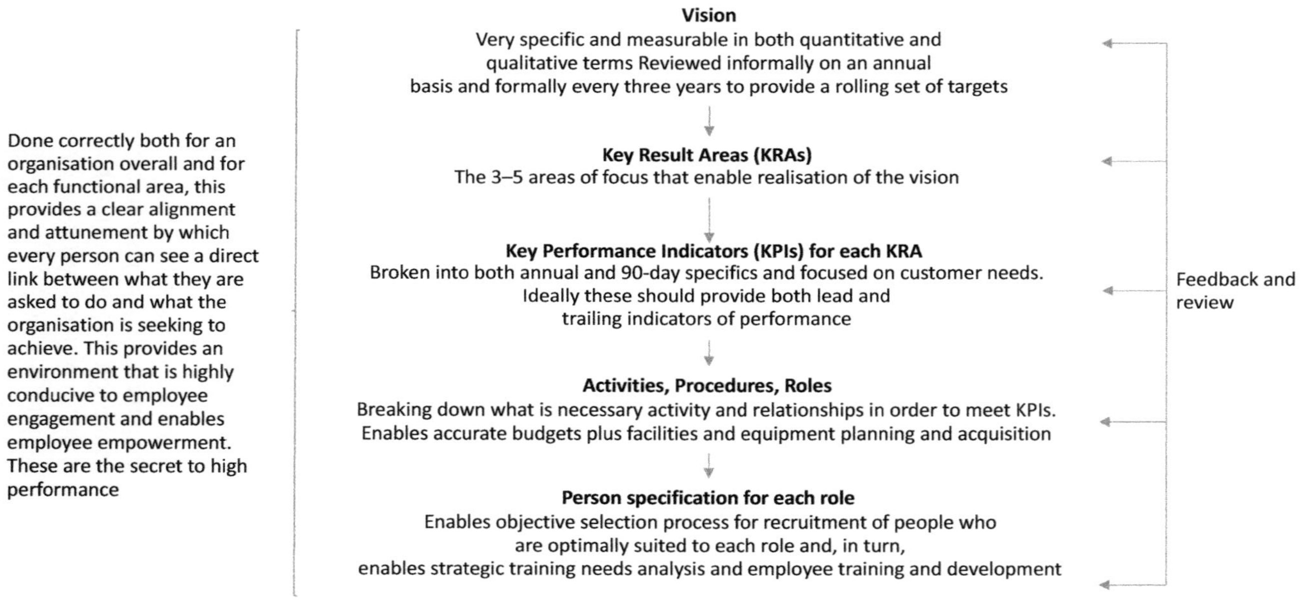

Vision
Very specific and measurable in both quantitative and
qualitative terms Reviewed informally on an annual
basis and formally every three years to provide a rolling set of targets

Key Result Areas (KRAs)
The 3–5 areas of focus that enable realisation of the vision

Key Performance Indicators (KPIs) for each KRA
Broken into both annual and 90-day specifics and focused on customer needs.
Ideally these should provide both lead and
trailing indicators of performance

Activities, Procedures, Roles
Breaking down what is necessary activity and relationships in order to meet KPIs.
Enables accurate budgets plus facilities and equipment planning and acquisition

Person specification for each role
Enables objective selection process for recruitment of people who
are optimally suited to each role and, in turn,
enables strategic training needs analysis and employee training and development

Feedback and
review

Done correctly both for an
organisation overall and for
each functional area, this
provides a clear alignment
and attunement by which
every person can see a direct
link between what they are
asked to do and what the
organisation is seeking to
achieve. This provides an
environment that is highly
conducive to employee
engagement and enables
employee empowerment.
These are the secret to high
performance

Figure 9.7 The process for accountability

When this is done, no matter where a person may be in the organisation, they are able to see a direct link between what they are asked to do and what the organisation seeks to achieve.

This is different from any traditional 'performance management' system that may be used to correct unsatisfactory performance and which, very often, results in an employee involuntarily leaving the organisation. The process set out above is a positive, results-orientated approach that can be readily understood and used by any person. However, it only works when the Key Performance Indicators (KPIs) always reflect matters over which the person has control. Metrics are important for good management, but we need to ensure we measure the right things in the right way.

Across the world, there is increasing disquiet about both how we establish KPIs and how we manage them. The issue centres on whether people can actually exert any influence on the KPIs for which they are held accountable. Is it fair and equitable for a person to be measured over things they cannot control or impact? If people are unable to exert any influence on their results then an organisation is highly unlikely to be better off for utilising that measure of performance. In such a situation (and such situations are far too common) the process becomes demotivating and any anticipated increase in productivity can often prove to be a chimera. KPIs in which a person has only a random probability of success become demotivating rather than motivating management tools.

A further issue that can demotivate is when KPIs become unrealistic. Most people want to do a good job and, initially, set out to achieve their goals with a degree of optimism. They know what they want or need to do. They know how to do it. They have the resources available to do it. But then something unexpected happens. Circumstances beyond the individual's control change and their goal is no longer important or even relevant. People fall sick or are injured. Management decides the available resources must be diverted to some other cause. Something totally outside an individual's control has happened and the goal is no longer realistically capable of achievement. If a person is still expected to achieve the same KPI and is still assessed against this KPI then a downward spiral of motivation quickly evolves.

When this happens, once highly committed employees can morph back into instrumentally compliant employees in a short space of time. Invariably the result is a drop in productivity and, possibly, the loss of a person who was once an extremely good employee. Sometimes it is easy to forget that the attainment of organisational goals is a combination of factors over which we have some control and factors over which we have no control. In high-performing organisations people have some control over virtually all the factors that impact their performance.

Individuals can and should be held accountable for their performance. However, such accountability starts at the very top. If the people at the top are not seen to be held accountable for what they do, it is both hypocritical and dysfunctional to expect people at the bottom of the organisation to accept accountability. It is also totally dysfunctional to hold people accountable for results over which they have only a random chance of achieving. (This, of course, does not always apply. In too many cases, if you are at the top of an organisation, there is a high probability you will receive your desired rewards regardless of the results achieved. Because of your status and associations, excuses that would be deemed totally unacceptable from lower echelon personnel are now deemed 'reasons'.)

It is extremely important, however, that this accountability applies to both legal and ethical issues. While *The Ethical Kaleidoscope*[41] is primarily directed at Company Directors, the message about operating ethically as well as within the law applies across the entire organisation. To optimise the probability of this eventuating, a series of questions is suggested:

a   Am I prepared for it to be on the front page of the newspaper?
b   Will I be proud to tell my family and friends about this decision?
c   Will I feel or experience any possible personal embarrassment if I have to defend this action?

These are applicable to every employee, no matter their position. They can be used to develop a KPI that specifically looks at this quality issue of 'how' results are achieved. Such a KPI can complement the more frequently encountered KPIs. If the values of the organisation are expressed in behavioural terms, then inclusion of such a KPI is a natural and easily developed part of the chain of accountability.

This then leads to the issue of control versus empowerment.

The concept of scientific management is predicated on the belief that a manager can control performance by breaking every activity down into its component parts and then tightly managing the process so that people do a limited number of tasks with no freedom as to the rate at which they work or they manner in which they do it. This is a very mechanistic approach that encourages impersonal interaction with people. In this approach, people are resources in exactly the same way as are facilities, finance, tools and equipment. They can be used and discarded at will and, while being used, should cost the absolute minimum possible.

Control and empowerment are the two extremes on a continuum. Where the balance moves too far in either direction, chaos can occur. The further movement occurs to the 'control' end, the greater the probability of instrumental compliance, groupthink, unacceptably high labour turnover and other dysfunctional behaviours occurring. The further movement occurs to the 'empowerment' end, the greater the probability of individual agendas and personal aggrandisement occurring. High-performing organisations continuously work on optimising the balance practiced.

This balance is usually found as an extension of the chain of accountability that was earlier discussed (see Figure 9.5) and involves the concept of 'degrees of discretion'. 'Discretion' is judgement applied to decisions with one or more resolutions and frequently involves unilateral decision making without consulting others. 'Degrees of discretion' refers to the parameters within which an individual is permitted to exercise their own judgement or 'discretion'.

There are no 'absolutes' when it comes to degree of discretion. The parameters within which personal judgement may be made can be imposed by ourselves or the organisation within which we are involved. For example, a person with an external locus of control may self-impose (even if unconsciously) parameters that relate to the response the feel they will receive from other people. If they feel their actions will garner approval, they may be far more likely to act than if the opposite is true. The reality of what might occur is irrelevant. All that matters is the perception of how others *might* react.

The parameters within which we operate will also vary depending on the stratum we are at in our particular organisation. The degrees of discretion available at the top of an organisation will almost certainly be greater than those available to people at the lower levels. Additionally, if I own the organisation or am its major stockholder then I will have greater flexibility than if I am an employee. Or, as Donald Trump is discovering, if I am running a privately-owned business then I have far fewer restrictions than if I am President of the USA. Much of his Twitter output is focused on seeking to remove restrictions that are imposed by the Constitution and the facts of history.

In many organisations, degrees of discretion are clearly stated in terms of financial responsibility. Managers at different levels will have different financial 'delegations' that state explicitly what discounts or other inducements they may offer in order to obtain business or the maximum amount of money they may spend without recourse to another stratum. This clarity generally also applies as to whether competitive quotes for goods and services are required and, if so, whether these must be in writing or even must be done by a tender process. The same may be true with issues such as employment of new staff. Managers are generally aware of their maximum 'headcount' and whether this refers to full-time, part-time, casual, or 'full-time equivalent' (FTE) numbers.

But the parameters may not be so clear when it comes to other decisions or if you are outside of the management strata. This is where confusion and conflict are most likely to occur. I am faced with the need for a decision to be made. I have never been explicitly told the parameters within which I have discretion to act. I know precedents because of my time in the organisation and, in order to achieve my understanding of desired results, I use my own judgement. However, unbeknown to me, other factors are now in play. Accordingly, when my manager learns of my decision, a crisis ensues and I suffer the consequences. When this happens, initiative and innovation are quickly stifled, and the probability of organisational high performance is impaired.

'Degrees of discretion' enable an organisation to operate within the optimum range of the 'control-empowerment' continuum. Properly linked to a person's KPIs they provide clarity as to when I may, myself, make a decision; when I need to check with my manager regarding the decision before implementation; and when I need to refer the decision to the next stratum. In other words, it makes clear the 'white', the 'grey' and the 'black'. I may or may not choose to discuss with my boss the possible options available prior to making the decision but, so long as I make my decision within the defined parameters then even if my decision is different from what my boss may have decided, I will not suffer career-limiting consequences. When this happens, self-confidence is fostered along with innovation and creativity. Should the decision later prove to have been 'wrong' then the probability for learning can take precedence over punishment. The probability of both personal and organisational high performance is enhanced.

Notes

1 Douglas G. Long (2013), *Delivering High Performance: The Third Generation Organisation*. Farnham: Gower Publishing Ltd.
2 Douglas G. Long and Zivit Inbar (2017), *The Ethical Kaleidoscope: Values, Ethics and Corporate Governance*. Abingdon: Routledge.
3 Douglas G. Long (1998), *Leaders: Diamonds or Cubic Zirconia? Asia Pacific Leaders on Leadership*. Sydney: CLS.
4 See, for example, Jay H. Conger, Robindra N. Kanungo, and Associates (1988), *Charismatic Leadership: The Elusive Factor in Organizational Effectiveness*. San Francisco: Jossey-Bass.
5 Richard Wike, Bruce Stokes, Jacob Poushter and Janell Fetterolf, 'U.S. images suffers as publics around the world question Trump's leadership', 26 June 2017. Available at http://www.pewglobal.org/2017/06/26/u-s-image-suffers-as-publics-around-world-question-trumps-leadership/.
6 Chris Cizzilla, 'Trump just held the weirdest cabinet meeting ever', 13 June 2017. Available at http://edition.cnn.com/2017/06/12/politics/donald-trump-cabinet-meeting/index.html
7 'Donald Trump has a fake Time magazine cover on display in his golf clubs', 28 June 2017. Available at http://www.abc.net.au/news/2017-06-28/trumps-framed-time-magazine-cover-revealed-as-fake-news/8658432.
8 David C. McClelland and David H. Burnham (2008), *Power is the Great Motivator*. Boston, MA: Harvard Business Press (First published in *Harvard Business Review*, 1976).
9 Tasha Eurich (2017), *Insight: Why We're Not as Self-Aware as We Think, and How Seeing Ourselves Clearly Helps Us Succeed at Work and in Life*. New York: Penguin Random House.
10 See Long, *Diamonds or Cubic Zirconia?*
11 In *Leaders: Diamonds or Cubic Zirconia?*, distinction is drawn between 'genuine' leaders (diamonds) and their imitators (cubic zirconia). Genuine leaders have at their core a real belief in the importance and value of every person. They seek to treat every person with unconditional respect while drawing a distinction between the person and the behaviour. They will address improper behaviour very directly and strongly while still maintaining respect for the person per se. Cubic zirconia leaders tend to be manipulative and discriminatory.

12 Rita Gunther McGrath, 'The pace of technology is speeding up', 25 September 2019. Available at https://hbr.org/2013/11/the-pace-of-technology-adoption-is-sp eeding-up.
13 Lynda Gratton and Andrew Scott (2016), *The 100-Year Life*. London: Blooms-bury Information.
14 Mrs Patrick Campbell (who was renowned for her platonic association with thea-tre critic and playwright George Bernard Shaw) was a socialite and actress infa-mous for her sharp wit. Her best-known remark, reputed to have been uttered upon hearing about a male homosexual relationship, was 'My dear, I don't care what they do, so long as they don't do it in the street and frighten the horses'. This quote has also been attributed to other people, most notably Queen Victoria, but it seems more likely that it originated with Mrs Campbell.
15 Shannon Greenwood, Andrew Perrin and Maeve Duggan, 'Social media update 2016', 11 November 2016. Available at http://www.pewinternet.org/2016/11/11/social-media-update-2016/.
16 Adam Mitchinson and Robert Morris (2014), *Learning About Learning Agility*. Greensboro, NC: Center for Creative Leadership.
17 Mitchinson and Morris, *Learning About Learning Agility*.
18 Mitchinson and Morris, *Learning About Learning Agility*.
19 A Luddite is a person who dislikes and opposes technology in general.
20 A good summary of MBTI can be found in David Keirsey and Marilyn Bates (1978), *Please Understand Me: Character and Temperament Types*. Del Mar, CA: Prometheus Nemesis Books. It should be noted, however, that there are many criticisms of the con-cept as can be noted in https://www.forbes.com/sites/toddessig/2014/09/29/the-myster ious-popularity-of-the-meaningless-myers-briggs-mbti/#1c093d6b1c79; https://www.psy chologytoday.com/blog/give-and-take/201309/goodbye-mbti-the-fad-won-t-die, and indi ana.edu/~jobtalk/Articles/develop/mbti.pdf.
21 J.M. Digman (1990), 'Personality structure: Emergence of the five-factor model'. *Annual Review of Psychology, 41*: 417–40.
22 OCEAN stands for Openness, Conscientiousness, Extraversion, Agreeableness, Neuroticism.
23 The Enron scandal, publicised in October 2001, eventually led to the bankruptcy of the Enron Corporation, an American energy company based in Houston, Texas, and the *de facto* dissolution of Arthur Andersen, which was one of the five largest audit and accountancy partnerships in the world. Enron was formed in 1985 by Kenneth Lay after merging Houston Natural Gas and InterNorth. Several years later, executives used accounting loopholes, special purpose entities, and poor financial reporting to hide billions of dollars in debt from failed deals and projects. Chief Financial Officer Andrew Fastow and other executives not only misled Enron's Board of Directors and Audit Committee on high-risk accounting prac-tices, but also pressured Arthur Andersen to ignore the issues.
24 Troy Segal, 'Enron scandal: the fall of a Wall Street darling', (updated) 29 May 2019. Available at https://www.investopedia.com/updates/enron-scandal-summary/.
25 Long and Inbar, *The Ethical Kaleidoscope*.
26 Institute for Health and Human Potential, 'What is emotional intelligence?', n.d. Available at http://www.ihhp.com/meaning-of-emotional-intelligence.
27 Changing Minds, 'Locus of control'. Available at http://changingminds.org/explana tions/preferences/locus_control.htm.
28 Carol Dweck (2017), *Mindset: Changing the Way You Think to Fulfil Your Potential*. London: Little, Brown. See also Carol Dweck, 'The power of believing that you can improve'. Available at https://www.ted.com/talks/carol_dweck_the_p ower_of_believing_that_you_can_improve.
29 See, for example, Douglas G. Long (2012), *Third Generation Leadership and the Locus of Control*. Farnham: Gower Publishing Ltd.

30 B.F. Skinner (1938), *The Behavior of Organisms: An Experimental Analysis.* New York: Appleton-Century-Crofts. See also B.F. Skinner (1953), *Science and Human Behavior.* New York: Macmillan.
31 William Robert Johnston, 'Terrorist attacks and related incidents in the United States', updated 30 December 2019. Available at http://www.johnstonsarchive.net/ terrorism/wrjp255a.html. Between 1865 and 11 September 2001, there had been 217 incidents involving unconventional weapons, politically-motivated murders, and other incidents of terrorism, political or methodological significance in the USA – with virtually all of them committed by US citizens. Since 11 September 2001 and up to 17 June 2017 there had been 119 further attacks – again most committed by US citizens.
32 Elliott Jaques, with Stephen D. Clement and Ronnie Lessem (1994), *Executive Leadership: A Practical Guide to Managing Complexity.* Oxford: Blackwell Publishing.
33 'C-suite' refers to the Chief Executive and those people at the organisational level immediately reporting to the CEO.
34 Statement by Professor Warren Bennis while he was at University of Southern California.
35 Long, *Third Generation Leadership.*
36 'Malaysia as a fully developed country: one definition', n.d. Available at http:// www.wawasan2020.com/vision/p2.html.
37 See http://www.nationalanthems.us/forum/YaBB.pl?num=1115905209.
38 *Encyclopaedia Britannica*, entry, 'Abraham Maslow, American psychologist'. Available at https://www.britannica.com/biography/Abraham-H-Maslow.
39 Bertrand Russell (1938), *Power: A New Social Analysis.* London: Allen & Unwin.
40 Adrian Cadbury (1995), *The Company Chairman.* Hemel Hempstead: Director Books.
41 Long and Inbar, *The Ethical Kaleidoscope.*

Conclusion: Quo Vadis?

As at the end of 2019 we are at a possibly pivotal place in history. There are many parallels with the world of 100 years ago. As in 1919, today we have political leaders who are more interested in their own power than they are in the overall future of mankind. In this they are aided and abetted by those with great wealth – much of which has been obtained through exploitation of one sort or another – and we are all-too-frequently assailed by tales of unethical corporate behaviour in the quest to acquire even more wealth.

President Trump is in a long line of leaders who have demonstrated you do not need to be a 'good' leader in order to further your personal agenda. Creating a culture where people fear to contradict you – a culture based on the exercise of raw power – can be effective. Such power can be even more effectively exercised if you are also perceived as having great wealth, no matter how this may have been obtained. Most politicians, no matter what idealism with which they enter politics, become seduced into a power game of retaining their seat (and income), along with being part of (or controlling), the government of the country, state, or local authority. In order to do this, most (no matter what their political affiliation) are past masters in using real or imagined threats to garner votes. Power and money are extraordinarily effective in the methods of persuasion.

But leaders, no matter their arena of influence, do not need to follow this example. Today there are many economists and others who are concerned about greater global challenges and are challenging our current dominant economic approaches. They recognise the importance of economics as a tool, but reject it as a religion. Rather than seeing the economy as the *sine qua non* of society, they see economics as something that interacts with every other aspect of society. Using an open system approach their considered perspective requires that we look at the impact of every component part of society in the context of society's entirety. This then demands a very careful look at inequality of opportunity as well as at the equitable distribution of rewards. It requires, too, that the full gamut of environmental issues is taken into account both for the present and for the future. While today's dominant shareholder value approach argues that nations must balance their budgets, so as to not load future generations with the debt burden, these people want to also ensure that there will be a viable environment around when the future generations arrive. It wants to return the 'socio' to socio-economic.

Making this shift will not be easy. For some 40 or so years the western world has been rolling back legislation that would protect society. We have seen increasing moves to individual employment contracts where, especially in the case of lower level workers, the might of a corporation is pitted against the weakness of an individual in a 'divide and conquer' exercise. Returns to shareholders are king. Trade unions have been emasculated and the employer remains firmly in control of an unbalanced system. The result has been significant reduction in full-time jobs and a corresponding increase in part-time or casual employment. Remuneration increases, when provided, have been strenuously opposed and, as far as possible, kept to below the level of inflation. We have seen a reduction in government oversight in areas such as building and construction with the result that, as evidenced in the 2017 Grenfell Tower disaster in the UK, sub-standard materials were utilised because developers had few checks and balances. We have seen public assets sold off to private industry with the result that, instead of returning public sector 'profits' to either the state or using them to keep prices low, tolls on roads and highways, utility prices, and transport costs have increased in order to improve profits to private sector shareholders. The concept of 'the commons' in which the public at large own and benefit through common ownership has been ridiculed and denigrated as being 'inefficient' and/or as 'holding back the economy'. We have managed to get ourselves in a mess and it is against this situation that people are now protesting.

It is becoming increasingly obvious, even if not to politicians and business executives, that the shareholder theory consensus of small government, reduction of legislated controls on business practices, ever decreasing business and personal taxes, privatisation, surplus budgets and an internationalism headlined by free trade, has now run its course.

Eventually, even orthodox extremists in the economic faith of shareholder value may have to face the new reality that economic practices and governments really are servants of society and that there is a responsibility to exercise 'good' leadership that is truly creating an environment in which everyone can be successful. Organisations, be they government or any other sector, need to face the reality that stakeholders are increasingly advocating for business to once more recognise that they operate as part of a social contract.

Since 2017, President Donald Trump has demonstrated a leadership which is the end result of ignoring this social contract. All the indications are that Donald J. Trump will be re-elected in 2020 and that, in the US, in common with other countries that have tilted towards protectionism and reactionary political leaders, he will continue their quest for personal power. Since 2016 Donald Trump has demonstrated the sort of leadership the world does not need as we move into the future. Almost certainly he will continue to do this until 2024. Learning from the Trump event can enable us to avoid perpetuating this while developing and working towards the leadership our world *does* need as we move forward.

In the next four years we must initiate and foster the process of moving forward.

We will never, and should never, have a world in which wealth, power, and the like are shared equally. Communism has been proven to be an abject failure. (And it did not ensure equal distribution, anyway!). Capitalism has been a very positive force in the past and it can be again. The evidence is clear that the right sort of capitalism can be of benefit to everyone. All that we need in order to have strong, vibrant, successful economies is to have a society in which the benefits are shared equitably and in which we operate in an ethical manner.

To obtain this we need a leadership that works towards enabling everyone to be successful even if they do not seek success that is synonymous with wealth and power. This will require that those we endorse in leadership roles (no matter whether politics, business, education, or anywhere else) are people who have the ability and willingness to deal with the ever-increasing ambiguity and complexity that will exist in coming days. The evidence is clear. Simplistic answers to complex issues only create a short-term solution that almost invariably later becomes another problem to be solved.

As the ancient Chinese general, military strategist and philosopher, Sun Tzu is reputed to have said: 'The bad leader is he who the people fear. The good leader is he who the people revere. The great leader is he of whom the people say: "we did it ourselves"'.

Index

For Product Safety Concerns and Information please contact our EU
representative GPSR@taylorandfrancis.com
Taylor & Francis Verlag GmbH, Kaufingerstraße 24, 80331 München, Germany

www.ingramcontent.com/pod-product-compliance
Ingram Content Group UK Ltd.
Pitfield, Milton Keynes, MK11 3LW, UK
UKHW021122180425
457613UK00005B/187